VCs
OF THE FIRST WORLD WAR

SOMME 1916

GERALD GLIDDON

LIBRARIES NI
WITHDRAWN FROM STOCK

The
History
Press

LIBRARIES NI	
C700992136	
RONDO	27/02/2012
940.460922	£ 9.99
ARDOY	

First published 1991
This edition published in 2011

The History Press
The Mill, Brimscombe Port
Stroud, Gloucestershire, GL5 2QG
www.thehistorypress.co.uk

© Gerald Gliddon, 1991, 1994, 2000, 2011

The right of Gerald Gliddon to be identified as the Author
of this work has been asserted in accordance with the
Copyrights, Designs and Patents Act 1988.

All rights reserved. No part of this book may be reprinted
or reproduced or utilised in any form or by any electronic,
mechanical or other means, now known or hereafter invented,
including photocopying and recording, or in any information
storage or retrieval system, without the permission in writing
from the Publishers.

British Library Cataloguing in Publication Data.
A catalogue record for this book is available from the British Library.

ISBN 978 0 7524 6303 2

Typesetting and origination by The History Press
Printed in Great Britain

CONTENTS

E.N.F. Bell	17
G.S. Cather	22
J.L. Green	26
S.W. Loudoun-Shand	31
W.F. McFadzean	36
R. Quigg	41
W. Ritchie	46
G. Sanders	49
J.Y. Turnbull	54
A Carton de Wiart	58
T.G. Turrall	64
T.O.L. Wilkinson	68
D.S. Bell	71
W.E. Boulter	77
W. F. Faulds	80
W. La T. Congreve	85
J.J. Davies	90
A. Hill	94
T.W.H. Veale	98
J. Leak	103
A.S. Blackburn	107
T. Cooke	113

A. Gill	116
C. C. Castleton	119
W.J.G. Evans	123
J. Miller	127
W.H. Short	130
G.G. Coury	133
N.G. Chavasse	140
M.O'Meara	149
W.B. Allen	153
T. Hughes	157
J.V. Holland	160
D. Jones	164
L. Clarke	168
D.F. Brown	171
F. McNess	174
J.V. Campbell	180
J.C. Kerr	184
T. A. Jones	187
F.J. Edwards and R.E. Ryder	193
T.E. Adlam	201
A.C.T. White	207
R. B. Bradford	211
H. Kelly	217
J.C.Richardson	221
R. Downie	225
E.P. Bennett	228
J. Cunningham	232
B.C. Freyberg	238
Appendices	247
Bibliography	257
Index	261

Acknowledgements

I would like to thank the following institutions and individuals for their very kind co-operation and assistance during the preparation of this book: Australian National Memorial Canberra, Commonwealth War Graves Commission, Gallahers, Imperial War Museum, National Archives of Canada, National Army Museum, Public Record Office, now The National Archives, and the Western Front Association. Peter Batchelor, the late Lady Joan Carton de Wiart, Richard Denyer, Denis Pillinger, Steve Snelling, the late Tony Spagnoly, Martin Staunton, Iain Stewart, Ian Uys and Lieutenant Colonel R.J. Wyatt. My wife Winifred has, as always, been of great support.

Preface

This book grew out of my earlier book on the Battle of the Somme called *When the Barrage Lifts* in which all fifty-one Somme VCs make a brief appearance.

I decided to explore the lives of this group of men who won for themselves the highest award for gallantry that their country could bestow. I wanted to try and find out what sort of men they were, and also if they survived the war, what sort of lives that they led after it was over.

The first place to start was with the Canon Lummis collection of material on the lives of all VC holders, which is held at the National Army Museum under the stewardship of the Military Historical Society. Although these files are by no means complete, they do point researchers in the right direction. I wrote to all the regiments associated with the men and to all the local newspapers in their home towns. I contacted the Imperial War Museum, Commonwealth War Graves Commission and Public Record Office (now National Archives, Kew) in addition to the appropriate agencies in Canada, Australia, New Zealand and South Africa. I also, of course, read all that I could get hold of about the lives of these men that had been already published and contacted the families where possible.

I have only set out to write a biographical portrait of each man and not a full blown life story and the average entry is roughly 1,250 words. I have tried to expand on all previous biographical accounts and in most cases I have written more than has been published before. However a number of the men have had whole books devoted to them, i.e. Second Lieutenant D.S. Bell, Sergeant W.E. Boulter, Lieutenant Colonel R.B.

Bradford, Captain N.G. Chavasse, Lieutenant Colonel Carton de Wiart, Major W. La T. Congreve, Lieutenant Colonel B.C. Freyberg and Private T.A. Jones. Each section begins with the appropriate action in 1916 when the deed for which the Victoria Cross was awarded took place, and then the story reverts to the soldier's early life.

I have listed my main sources at the back of the book under bibliography and appendices. The bibliography covers all the men that I have written about and the appendices with sources give some details of where I obtained much of the rest of the information.

I would be very grateful to hear from any reader who may have any suggested corrections to make or who might have additional information.

INTRODUCTION

British troops first began to arrive in the Somme region in July 1915 when they took over from the French Army who had been in the area since 1914. At the beginning of 1916 General J. Joffre, Commander-in-Chief of the French Army and General Sir Douglas Haig agreed that the British and French armies should carry out a joint offensive north of the River Somme at the beginning of July.

After a two-day postponement caused by poor weather, the Battle of the Somme began at 7.30am on 1 July after a massive seven-day Allied bombardment. Fourteen British divisions with two French divisions on their right climbed out of their trenches on an 18 mile front to the north of the River Somme, and slowly advanced on the strongly held German positions. By the end of the day the advance on the British front had failed everywhere except for small gains at the southern end of the battlefield. There had been 57,000 British casualties either killed or wounded on that disastrous first day and by 18 November, when the battle officially ended, nearly a million men from the Allied and German armies had become casualties.

The Victoria Cross was instituted in 1856 and is still made from Russian cannons captured at Sebastopol. The decoration weighs 430 grams and is 1½ inches square.

During the Great War no less than 634 awards of the VC were made, of which fifty-one were for the Battle of the Somme. The spread of ranks who won the medal is a fairly wide one, with twenty going to officers, twelve to non-commissioned officers, and nineteen going to privates or their equivalent. In order to qualify for a medal it was of course very important to be seen carrying out the deed itself. No doubt there were many cases when a man deserved a Victoria Cross, yet went unrewarded. However, I have no qualms about the merits of the Somme VC holders, although it is true to say that many of the men did not feel themselves justified in accepting such a high honour when they had seen similar acts of bravery performed around them on the battlefield.

Many of the awards were for the saving of life and not just for rushing forward in the heat of battle with a Lewis gun to an enemy-held trench and spraying it with fire. Indeed many VC winners did both, killing Germans and saving their compatriots' lives in equal measure. Surely the most heroic figure was Pte W.F. McFadzean who in smothering some grenades that had spilt their pins truly gave his life for those of his friends. On the other hand it can be argued that no battle could possibly be won if the momentum was to be continually interrupted by the saving of the lives of casualties. As the Somme battle progressed, the job of saving lives was reserved for the stretcher bearers who accompanied the advance or battle.

I am not going to speculate here on the meaning of bravery and where a line can be drawn between heroism and foolhardiness, all I will say is that valour and personal sacrifice are two of the good things that come out of any war.

A third of the Somme VCs were awarded posthumously and only thirty-three men survived the war. If the VC holder survived then very often he received a considerable amount of what was probably unwanted publicity. He was often invited back to his home town by the local council who then presented him with gifts or an Illuminated Address, among other things. Some men were also given a gift of money until the War Office cracked down on the practice. It is difficult not to regard all this local attention as an exercise in exploitation and one that helped to encourage local belief in the war effort and in turn help with industrial output in the form of munitions and other vital war materiel. There are many photographs of men who have won the VC looking downright embarrassed by the whole business.

The winning of the coveted award also brought other problems in that each man was marked out as something special, and if he digressed then it would almost certainly be written up by the press, for example Cunningham and Kelly. Others too, could never settle down after the war, although the award of the VC could not be given as the reason but rather the effect of the war itself. Captain W.B. Allen's health was permanently destroyed and he had to resort to alcohol and opium, Private T. Hughes took to the bottle, Private M. O'Meara never regained his sanity, Private J. Cunningham beat up his wife and Lieutenant Sergeant F. McNess committed suicide.

On the other hand, several men seemed almost to qualify for the award of the decoration as if by right, men such as Lieutenant Colonel A. Carton de Wiart, Major W. La T. Congreve, Lieutenant Colonel R.B. Bradford and Lieutenant Colonel B.C. Freyberg, who were all brilliant and courageous soldiers. It would surely only be a matter of time before they qualified for the highest of military honours? Others had no problems with the award and took its ownership in their stride. I am thinking here of men like Second Lieutenant T.E. Adlam, Captain A.C.T. White, Private R.E. Ryder and Private T.A. Jones. 'Todger' Jones, who rounded up 102 Germans single handed, even had correspondence with a film company based in Wardour Street about plans to make a film out of the heroes of the Somme. He wasn't expecting to co-operate without payment either!

I cannot pretend to have got 'inside' every man that I have attempted to write about, and only a fuller biography could achieve this. This book is meant to be a biographical portrait of the fifty-one men who won the Victoria Cross on the Somme, and I am afraid that all too often readers will be left to guess the inner man from the external circumstances. I only hope that I have left enough clues.

Introduction to
the 2011 edition

The History Press have decided to reissue *VCs of the First World War: Somme 1916* and plan to re-publish the rest of the VC series in new editions and I have taken advantage of this decision by revising and updating the text. Indeed many of the biographical portraits have been completely re-written.

Since the initial research for this book was carried out more than twenty years ago, there has been an increasing amount of interest and awareness of the stories and lives of the men who were awarded the nation's highest military honour. Evidence of this can be found in the amount of new books being published on the subject; the reissuing of servicemen's records by the National Archives and the accessibility of other records of family history which are now available through *Ancestry*, the family history magazine. The Internet has also played a very significant role, although such material can be very varied and if used should always be verified by cross-checking with a reliable source.

In 2002, the Victoria Cross enthusiast, Brian Best, founded The Victoria Cross Society which has encouraged further research and publication of important and informative articles. Finally the Victoria Cross gallery at the Imperial War Museum was opened as the Lord Ashcroft Gallery on 11 November 2010 by the Princess Royal. This collection houses 164 VCs which at the the time of writing are worth at least £30 million and were put on display together with forty-eight in the ownership of the museum and with the thirty-one George Crosses which are also in the museum's care.

One of the really heartening consequences of this renewed interest in the subject is in the erection of new or replacement headstones on some of the graves of these brave men, and it is hoped that in time every man who has a grave should have it properly marked.

When dealing with the first day of the Battle of the Somme the author could have arranged the appropriate deeds of gallantry in an order of right to left of the line, but he felt that this would only confuse the reader and instead a straight forward alphabetical choice has been followed, as with many other books written about Victoria Cross heroes.

Gerald Gliddon, Brooke, Norfolk, May 2011

E.N.F. BELL

No fewer than nine men were to win a Victoria Cross on 1 July 1916, the first day of the Battle of the Somme, and four of these were members of the 36th (Ulster) Division which was formed in October 1914. The great majority of the members of this new division had already formed themselves into a Northern Ireland group called the Ulster Volunteer Force.

The year of 1914 was a dangerous and volatile one in the province with two groups threatening to split the country into two factions. The dispute between the two sides was of those who wished to break away from London-based control and to join the south in a unified Ireland and those, usually Protestants, who remained loyal to the King and to Great Britain. What was known as the Home Rule Bill was going through its various stages in the Houses of Parliament but after the assassination of the Archduke Franz Ferdinand, heir to the Austro-Hungarian throne and inspector of the army in Sarajevo, Serbia on 28 June 1914, events in Europe moved downhill fast and led to any dreams of self-government being put on hold for the foreseeable future until the end of hostilities.

Initially the Ulster Division was formed as a result of the Secretary of State for War, Lord Kitchener's appeal for volunteers to form a 'New Army' to supplement the small professional army which Great Britain possessed. This appeal for volunteers was aimed at the average man in the street and the response in Ulster was similar to that on the British mainland when a large number of men came forward from all ranks of society including city clerks, factory workers, miners and university students. The main areas associated with volunteers and their military formation was Belfast in County Antrim, together with the other eight counties of the province. A strong factor in the forming of an Ulster Division was the Orange Order, a Protestant organisation with its origins in the Battle of the Boyne in 1690. Basically this conflict had been a battle for the possession of the thrones which made up the countries of Great Britain. In 1688 the Protestant William of Orange had deposed the Catholic King James from the English throne and later made an unsuccessful comeback in Ireland.

In 1914 Catholic or Nationalist supporters of a Dublin-based government in the south mainly joined the 16th (Irish) Division, while a third Irish division, the 10th was soon to be formed.

Thirteen battalions were raised for the three Irish regiments, including the Ulster-based Royal Inniskilling Fusiliers, Royal Irish Fusiliers and Royal Irish Rifles, and they were formed into three infantry brigades: the 107th, 108th and 109th. After initial training the 36th (Ulster) Division, mostly formed of the newly formed battalions, set foot on the continent for the first time in 1915.

The 9th (Service) Battalion, Royal Inniskilling Fusiliers from County Tyrone were formed from the Tyrone Volunteers in Omagh in September 1914, and in early November were sent to Finner Camp for training and became part of the 109th Brigade. After further training they arrived in France in early October 1915, with the first members of the Ulster Division arriving in the Somme region on the 4th.

Nine months later, on 1 July, the 9th Royal Inniskilling Fusiliers of the 109th Brigade were the right-hand attacking battalion on the edge of Thiepval Wood. They faced the Thiepval Road and beyond was their objective, the German-held Schwaben Redoubt – a defensive position on high ground with an excellent view overlooking the Ancre Valley below it. The redoubt was shaped like a parallelogram and consisted of dugouts, trenches and fortified machine-gun posts.

Temporary Captain Eric Bell was an officer with the 9th Battalion and on 1 July was attached to the Trench Mortar Battery, 109th Brigade and led this battery with particular courage, losing his life and gaining a posthumous VC in the process. The citation for the Somme decoration was one of the earliest to be announced and was published in the *London Gazette* of 26 September 1916. It tells the story of Bell's gallantry as well as any other source does:

For most conspicuous bravery. He was in command of a Trench Mortar Battery, and advanced with the infantry in attack. When our frontline was hung up by enfilading machine-gun fire Captain Bell crept forward and shot the machine-gunner.

Later, on no less than three occasions, when our bombing parties, which were clearing the enemy's trenches, were unable to advance, he went forward alone and threw trench-mortar bombs among the enemy. When he had no more bombs available he stood on the parapet, under intense fire, and used a rifle with great coolness and effect on the enemy advancing to counter-attack.

Finally he was killed rallying and reorganising infantry parties which had lost their officers.

All this was outside the scope of his normal duties with his battery. He gave his life in his supreme devotion to duty.

Bell's body was never found and his name is listed on the panels of the Thiepval Memorial to the Missing, Pier 4-5, Face D-B. He was 20 years of age.

Eric Norman Frankland Bell was born at Alma Terrace, Enniskillen, County Fermanagh, Northern Ireland on 28 August 1895. He was the youngest of three sons of Edward Henry Bell and of Dora Algeo Bell, née Crowder. At the time of Eric's birth his father was serving with the 2nd Royal Inniskilling Fusiliers at Thayetmyo, Burma as a lieutenant quartermaster, and when his battalion returned home the family were reunited in Warrington, Cheshire. Eric began his education at an elementary school named the 'People's College' in Arpley, Warrington. Later the family moved to 114 Huskisson Street, Liverpool. On 18 August 1902 Eric joined St Margaret's School in Prince's Road, Toxteth, Liverpool as by then the family had moved to 18 Prince's Avenue. Later they upped sticks once more and moved to Bootle where they lived at 22 University Road. At this point Eric continued his education at the Liverpool Institute and then switched to Liverpool University where he began training for a career in architecture under the guidance of Professor Sir Charles Reilly. At the time it was noted that he was a student who 'made rapid progress in his studies'. He also became a keen musician and linguist and was described as 'being reserved and unpretentious'.

On the outbreak of war in 1914 Bell joined the Royal Inniskilling Fusiliers and applied for a commission on 28 August with the written support of a reference from the head of the Liverpool Institute. Three weeks later he was commissioned as a second lieutenant on 22 September as an officer in the 6th Battalion. He was later transferred to the 8th Battalion and then to the 9th where his father was adjutant. He was 19 years of age. Eric had two brothers, Alan George Frankland Bell and Haldane Frankland Bell who came respectively from Australia and America to join up. So Captain Bell, their father, had three sons in the same regiment.

After the VC award was published in the *London Gazette* the King wrote a letter of commiseration to Captain Bell, concerning his younger son:

> It is a matter of sincere regret to me that the death of Captain E.N.F. Bell deprived me of the pride of personally conferring on him the Victoria Cross, the greatest of all rewards for bravery and devotion to duty.

The decoration was presented to Captain Bell senior on 29 November 1916 at Buckingham Palace. Colonel Ambrose Ricardo, leader of the Tyrone Volunteers and CO of the 9th Royal Inniskilling Fusiliers also wrote a letter of sympathy to Bell's parents.

Both Alan and Haldane Bell were seriously wounded in the war, but after the war was over they were able to return to Australia and America respectively. Alan was his dead brother's executor and there was a fourth member of the family, Irene, who lived in Wellington, New Zealand. Eric had died intestate and his records show that his father was credited with £198 from his estate. Dora Bell, their mother, died in 1919 and Edward, their father, in 1920.

On 19 November 1921 the by now Brigadier General Ambrose Ricardo planted one of the tress at Ulster Tower in memory of members of his former battalion. Having survived the war Ricardo died a mysterious death and was found floating in a reservoir by his wife in 1923.

According to Bell's file in the National Archives (WO339/14809) his memorial plaque had to be claimed, as by 1931 it still hadn't been issued to the family. His brother Alan lived in Sydney at the time, but the error was pointed out to the War Office by Irene when she wrote to them in 1930 informing them that she had her late brother's VC and Mons Star but none of his other campaign medals.

Apart from the Thiepval Memorial, Bell's memory is commemorated in a number of ways including being listed on the Regimental Memorial at St Anne's Cathedral, Belfast. He is also remembered on the King's Garden Memorial in Bootle, Liverpool, which was his parents' home town, and with a plaque on his parent's home at 22 University Road. Together with those of other men in his regiment, the Royal Inniskilling Fusiliers, his name is also listed on the County Fermanagh War Memorial (Enniskillen War Memorial) in Belmore Street in County Fermanagh. The memorial, dedicated to the 650 fallen County Fermanagh Servicemen, was blown up by the IRA on 8 November 1987 at a service of remembrance, killing eleven and badly wounding many others. It was rebuilt four years later and rededicated in 1991. Never one to be scared of the threats of Irish terrorists, Prime Minister Margaret Thatcher attended the service. Eleven doves representing the dead and wounded from the 1987 tragedy had been added to the design of the rebuilt memorial. In addition an extra inscription was also added to 'Our Glorious Dead, 1914–1918'. Bell's name is the very first listed in the section which lists the dead from the 9th Royal Inniskilling Fusiliers. His name is also the first mentioned on the VC Memorial Stone at Ulster Tower, unveiled by the Duke of Kent in July 1991.

Bell's VC remained for seventy years with Bell family relatives in New Zealand until 2001. It was then transferred to the Royal Inniskilling Fusiliers Museum in the Castle Keep of Enniskillen Castle.

G.S. CATHER

The 36th (Ulster) Division won four VCs on 1 July 1916; two of them went to the 109th Brigade and two to the 108th Brigade. Three out of the four winners were not to survive the first days of the Somme battle and Lieutenant Geoffrey St George Shillington Cather of the 9th (Service) Battalion, The Royal Irish Fusiliers (County Armagh), 108th Brigade was one of them.

This brigade was the furthest left of the Ulster Division and was also on the north side of the River Ancre. The brigade objective was Beaucourt Station and to the north of it towards Beaucourt village. The station building was, and still is, at the fork of Station Road and Railway Road, with the railway line running parallel to the river. Though some elements of the Ulster Division were to make great progress on this otherwise disastrous day, they were on the south side of the Ancre and then only forced to withdraw through lack of support in their attempts even to reach Grandcourt.

With the 12th Royal Irish Rifles on their left, the 9th Royal Irish Fusiliers began their advance over some 600 yards of no man's land at 7.28am, two minutes before zero hour. Tragically they suffered high casualties even before reaching the gaps in their own wire and follow-ing waves faired no better as they were mown down when their turn came to attempt to reach the ravine. The 12th Royal Irish Rifles were also met with murderous fire in their bid to capture Beaucourt Station. Within two hours the enemy had been restored to their original posi-tions and the battlefield was strewn with the Irish dead and wounded of the 108th Brigade. According to a footnote in the *Official History*:

It was subsequently discovered that a machine-gun which had done much damage was used from the top of a shaft, entered by a tunnel from the bank alongside the railway line in the Ancre valley, like many others, this emplacement was not unmasked until the attack had been launched.

The abortive attack had come to a halt even by 8.00am and it withdrew to its starting positions. It was for his supreme efforts to retrieve wounded men lying out in no man's land and his subsequent death while carrying out this work that 25-year-old Temporary Lieutenant Geoffrey St George Shillingon Cather was later to be awarded a posthumous Victoria Cross. At roll call there were no officers left and only eighty men to respond. Nine officers and 244 other ranks had been either killed or wounded and those who survived returned to Martinsart the next day.

Lt Cather, the battalion adjutant, had gone out in no man's land at night to bring in the wounded. While he worked, heavy German fire continued but by midnight he had brought three men into safety. The next morning he went out again in order to give succour and comfort, but this time was killed at around 10.30am by machine-gun fire. He was buried where he fell, but his body was not recovered after the war and his name is listed on the Thiepval Memorial to the Missing on Pier and Face 15A.

His citation which appeared in the *London Gazette* of 9 September 1916 read as follows:

> For most conspicuous bravery. From 7pm till midnight he searched 'No Man's Land', and brought in three wounded men.
>
> Next morning at 8am he continued his search, brought in another wounded man, and gave water to others, arranging for their rescue later. Finally, at 10.30 am, he took out water to another man, and was proceeding further when he was himself killed.
>
> All this was carried out in full view of the enemy, and under direct machine-gun fire and intermittent artillery fire.
>
> He set a splendid example of courage and self-sacrifice.

George Cather was the son of Mr R.G. Cather of Limpsfield, Surrey and Mrs Margaret Matilda Cather of 26 Priory Road, West Hampstead, NW6. He was born at Christchurch Road,

Streatham Hill on 11 October 1890. He attended Hazelwood School, Limpsfield in September 1900 and after about three years his academic record improved before he went on to Rugby in 1905. He was never prominent at the school and in 1908, when in the Upper Fifth, he had to leave the school when his father died and was unable to complete his studies. The impression that he left was of a shy, retiring and earnest young man. He joined the firm of Joseph Tetley and Co. in the City of London where his father had been a partner.

In January 1909 Cather enlisted as a private in B Company of the 19th (2nd Public Schools) Royal Fusiliers, but resigned in February 1911 having bought himself out as he wished to travel to America for business reasons, and in the following year he visited the United States and Canada and returned in May 1914. On 3 September he was attested and gave his profession as tea planter and was posted to the 2/28th (County of London) Battalion (Artists Rifles). However, as his parents were both from Northern Ireland he applied for a temporary commission on 3 May 1915 with the 9th Battalion, Royal Irish Fusiliers and on the 22nd was discharged having been awarded a commission. The 9th Battalion had originally been The Armagh, Monaghan and Cavan Volunteers and he left with them for France as part of the 36th (Ulster) Division, arriving in Boulogne in October. In November, by now a lieutenant, he became assistant adjutant and full adjutant in December.

By the end of June 1916 his battalion, as part of the 107th Brigade to the north of the River Ancre was in position in front of the village of Hamel.

After his death Cather's colonel wrote to the family as follows:

He heard a man calling out and went over the parapet in broad daylight, gave him water, called out to see if there was anyone else within hail, saw a hand waving feebly, went on and was shot through the head by a machine-gun and killed instantaneously.

So brave and fearless: such a fine character. As an adjutant he was perfectly wonderful, and the battalion has sustained a severe loss by his death....

The battalion chaplain wrote:

...He was one who lived on a very high level, and yet he was always in full sympathy with his fellow creatures, and ready at all times to extend a kindly hand.... We all very much hope that his name will be added to the list of gallant heroes who have gained the VC.

On 31 March 1917 at Buckingham Palace the King presented the decoration to Cather's widowed mother, who was also her son's executrix, and in 1979 Cather's brother, retired Captain Dermot Cather (RN) presented his brother's VC and medals to the Regimental Museum in Armagh. Cather's name was commemorated at Hazelwood School on a plaque in the school chapel until the building was destroyed in the October Hurricane of 1987. The plaque has now been remounted on the wall of the main school building where the chapel once stood. Hazelwood School also has another holder of the VC amongst its former pupils, Captain Percy Howard Hansen who won a VC during the Gallipoli Campaign in August 1915.

Apart from at Hazelwood School, Limpsfield, Surrey, George Cather's memory is also honoured on the VC Memorial in the grounds of the Ulster Tower in Thiepval, the Regimental Memorial in St Anne's Cathedral, Belfast and his VC and medals are held in The Royal Irish Fusiliers Museum.

J.L. GREEN

Going from right to left of the Somme battlefield, Captain John Leslie Green was the last man to be awarded the VC for a deed carried out during the first thirty-six hours of the battle. Green was a medical officer who was attached to the 1/5th Battalion (TF), The Sherwood Foresters (Nottinghamshire & Derbyshire Regiment), 139th (Notts and Derby) Brigade, 46th (North Midland) Division (TF).

The task of the division was to capture Gommecourt Wood on the northern side of Gommecourt village. At the same time the 56th (1/1st London) Division (TF) was to take Gommecourt Park to the south. The two divisions were then to meet up. Although this was the plan, the whole attack was in fact a diversionary attack in order to relieve enemy pressure on the battlefield further southwards. Like most British attacks on 1 July 1916 it ended in total disaster.

On the eve of the battle the 1/5th Sherwood Foresters left Pommier for Fonquevillers, and at midnight moved up into the muddy assembly trenches. On 1 July at 6.25am they moved up to advance trenches and after throwing smoke bombs at 7.25am the battalion moved off in three waves. The fourth wave was delayed, partly because of the density of the smoke and partly because of the withering enemy machine-gun fire from the wood. On the right were the 1/6 Battalion (TF), The Prince of Wales's (North Staffordshire) Regiment and on the left was the 1/7th (Robin Hood) Battalion (TF), The Sherwood Foresters (Nottinghamshire & Derbyshire) Regiment and the two battalions had great difficulty in advancing at all. Many men in the three lines of the 1/5th Sherwood Foresters reached the second line but as the first line had not been cleared it meant that the troops could be shot from behind as well as from the front. Captain Green advanced in the rear of his battalion and on reaching the German wire found a brother officer lying seriously wounded. The officer's name was Captain Robinson and he was the 139th Brigade machine-gun officer. His task was to be responsible for two machine-gun sections of the 1/5th Sherwood Foresters attached to the 139th Machine Gun Company. The machine-gunners were wiped out before covering more than 150 yards and Robinson had gone on and reached the enemy wire where he was wounded and became entangled. Green moved Robinson when they were both under very heavy fire and dragged him into a shell hole where he dressed his wounds. He then carried him back to the British positions and on reaching the advanced trench Robinson was hit again. Once more Green dressed his wounds when he himself was shot in the head and killed. Robinson was eventually brought in but was to die two days later. The 1/5th Sherwood Foresters were relieved at 6.10pm after a day of disaster, their casualties being 491 out of the 734 men that they began the day with. Those men remaining returned to Bienvillers and were in the Bellacourt area for the rest of July.

The chief witness of Green's heroism was Captain Frank Bradbury Robinson of the 1/6th Battalion (TF), The Sherwood Foresters before he died of his wounds on 3 July. He was buried at Warlincourt Halte British Cemetery in Plot I, Row F, Grave 6. The citation for Green's VC was published only five weeks later in the *London Gazette* of 5 August and read:

> For most conspicuous devotion to duty. Although himself wounded, he went to the assistance of an officer who had been wounded and was hung up on the enemy's wire entanglements, and succeeded in dragging him to a shell hole, where he dressed his wounds, notwithstanding that bombs and rifle grenades were thrown at him the whole time.
>
> Captain Green then endeavoured to bring the wounded officer into safe cover, and had nearly succeeded in doing so when he was killed himself.

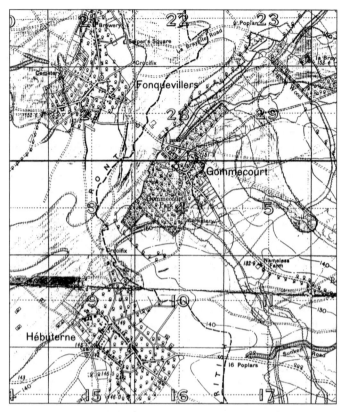

Detail from OS sheet 57D N.E. The 56th Division attacked between the southern edge of Gommecourt Park and the Sunken Road, south of Nameless Farm. (TM 453)

The general commanding 139th Brigade wrote to Green's widow:

Dear Mrs Green,

I have seen the letter you wrote to the officer commanding the 5th Sherwood Foresters, asking for news of your husband. I am deeply grieved to have to tell you that I am afraid that there is no doubt that your husband was killed on 1 July, and that I should like to say how much I feel for you in your sorrow, but at the same time I must express my intense admiration for the manner in which he met his death....

Green was 27 years old when he was killed and his body was buried in Fonquevillers Cemetery Plot III, Row D, Grave 15. His widow, who had been on the staff of Nottingham Hospital, collected the VC from the hands of the King on 7 October. She later remarried and presented her first husband's medals to the RAMC in Aldershot.

Green had a sister and a younger brother, Second Lieutenant Edward Alan Green, who was with the 1/5th South Staffs. He had been killed the previous year on 2 October during the Battle of Loos.

John Leslie Green was born in a house named Coneygarths, which is in the High Street at Buckden in the former county of Huntingdonshire, now part of Cambridgeshire. He was the son of Mr John George Green and Florence May Green. John George was a local landowner and Justice of the Peace.

St Mary's Church, Buckden contains the tombs of many of the Green family. John Leslie Junior was baptised in Buckden Church on 12 January 1889 and was known as Leslie in order to distinguish him from his father. Leslie attended Felsted School (1902–1906) in north Essex and then went up to Cambridge where he studied at Downing College. He obtained Honours in Part 1 of the Natural Sciences Tripos in 1910. He was a keen rower who rowed for his college and an all-round sportsman. He trained for a career in medicine at St Bartholomew's Hospital, London and became house surgeon at Huntingdon County Hospital. In 1913 he qualified and on the outbreak of war in 1914 was commissioned into the Royal Army Medical Corps. He was at first attached to the 1/5th South Staffs and then the Field Ambulance, before transferring to the Sherwood Foresters. On 1 January 1916 he married Miss Edith Mary Nesbitt Moss, who was a fellow doctor and daughter of Mr F.J. Moss of Stainfield Hall, Lincolnshire.

In 1920 Green's father wrote to the Buckden Parish Council and suggested that he would freely donate a memorial to the men of the village who had been killed in the war. For some reason this offer was rejected, but Green went ahead anyway and on land that he owned next to Coneygarths, the family home, he erected a memorial stone in 1921 dedicated to his two sons and also the dead of the village, although only the two names are listed. This memorial fell into decay but was later 'rediscovered' and repaired in time for a service of rededication on 1 July 1986, the 70th anniversary of the Battle of the Somme and Green's death. Opposite the memorial stone and birthplace of Green is Buckden Towers, a former home for the use of the bishops of Lincoln. In the Great War it was used as a military hospital, St Mary's Church where Green was christened has a memorial to the village dead of both wars and so the Green brothers are commemorated twice in the village. Leslie is also listed on the memorial at Downing College, Cambridge.

Felsted School has two former pupils who gained the VC, Walter Hamilton from the Afghan War in 1879 and Leslie Green. There used to be a plaque to their memory in the school chapel, but when the building was modernised in the 1960s the plaque, along with part of the wooden school war memorial, was lost. In the mid-1980s it was felt that the two Felsted VCs should once more be remembered and funds were collected and a new plaque to both men was rededicated on Remembrance Sunday in 1986. One other reminder of Green is the former Huntingdon County Hospital building, which has changed its use but still stands on the outskirts of the town. A plaque to his memory was also put up in the RAMC College, Millbank, London.

S.W. LOUDOUN-SHAND

On 1 July 1916 the 10th (Service) Battalion, The Princess of Wales's Own (Yorkshire) Regiment, 62nd Brigade, 21st Division, known as the Green Howards, was to take part in attempts to capture the enemy-held village of Fricourt. They had been billeted for two days in Buire, south-west of Dernancourt, and on the night before the attack were in reserve positions in front of a copse called Queen's Redoubt, south of Bécourt Wood.

In the initial advance at 7.30am the 62nd Brigade was in frontal positions ready to move forward, but taking part in the second wave of attack was B Company of the 10th Green Howards, led by Temporary Major S.W. Loudoun-Shand. He realised that his men were in difficulty or perhaps plainly reluctant to leave their trenches, and so he immediately leapt onto the parapet to assist them over the top. Moving forward under heavy machine-gun fire Shand helped and cajoled his men, but was soon mortally wounded himself in what were very congested conditions. B Company suffered very heavily during this abortive attack close to Queen's Redoubt, and of five officers and 117 other ranks who had gone into action, only one officer and twenty-seven other ranks survived being killed or wounded. The 12th (Service) Battalion, The Northumberland Fusiliers, a sister battalion of the 10th Green Howards, was ordered forward at midday when they found the ground full of casualties from B Company. The surviving Green Howards moved north-eastwards towards Crucifix Trench where they were to be relieved in the early evening by the 15th (Service) Battalion, Durham Light Infantry, 52nd Brigade, 17th (Northern) Division in Shelter Wood. No real progress

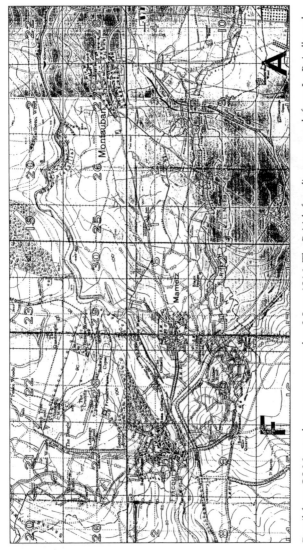

Detail from OS Montauban map, corrected to 2 June 1916. The British frontline runs south from La Boiselle and Sausage Valley to turn east before Fricourt. Montauban is in square S27 (upper right area of the map), Mametz Wood is in S19, and Bernafay Wood is in S28. (TM 442.6 [3])

had been made on the left of the 21st Division, with the 63rd Brigade failing in their attacks against the enemy line to the north of Fricourt and leaving their flanks in the air. However, in the end it made no real difference as on the following day the 17th (Northern) Division entered Fricourt unopposed, only to find the enemy had flown.

In an article which appeared in *The Legion*, former Corporal Harry Fellows of the 12th Northumberland Fusiliers paid tribute to the deeds of Loudoun-Shand:

> The Green Howards led the attack north of Fricourt, with my own battalion in support, some 400 yards to the rear. When the barrage lifted, the German machine-gunners had scrambled from their dugouts, manned the guns and swept a murderous hail of fire across no man's land. With such a savage fire overhead the Green Howards had shown a reluctance to leave the trench. But the major mounted the parapet and urged his men over the top.
>
> Had the Green Howards faltered we should certainly have been called into action to advance over the open ground. It was then that we Northumberland Fusiliers realised the great debt we owed to that one gallant officer. Since that day he has remained my hero of the Great War.

With the circumstances of the day it would have come as no surprise for Loudoun-Shand to be awarded what was a posthumous VC, and the citation for it was published in the *London Gazette* of 9 September 1916:

> For most conspicuous bravery. When his company attempted to climb over the parapet to attack the enemy's trenches, they were met by very fierce machine-gun fire, which temporarily stopped their progress. Major Loudoun-Shand immediately leapt on the parapet, helped the men over it and encouraged them in every way until he fell mortally wounded. Even then he insisted on being propped up in the trench, and went on encouraging the non-commissioned officer and men until he died.

Loudoun-Shand's father attended an investiture at Buckingham Palace on 31 March 1917 in order to receive his son's posthumous VC from the King.

Loudoun-Shand's body was brought back from the line and is buried in Norfolk Cemetery, Becourt. It is in Plot I, Row C, Grave 77. In July 1984 Harry Fellows visited the major's grave and placed a wreath there. This tribute was to be repeated over the following years and the tradition was taken over by his son Michael after his father's death. Harry also wrote verse which included a tribute to Shand's memory and during the early 1980s was a regular attendee at the annual act of remembrance every 1 July at Lochnager Crater, where he used to read his poetry. When he died in 1987 he requested that his ashes should be placed in Mametz Wood.

Stewart Loudoun-Shand was born in Ceylon on 8 October 1879, the second son of Mr and Mrs J. Loudoun-Shand who had five sons and five daughters. The family, whose fortune was derived from tea, had moved to Dulwich in South London and lived at Craigelie, 24 Alleyn Park. The boys went to Dulwich College and Stewart became a distinguished athlete and cricketer. His youngest brother E.G. Shand was later to play for Oxford University Rugby Team and then for Scotland. Stewart left college early and took up an appointment with William Deacon's Bank. When the South African War broke out Stewart enlisted with the London Scottish but was considered too young for active service. He then managed to switch to the Pembroke Yeomanry and served with them throughout the war. In 1901, after eighteen months, he then accepted a post in Port Elizabeth with a mercantile company and stayed three years before returning to a position in Ceylon which his father had procured for him as a tea merchant. When war broke out in 1914 Loudoun-Shand hurried home to England to volunteer and was commissioned into the 10th Yorkshire (Service) Battalion with rank of lieutenant, and the battalion trained at Halton Park and Witley Camp, Godalming, Surrey. He was promoted to captain on 14 June 1915 and temporary major in December and given command of B Company. The battalion landed in France in September and took part in the Battle of Loos, with the result that very heavy casualties led to rapid promotion for Loudoun-Shand, his colonel and two majors having been killed. The orders for the battalion for 1 July 1916 were to attack to the north of Fricourt as part of a planned encircling movement.

Although his VC and war medals, which included the Queen's South Africa Medal (1899–1902) with two Clasps, have been shown in public they are retained by the family; however, the Green Howards Museum is fortunate enough to own the medals of their other three Somme VC holders. Loudoun-Shand's name is listed on the Dulwich College War Memorial and on the family memorial in West Norwood Cemetery.

W.F. McFadzean

During the night of 30 June the 14th (Service) Battalion (Young Citizens), The Royal Irish Rifles(RIR), 109th Brigade, 36th (Ulster) Division moved from Forceville, across the southern causeway over the River Ancre, into Thiepval Wood and up into their assembly trenches known as Elgin Avenue. Arriving there at about 1.00am the battalion was about a 100 yards into the wood behind the divisional frontline on the northern edge of the wood. The frontline faced the German defensive stronghold of the Schwaben Redoubt, which was their objective on high ground looking down in to the valley of the River Ancre.

At about 6.45am and with about forty-five minutes left before the Allies were to lift off their seven day artillery barrage, there occurred what was to be one of the first acts of supreme sacrifice of the first day of the Battle of the Somme. When bombardiers from the Young Citizens were busy priming supplies of grenades, Private William (Billy) McFadzean lifted an ammunition box by its handle, only for it to overturn and spill out some of its bombs onto the ground, two of which lost their pins in the process. It later appeared that some of the boxes had had their ropes cut in order to facilitate speed of distribution, but presumably McFadzean had been unaware of this action. Enemy shells were falling in the vicinity and seemingly without a moment's hesitation and knowing there would be an explosion within four seconds, this gallant young man threw himself down to cover the bombs in order to reduce the impact of the inevitable explosion in the crowded trench. McFadzean was killed instantaneously but in giving his life he had saved the lives of many of his comrades. Even so, the explosion did badly wound two men, including Private George Gillespie who was on McFadzean's left when the incident occurred and later had to have a leg amputated. Some accounts of McFadzean's death state he was blown to pieces and, in addition, when what was left of him was carried away on a stretcher, men removed their helmets in salute to their brave colleague. Many also openly wept.

Half an hour later the battalion moved into the trenches vacated by the 10th Royal Inniskilling Fusiliers and the first or leading groups of the assault did manage to reach the German frontline, but were ruthlessly cut down by enemy machine-gun fire. The Young Citizens witnessed the terrible slaughter in front of them and ten minutes later it was their turn to clamber out of their trenches and go towards their almost certain death.

Not surprisingly Pte McFadzean was awarded a posthumous VC, although he may have only saved some lives for a short time in the light of the high number of casualties recorded that day. The citation for the decoration was published two months later in the *London Gazette* of 9 September 1916 and read:

> For most conspicuous bravery. While in a concentration trench and opening a box of bombs for distribution prior to an attack, when the box slipped down into the trench, which was crowded with men, and two of the safety pins fell out. Private McFadzean, instantly realising the danger to his comrades, with heroic courage threw himself on the top of the bombs.
>
> The bombs exploded blowing him to pieces but only one other man was injured. He well knew the danger, being himself a bomber, but without a moment's hesitation he gave his life for his colleagues.

McFadzean's body was never found and he is commemorated on the Thiepval Memorial (Pier 15 Face A/B).

William Frederick McFadzean was born at Lurgan, County Armagh on 9 October 1895. He was the eldest son of William McFadzean and Mrs McFadzean of Rubicon, Cregagh, Belfast.

The family lived at Cregagh, a Belfast suburb. McFadzean was always known as Billy and he went to school at Mountpottinger National School, and the Trade Preparatory School of the Municipal Technical Institute. He was not considered a model pupil as records show that he was reprimanded for bad conduct no less than thirty-four times during his second year.

On completing his education he was apprenticed to the linen manufacturer, Spence, Bryson & Co., of Great Victoria Street, Belfast, and was paid £20 a year. He was a very keen junior rugby player for the Collegians' Rugby Football Club. Being 6ft in height and weighing 13st, he was ideally suited for the sport.

He became a keen member of the Ulster Volunteer Force, No. 1 Battalion Ballynafeigh and Newtownbreda, East Belfast Regiment, and on 22 September 1914 he joined the 14th Battalion Royal Irish Rifles (Young Citizens) as a private. This was in response to the call to the Volunteers to join a division which was to become the 36th (Ulster) Division. His battalion trained at Finner Camp, Prandalstown before going to England for further training at Seaford and Liphook. The division sailed for France in October 1915.

After Billy's death on 1 July 1916 his father, who was a Belfast JP, received many letters including one from the CO of the 14th Royal Irish Rifles, Lt Col F.C. Bowen dated 16 September 1916:

> It was with feelings of deep pride that I read the announcement of the granting of the VC to your gallant son, and my only regret is that he was not spared to us to wear his well-earned decoration. It was one of the very finest deeds of a war that is so full of big things, and I can assure you that the whole battalion rejoiced when they heard it...

On 15 September 1916 Lt Col R.D. Spencer Chichester, who raised the 14th RIR also wrote:

> I was greatly grieved to hear of his death at the time that I heard of his magnificent and heroic deed. I did not write you then as I knew he was recommended for the Victoria Cross, and I waited to do so till it should have been definitely conferred on him...

The King also wrote on 18 December 1916 and William McFadzean senior was presented with a return third class ticket from Cregagh to London to collect his son's medal. The ceremony took place on 28 February 1917 at Buckingham Palace when the King said:

> I have very great pleasure in presenting to you the Victoria Cross for your son, the late Private McFadzean. I deeply regret that he did not live to receive it personally, but I am sure you are proud of your son; nothing finer has been done in this war for which I have yet given the Victoria Cross, than the act performed by your son in giving his life so heroically to save the lives of his comrades.

Exactly a year after Billy's death a service was held at his church, the Newtownbreda Presbyterian Church, on the outskirts of Belfast in order to commemorate his life. A plaque was also unveiled by Colonel Barlow, DSO, General Staff Officer, Northern District Irish Command. The church service was taken by Reverend Dr Workman, who quoted these words from St John's Gospel: 'Greater love hath no man than this that a man lay down his life for his friends.' In addition to two plaques in St John's Church, Newtownbreda, his name is also included on the war memorial outside the church.

Billy was said to have been a very popular soldier and one to keep up a spirit of cheerfulness, and apparently his favourite song was 'My Little Grey Home in the West' which he was said to have been singing shortly before his death.

His Victoria Cross decoration is usually kept in a bank vault but in 1989 his nephew, also a William, took it to France with him when on a short trip to the battlefields.

Over the years McFadzean has become a folk hero in Ulster and is certainly by far the most well-known member of the Ulster Division to win a VC. It is comes as no surprise then to learn that his brief life has been commemorated in so many ways. Apart from having his name listed on the panels of the Thiepval Memorial to the Missing, he has been remembered in ballad form and in other ways as well. In 1997 a plaque to his memory was erected on his parents house in Cregagh Road by the Castleneagh Council of County Antrim; his name is included on a memorial stone to VC holders from the 36th (Ulster) Division erected at Ulster Tower in Thiepval and unveiled on 1 July 1991; he has a plaque in the Castlereagh Council Offices; and his name is one of those listed on the Regimental Memorial in St Anne's Cathedral in Belfast. In Lurgan, as well as being included in the memorial in the old town hall, he is also remembered elsewhere in the town with a room named after him in the Royal British Legion Home. A mural linked with his death is also to be found in East Belfast. Lastly his VC and medals are in the collection of the Royal Ulster Rifles Museum.

In the 1920s Billy's parents desperately searched for their son's grave but without success. Seventy years later in a conversation with the author, when we were both billeted in Grandcourt in 1991, Billy's nephew, named after his famous uncle, always assumed that his uncle's remains were in Connaught Cemetery, Thiepval but there is no proof that this was so nor can the Commonwealth War Graves Commission provide any evidence to support the theory. Finally in recent years attempts have been made in Thiepval Wood to identify the spot where Billy McFadzean gave his life for his colleagues.

R. QUIGG

The fourth man of the 36th (Ulster) Division to win the Victoria Cross and the only one of the four who lived to wear it was Robert Quigg. Like Cather and McFadzean he was involved with saving life rather than with killing the enemy. He was a member of the 12th (Service) Battalion (Central Antrim), The Royal Irish Rifles, 108th Brigade, 36th (Ulster) Division, who were left of Thiepval Wood and attacked a section of the line on the north side of the River Ancre. The battalion was without B Company who were attached to the 9th (Service) Battalion, The Royal Irish Fusiliers (Princess Victoria's). Leading waves of the 12th Battalion moved forwards in a north-easterly direction towards their objective, Beaucourt Station, but were severely hampered by enemy machine-gun fire. Quigg, having advanced three times with his platoon, learnt early next morning that Sir Harry Macnaghten, whose batman he was as well as platoon commander, had twice regrouped his remaining men in no man's land and lead them against gaps in the enemy wire before falling himself. Quigg immediately went out into no man's land to search for Sir Harry and although he went out seven times he failed to find him. Instead, on each occasion he brought in a wounded man, the last being on a waterproof sheet. Sir Harry's body was never found.

Quigg's citation for the VC was published in the *London Gazette* of 9 September as follows:

For most conspicuous bravery. He advanced to the assault

with his platoon three times. Early next morning, hearing a rumour that his platoon officer was lying out wounded, he went out seven times to look for him under heavy shell and machine-gun fire, each time bringing back a wounded man. The last man he dragged in on a waterproof sheet from within a few yards of the enemy's wire.

He was seven hours engaged in this most gallant work, and finally was so exhausted that he had to give it up.

As has previously been noted, Quigg was one of four men from the Ulster Division to win a VC on 1 July 1916, and the deeds and heroism of the Ulster battalions have gone down in history as one of the finest achievements in what had been a day of disaster for the British Army – a day which had no precedent with previous military disasters.

Robert Quigg was born on 12 March 1885 at Ardihennon, Cornkirk, Giants Causeway, Northern Ireland. His father, whose name was also Robert, was a boatman and tourist guide on the Causeway. Robert junior attended the Giants Causeway National School and became a farm labourer on the Macnaghten Estate. Sir Harry, whose life Robert was to try and save on 1 July 1916, was born in 1896. In September 1914 Quigg joined the Royal Irish Rifles (Central Antrim) as a private and Macnaghten joined as a second lieutenant. They left for England with the rest of the 36th (Ulster) Division in October 1915 and unlike most recipients of the VC Quigg did not go to Buckingham Palace but to York Cottage, Sandringham, Norfolk on 8 January 1917. It was reported that the King, after congratulating him, asked Quigg whether he was married and received the reply: 'No Sir, but after what has happened to me I suppose I soon will be.' This rejoinder very much amused the King, who Quigg was later to have described 'as a brave wee man'. On his return to Bushmills, his parish, he was given a great reception for not only trying to save the life of the local squire but also of course for winning what was to be one of the four Somme VCs for the Ulster Division. At a reception at Hamill Hotel, Bushmills, Quigg was presented with £200 in Exchequer Bonds. Sir Harry's mother, Lady Macnaghten presented him with a gold watch as a mark of appreciation. Later when he was hard up he was to sell this watch for £100.

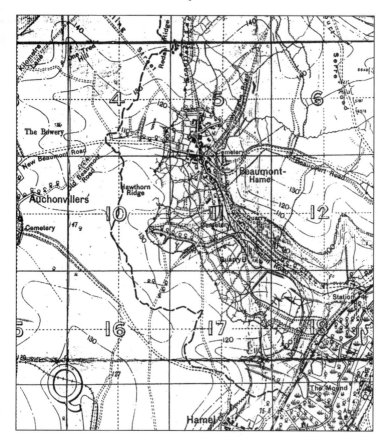

Detail from OS sheet 57D N.E, 16 May 1916, west of Beaumont Hamel. Y Ravine is in the lower right of square 10. (TM 453)

After 1916 Quigg served in Mesopotamia and Egypt, reaching the rank of sergeant. He served in the whole of the war but later was declared as not reaching Army Physical Requirements. In 1926 he had an accident which left him partially paralysed, having fallen 50ft from a third storey window in a soldiers' home in Belfast. He was finally discharged in 1934 and continued working as a civilian in the Regimental Depot in Armagh. He then became a boatman on the Causeway as his father had been before him, dealing with the many visitors who still visited the area. After the war his figure was used as a model for the local war memorial and he spent the rest of his life in a cottage on the Macnaghten estate. He never married.

He did attend Armistice Day services and in 1929 travelled to London to attend the VC Reunion Dinner held in the House of Lords.

In 1953 Queen Elizabeth II visited Ulster when Quigg was presented to her. In May 1954 at Ulster Hall he was one of five Northern Irishmen who had won the VC to be presented with a silver tankard. A picture of this group taken by a local newspaper tells us more about what sort of man Quigg was than a hundred words does! He died at the age of 70 at Dalriada Hospital, Ballycastle, on 14 May 1955 and was buried close to Billy Parish Church in the Protestant Cemetery (Church of Ireland) near Bushmills, on the Portrush side. At his funeral there was an escort party of fifty men from the Royal Ulster Rifles Depot. Quigg's oak coffin was draped with the Union Jack and his decorations were carried separately. A bugler played the Last Post and Reveille. At the time of his death Quigg was survived by a brother and four sisters.

In 1958 at the instigation of the Royal British Legion a simple granite headstone was placed on Quigg's grave and unveiled by the Lord Lieutenant of County Antrim, Lord Rathcavan on 16 November. There was a large attendance of the Royal Ulster Rifles and of former comrades. His nine decorations included, apart from the VC, the 1914–15 Star, the British War Medal, Victory Medal, General Service Medal with Clasp, Silver Jubilee Medal 1935, Coronation Medals from 1937 and 1953, the Medal of the Order of St George of Russia (4th Class) and the Croix de Guerre. They are all held in the Royal Ulster Rifles Museum, Belfast.

Quigg's name is commemorated on the VC memorial at the Ulster Tower, Thiepval; the Victoria Cross memorial on the Regimental Memorial in St Anne's Cathedral, Belfast and on the Bushmills War Memorial.

As a postscript, not only did Sir Edward C. Macnaghten lose his 20-year-old son Sir E. Harry in the Battle of the Somme, but also his other son Sir A. Douglas, aged 19, who was a second lieutenant with the 8th Rifle Brigade and was killed on 15 Sept 1916 when leading his platoon near Delville Wood.

W. RITCHIE

On the extreme left of the positions of the 36th (Ulster) Division was the right flank of the 29th Division, whose task it was to capture the Y Ravine and the southern section of the village of Beaumont Hamel on 1 July. On their left was the 4th Division whose mission was to capture the ground to the north of this village and the Redan positions.

Drummer Ritchie was a member of the 2nd Battalion, The Seaforth Highlanders (Ross-shire Buffs), The Duke of Albany's, 10th Brigade, 4th Division. The other two brigades in the division were the 11th and the 12th. The 11th Brigade was to go forward with its immediate objective being Munich Trench, the last trench in the enemy frontline system. The 10th and the 12th brigades were to move forward slightly after having given the 11th brigade time to capture their objective. These following brigades were to go through the lines of the 11th – that was the plan.

For two hours prior to 7.30am, intense British artillery fire was concentrated on the German positions and at zero hour the 11th Brigade moved off in waves. An hour and a quarter later no message had been received by the following brigades and they moved off, including the 2nd Seaforth Highlanders. There was very heavy machine-gun fire from the enemy front and it became obvious to observers that the 11th Brigade had failed to reach its objective and had been ruthlessly cut down. Communication was almost non-existent and in mid-morning, when the third line was being evacuated, men of various units were drifting back to the Allied positions. Officer casualties were very high and the men became virtually leaderless.

Drummer Ritchie had disobeyed the standard instruction to leave all musical instruments behind before an attack and clambered onto the top of a German trench where he repeatedly sounded the 'Charge' in an attempt to stem the tide of British troops drifting back to their own trenches. This action together with his conduct throughout the day was to gain him the Victoria Cross. The necessary eyewitnesses of Ritchie's bravery were Captain J. Laurie and Lieutenant Colonel J.O. Hopkinson, who were the adjutant and the officer commanding respectively. At the end of the day these two officers, two wounded officers and about eighty other ranks were all the survivors left from the Seaforths. They had been relieved by the 1st Royal Irish Fusiliers at a position known as The Quadrilateral and withdrew to the sunken Beaumont Hamel–Serre Road and then to bivouacs behind the village of Mailly-Maillet. Casualties totalled 394. Next day they were inspected by the corps commander, Lieutenant General Sir Aylmer Hunter Weston.

Ritchie's VC citation was published in the *London Gazette* of 9 September:

> For most conspicuous bravery and resource, when on his own initiative he stood on the parapet of an enemy trench, and under heavy machine-gun fire and bomb attacks, repeatedly sounded the 'Charge', thereby rallying many men of various units, who, having lost their leaders, were wavering and beginning to retire.
>
> This action showed the highest type of courage and personal initiative.
>
> Throughout the day Drummer Ritchie carried messages over fire-swept ground, showing the greatest devotion to duty.

Later he commented 'that if things had gone the other way he would have been court-martialled and not decorated'. He received the VC from the hands of the King on 25 November 1916.

Walter Potter Ritchie was born at 81 Hopefield Road, Glasgow on 27 March 1892. His father's name was also Walter and his mother's maiden name was Helen Monteith Murphy. After leaving school he was apprenticed briefly to a blacksmith and was an ardent member of the Episcopal Church at Troon in Glasgow.

He joined the 8th Scottish Rifles when underage and in August 1908, at the age of 16, transferred to the 2nd Seaforth Highlanders as a drummer. He was a member of the original British Expeditionary Force and took part in the Battle of Mons and the Battle of the Aisne in September, and was wounded in October 1914 in a village just outside Armentières. Later in the war the battalion moved down to the Somme sector and spent a lot of time in the village of Mailly-Maillet before the 'Big Push'. After being presented with the VC in November 1916 Ritchie returned to Glasgow, arriving at St Enoch Station at 8pm on 26 or 27 November. He was met by a group of friends but did not want to expand on information about his exploit. 'If you were to drop a Jack Johnson at ma feet', he observed, 'you couldna' mak' me speak'.

He was wounded in 1917 and before the end of the war was gassed twice and wounded twice more. He always carried his bugle, although buglers had ceased to be employed early in the war. After the war he joined the 1st Seaforths at Belfast in July 1921 and was promoted to the rank of sergeant, and appointed drum major of the battalion. On 11 November he was a member of the VC Honour Guard for the Unknown Warrior at Westminster Abbey. He held the position of drum major until he left the Army in 1929 and later became a recruiting officer in Glasgow. He died at West Saville Terrace, Mayfield in Edinburgh on 17 March 1965 at the age of 72. He was c-remated three days later at the Warriston Crematorium and his ashes were placed in Niche C-20, which no longer exists. The bugle that he sounded the 'Charge' with is now at the Queen's Own Highlanders Museum, Fort George, Inverness. In 1970 his decorations came up for sale at Sothebys and were sold for £1,700. Eleven years later they were put on the market again, this time in Australia and are in private hands.

G. SANDERS

The 1/7th Battalion (TF), The Prince of Wales' Own (West Yorkshire) Regiment was part of the 146th Brigade, 49th (West Riding) Division (TF). At the beginning of the Battle of the Somme the role of the division was to provide support to the 36th (Ulster) Division and the 32nd Division.

The headquarters of the 1/7th West Yorks, together with its sister battalion the 1/8th West Yorks, was at Belfast City in Aveluy Wood. They were due east of the Leipzig Salient, which was to be the only position on the north side of the River Ancre that the British captured and then held on the first day of the battle.

During the opening day of the battle on 1 July, the 1/7th being one of the battalions from the 32nd Division that was ordered up to assist the 36th (Ulster) Division in its attempt to capture the extremely strongly-held position, the Schwaben Redoubt. At around 8.30pm, a company of the 1/7th and 1/8th West Yorks battalions provided a defensive flank that faced north at the Schwaben Redoubt in order to assist the 107th Brigade of the 36th (Ulster) Division already there. There was confusion and when darkness fell the two West Yorks companies withdrew. There had been many casualties amongst the officers and the other ranks.

During this withdrawal, a group of about thirty men under the leadership of Corporal George Sanders found themselves isolated in a position north-west of the Schwaben Redoubt near Thiepval Wood, which the frontline ran in front of. Sanders set about organising their defences and next morning the group drove off an enemy attack and even rescued some Allied troops, who had been previously captured, and gave sustenance to others. The men were relieved on the morning of the 3rd and the corporal managed to get his party back to safety in Aveluy Wood, and later Martinsart Wood. At this time Thiepval and Aveluy Woods had become an absolute nightmare of war and confusion. Many of the front-line trenches had been smashed by the German artillery and the wounded were clustered together for support.

Sanders was later awarded the VC and the citation for it was published in the *London Gazette* of 9 September:

> For most conspicuous bravery. After an advance into the enemy's trenches, he found himself isolated with a party of thirty men. He organised his defences, detailed a bombing party and impressed on his men that his and their duty was to hold the position at all costs.
>
> Next morning he drove off an attack by the enemy and rescued some prisoners who had fallen into their hands. Later, two strong bombing attacks were driven off. On the following day he was relieved, after showing the greatest courage, determination and good leadership during 36 hours under trying conditions.
>
> All the time his party was without food and water, having given all their water to the wounded during the first night. After the relieving force was firmly established, he brought his party, nineteen strong, back to our trenches.

George Sanders was the son of Thomas and Amy Sanders of 3 Shand Grove, Holbeck, Leeds. He was born at New Wortley, Leeds on 8 July 1894, the youngest in a family of seven, and his mother was to die when he was 9 years old. He attended Little Holbeck School and became a choirboy at St John's Church. When he left school he became a fitter's apprentice at the Airedale Foundry. On 9 November 1914 he enlisted in the Leeds Rifles, which was the 1/7th West Yorkshire Battalion, 49th (West Riding) Division, and he soon left for France. The division endured many casualties during an enemy gas attack to the south of Boesinge. From early February 1916 elements began to arrive on the Somme area. On 30 June the battalion arrived on the west side of the River Ancre and moved up to positions in

Aveluy Wood. They were north of the main track in the wood which led to Martinsart.

When Sanders' award of the VC was announced in September 1916 he became the third Leeds man to gain the distinction and the first Leeds Territorial to be awarded the decoration. On 14 November he returned to Leeds for the first time since his award was announced, and by this time he had been promoted from corporal to sergeant. His family were only warned of his arrival the day before and there was little time to organise a welcoming ceremony. Nevertheless, a large crowd turned out to greet the 'local hero' at the Midland Station platform including his family and his former colleagues at the Airedale Foundry. Sanders wore the ribbon of the VC on his breast and had a wound stripe on his arm. He was given three cheers and when he emerged into the City Square, the crowd was much larger. He was taken to the town hall where he was greeted by the Lord Mayor. He was, according to the *Yorkshire Evening Post*:

> Like most other heroes, not too willing to refer to the deed which won him fame, but he did mention that out of the thirty-two men who went into the trench only nineteen came out of it.... Five of them got Military Medals, however, and unfortunately one, Cpl Kirk, has since been killed.

Although on the 14th he was seemingly unaware of when he was to be awarded his VC, he actually travelled to London on the 18th in order to receive his decoration at Buckingham Palace. It emerged that he had been recommended for the VC by the commanding officer of the Royal Irish Rifles, whom Sanders' men were supporting, and not by his own commanding officer, Lieutenant Colonel A.E. Kirk who, nevertheless, was delighted when he heard the news of the award. He wrote as follows:

> They went up gallantly and suffered heavy losses. All the officers out of Sanders' platoon had gone, and he took command of the platoon and held on and organised a fine resistance.

A few days later Sanders was back in Leeds for a more formal reception from the City Council. This time he was greeted and thanked in public by the Lord Mayor on the steps of the Town Hall. There was again a large crowd which this time included a

Guard of Honour. The council were keen to award Sanders with a gift or donation, but at this time the War Office had forbidden soldiers from receiving gifts of money. The council were therefore going to think up an alternative.

Sanders was commissioned on 27 June 1917 and gazetted to the 2nd Prince of Wales' Own (West Yorkshire) Regiment, attached to the 1/6th Battalion. He was made acting captain on 15 December. By April his battalion were back in the Ypres sector and he became a prominent figure in the fighting during the German attack of April 1918 and was taken prisoner at Kemmel Hill on 25 April. Sanders had been wounded in the leg and right arm and had used his left arm for carrying his revolver, but was later posted missing. Three months later, however, his family heard from him at Limburg where he had been taken as a prisoner of war. He was repatriated on Boxing Day 1918 and demobilised on 20 March the following year. In his absence he had been awarded the MC.

After the war Sanders worked on the staff of the Meadow Lane gasworks, which was then under the management of Leeds Corporation and was later taken over by the North-Eastern Gas Board. On 13 November 1921 Sanders was invited to unveil a memorial to the memory of the Leeds Rifles which had been erected on the edge of the churchyard of St Peter's, Kirkgate, Leeds. The regiment was the only one to choose Sir Edwin Lutyens to design a memorial incorporating his War Cross. Captain Sanders was also one of eight Leeds pallbearers on 16 November 1929 at the funeral of John Raynes VC at Harehills Cemetery, Leeds. In the Second World War he was the officer commanding the Home Guard at the Gas Works.

Sanders died at the age of 55 at St James' Hospital, Leeds on 4 April 1950 after a long illness. His home was at Stratford Street, Dewsbury Road.

Sanders was given a full military funeral and four other VC holders attended the service. Three volleys were fired as the coffin left the chapel and two regimental buglers sounded the Last Post and Reveille. The coffin was draped with the Union Jack and Sanders' VC and medals were carried by his former sergeant major, Mr Frank Stembridge. Apart from his family, those present were the Leeds Rifles Old Comrades Association, the Home Guard, the British Legion and the Leeds Group of the North-East Gas Board. A firing party had been chosen from the 45th Battalion, Royal Tank Regiment (TA), who were descendants of the 7th (Leeds Rifles) Battalion, West Yorkshire Regiment. After the funeral on 6 April Sanders' body was cremated at the Cottingley Crematorium, Leeds and his ashes scattered on Lawn One.

His widow Nellie Sanders retained her husband's medals, which are in private hands. Sanders was commemorated in the New Leeds Rifles (TA) Museum at Carlton Old Barracks, Leeds.

In the memorial gardens in Leeds, on The Headrow side of Cookridge Street, are various memorials including one to the Victoria Cross holders who were born or buried in Leeds. It is outside the Henry Moore Institute and was unveiled in November 1992. Sanders' name is one of seventeen inscribed on it. The Leeds War Memorial had been moved to this site in 1937 from a site in the City Square and the original Winged Angel atop the cenotaph is a replacement.

J.Y. TURNBULL

By the eve of the first day of the Battle of the Somme, Sergeant James Turnbull had been a sergeant for seven or eight months serving with the 17th Battalion, The Highland Light Infantry, 97th Brigade, 32nd Division. The battalion had spent the night before billeted in huts in Bouzincourt, and then moved up to the frontline at 6.25am via trenches between Aveluy and Authuille Woods.

At the outbreak of war he had joined one of the Glasgow battalions, which in turn became the 17th Highland Light Infantry Battalion and owing to his pre-war training he rose rapidly to the rank of sergeant. He had a brother named Gavin who served with the Royal Engineers, and another was attached to the Canadian pay department in London.

The task of the 32nd Division was to capture and hold the Leipzig Salient, north of Authuille Wood, a position of great importance to the enemy and whose trenches overlooked the British positions from three sides. The task of capturing this position not only looked formidable but virtually impossible; nevertheless, the battalion did storm the position but were forced to retire later in the day. Sergeant Turnbull never wavered in his single-minded role which he played in the attempt to capture the Salient, but sadly he was not to survive the day.

We are fortunate in having an eyewitness account of what happened to Turnbull, which was first published in the *Glasgow Herald* of 28 November 1916. The article was based on an interview with a colleague of the sergeant, Lance-Corporal McKechnie:

It was during a recent attack that Turnbull performed his brave deed. He was one of the first to go over the parapet, and I was near him all the time, an eyewitness of what he did. We took the first line of German trenches fairly easily and when we were passing through there, Turnbull who was always on the alert, noticed a large German bomb store which had been abandoned. He indicated the store as we passed on and shouted out that in the event of our running short of bombs he would send some of the men back to the place. He was a fellow who always took charge of affairs, but we all had the greatest confidence in his judgement. We got held up at the second line trenches, which were flanked on either side by redoubts. Turnbull's party, of which I was a member, were told to attack the redoubt which was on our left flank. We met with considerable opposition. Turnbull had a splendid physique and was almost fearless. He was a fine cricketer, and it was possibly this that made him such an expert bomber. He could throw a bomb further than any other man in the battalion. At the beginning the fighting was pretty fierce, and we had to 'carry on' for about fourteen hours. Most of the men were exhausted by that time. The Germans were threatening to outflank us and this would have meant the cutting off of the complete battalion. Sergeant Turnbull however saved the situation by his initiative. He kept men carrying bombs to him, and he continued the bombing on his own until our own supply ran short. Then his foreknowledge of the German bomb store behind proved of value. Men were sent back to bring in bombs from this place. Occasionally if he ran short of bombs, and the men had not returned in time, he seized hold of a machine-gun and played it on the Germans. He kept this up for about sixteen hours, practically holding up the whole of the German flank and saving the battalion. Our position was held in this way until the battalion was relieved, and it was practically all due to Turnbull's courage and tenacity. His stamina was really remarkable, as most of the others were quite fagged out with what they had gone through. He was killed not long after that, during a momentary lull. With his usual activity he had been hustling around to see what was happening, and when he was crossing from the redoubt to behind a second line trench, a sniper got him.

The *Regimental History* tells a similar story:

> At 7.30am the 17th HLI on the right and the 16th HLI on the left crept out of their trenches and moved close up to the German wire under cover of the barrage. This was by order of the brigade commander, Brigadier General J.B. Jardine, as an alternative to the usual practice at that time of advancing in extended waves. The 17th HLI had no luck this day. When they rose up they immediately came under heavy enfilade fire from the ruins of Thiepval; the wire was intact but for the occasional gaps which were covered.... They had with them sappers, carrying Bangalore torpedoes, for it had been realised that the barrage had not been effective on the wire in this sector, but they were all shot down on the wire.... The 17th HLI pushed on towards the second line, but the failure on their left exposed their flank and the leading companies were all shot down. The remainder consolidated the first line, the Leipzig Redoubt, and held it. Their casualties were 22 officers and 447 other ranks. They gained a Victoria Cross, posthumous: Sergeant James Yuill Turnbull.

Turnbull was described as 'being very popular with the men' and as 'a strong forthright personality.' Lieutenant A.N. Drysdale in a letter to Turnbull's father paid a tribute to his abilities as a platoon sergeant, and referred to the deep regret felt by the whole battalion. The battalion withdrew to Crucifix Corner the following day, having suffered very high casualties and two weeks later the battalion moved northwards to the Bethune sector.

Turnbull was buried at the Lonsdale Cemetery close to Authuille Wood in Plot IV, Row G, Grave 9. His posthumous decoration was announced four months later in the *London Gazette* of 25 November.

> For most conspicuous bravery and devotion to duty, when, having with his party captured a post apparently of great importance to the enemy, he was subjected to severe counter-attacks, which were continuous throughout the whole day. Although his party was wiped out and replaced several times during the day, Sergeant Turnbull never wavered in his determination to hold the post, the loss of which would have been

very serious. Almost single-handed, he maintained his position, and displayed the highest degree of valour and skill in the performance of his duties.

Later in the day this very gallant soldier was killed whilst bombing a counter-attack from the parados of our trench.

His posthumous VC was presented to Turnbull's father and sister at Buckingham Palace on 2 May 1917.

James Turnbull, a master joiner and well known in Glasgow business circles, married Elizabeth Dunlop in the city on 29 December 1870. The couple were to have three sons, all of whom were to play a role in the Great War.

James Turnbull Junior was born on 24 December 1883 at 49 Park Road, Glasgow and given the family name of Yuill as his middle name. He was educated at Albert Road Academy, Glasgow and on leaving school was employed for a time by Wallace Scott & Co., a firm of wholesale specialist tailors. He later transferred to Messrs Wm. Chalmers of Oban. James grew up into a very tall man and was always known as 'Jimmy'. He was a keen amateur footballer and trained with the Glasgow Third Lanark Volunteers.

On the outbreak of war Turnbull joined the 3rd of the Glasgow battalions, which in turn formed the 17th Highland Light Infantry battalion and, assisted by his pre-war training, rose quickly to the rank of sergeant.

The whereabouts of the decoration is unknown but must be in private hands.

A. CARTON DE WIART

The village of La Boisselle was a very strongly held German position to the north-east of Albert and to the south of the main Albert–Bapaume Road. The French Army had lost control of the village in early 1915. Any troops attacking it from the direction of Becourt would have to advance along Sausage Valley, through no man's land and into the German trench system to the south-east of the village. Despite the blowing of a huge mine at Lochnagar just before the battle began on 1 July, as well as the previous seven days of Allied bombardment, the 34th Division was ruthlessly cut down in its attempts to capture the village. The enemy had not been visible to the naked eye as he had been sensibly concealed underground in strong dugouts.

After the subsequent retirement of the division, which had been in the frontline for two days, it was relieved by its supporting division, the 19th, which was also given the task of capturing the village. The division contained three infantry brigades: the 56th, 57th and 58th. The 8th (Service) Battalion, the Gloucestershire Regiment was part of the 57th Brigade, and their commanding officer was Adrian Carton de Wiart who already had the reputation of being very courageous soldier and was about to add to his reputation by winning a Victoria Cross.

At the start of the battle the 8th Glosters had moved from the village of Millencourt to the Intermediate Line to the north of Albert. Later on, on 1 July, they moved up to a valley close to the Albert–Pozières Road. At 10pm they moved again, to the trenches in the Tara–Usna Line where they remained for the night, and all through the next day. At 1.30am on the 3rd, when the line ran through the ruins of La Boisselle Church, the battalion moved forward to attack via St Andrew's Trench and at 3.15am they attacked La Boisselle and consolidated their positions. They remained there all day and night and in the bitter fighting for the village had six officers killed.

The other battalions in the 57th Brigade involved in the heavy fighting for the capture of the village had been the 10th (Service) Battalion, The Worcestershire Regiment, the 8th (Service) Battalion, The Prince of Wales's (North Staffordshire) Regiment and the 10th (Service) Battalion, The Royal Warwickshire Regiment. The brigade had attacked from the north of the village, whilst their sister brigade, the 58th, had attacked from the south.

At 11am the enemy, which had been considerably reinforced, attacked the 57th Brigade, and the Glosters were forced back to a line about halfway through the village. At around 12.30pm the situation for the British was absolutely critical, but the 57th Brigade were strong enough to hold onto the position which was marked by a hedge. It was felt that if the line had given way then the whole village would undoubtedly have been lost. That the line did hold was due in large measure to the gallantry of Lieutenant Colonel A. Carton de Wiart. He was not only the commanding officer of the 8th Glosters but, as the commanders of the 8th N. Staffs and of the 10th Worcesters had been killed and the commanding officer of the 10th Warwicks wounded, he had now become responsible for the whole of 57th Brigade. Carton de Wiart took a very active part in the fighting himself and this included drawing the pins out of grenades with his teeth! In time the 19th Division was to complete the capture of La Boisselle by the end of 4 July.

At 9am on the 4th, the 8th Glosters had moved into the support line called Ryecroft Street and at 5pm moved back into the village where they occupied the former German dugouts. On the 5th they held the support line all day before leaving by the main road for Albert, where they arrived at billets close to the railway station. Apart from their loss of six officers killed they also had fourteen wounded and the casualties amongst the other ranks were 302. On the 9th they returned to bivouacs at Millencourt.

Carton de Wiarts's citation was published in the *London Gazette* of 9 September 1916 and was as follows:

For most conspicuous bravery, coolness and determination during severe operations of a prolonged nature. It was owing in great measure to his dauntless courage and inspiring example that a serious reverse was averted.

He displayed the utmost energy and courage in forcing our attack home. After three other battalion commanders had become casualties, he controlled their commands, and ensured that the ground won was maintained at all costs.

He frequently exposed himself in all organisation of positions and of supplies, passing unflinchingly through fire barrage of the most intense nature. His gallantry was inspiring to all.

Carton de Wiart was presented his VC by the King at Buckingham Palace on 29 November 1916.

Adrian Carton de Wiart was the son of a Belgian lawyer, Leon Carton de Wiart and born on 5 May 1880. One of his cousins was Count Henri Carton de Wiart, a one time prime minister, and another was a political secretary to King Leopold II. In Adrian's childhood his father went to Egypt to practice law and became a naturalised British subject. The family then spent time in England while Count Henri waited to take up his post in Cairo in 1883, where he specialised in international law and becoming a British subject. In 1891 Adrian went to the Oratory School, Edgbaston where he became captain in most of the school sports. In the late 1880s Adrian's mother died and his father married again in 1888. By this time Adrian was already fluent in several languages and went to study law at Balliol College in 1898, having had to sit the entrance exams twice. He failed his preliminary law exams, but academic failure was expunged by the timely start of the South African War. By now he realised that his ambition was to be a soldier and having been born in Belgium, he was naturally on the side of the Boers. He was underage and his father forbade him to enlist, so Adrian decided to enlist anyway and, giving a false name, he joined the Middlesex Yeomanry (Duke of Cambridge's Hussars) in 1899 and left for Cape Town after training. He caught a fever but soon after was heavily involved in the conflict, where he was shot in the groin and stomach and was awarded the Queen's Medal with three Clasps. While in hospital the truth about his identity emerged and he returned to Balliol. By now his father realised for himself where his son's future lay and from then on supported his choice of a military career.

Adrian returned to South Africa and this time enlisted as a trooper in the Imperial Light Horse, and in 1901 was commissioned into the Second Imperial Light Horse, but six months later he switched to the 4th Dragoon Guards, joining them in India in March 1902. In 1905 he was made ADC to the lieutenant general in South Africa from 29 July 1905 to 21 October 1905 and then ADC to the GOC, Chief, South Africa from 1 November 1905 until 18 March 1908 when he returned to England and re-joined his regiment. In 1910 he was promoted to captain and became adjutant in the Gloucestershire Yeomanry from January 1912 to July 1914, when he left for Somaliland and joined the Camel Corps. It was during this period of his career that he lost an eye.

He was Mentioned in Despatches and on 5 May 1914 and appointed to the DSO for distinguished service in the field against the Dervish Forces at Shimber Beris, Somaliland.

Carton de Wiart had married the Contessa Frederica Fugger in 1908, by whom he was to have two daughters.

He was 34 years of age when the Great War began and he rejoined the 4th Dragoons in Flanders. Almost immediately he was wounded in the left hand, which had to be amputated. After leave to recover he returned to France and transferred to the Loyal North Lancs Battalion, and then took command of the 8th Glosters who were both part of the 19th (Western) Division.

After winning the VC at La Boisselle, his battalion was one of the many who were to be involved in the several attempts to capture High Wood. It was during the battalion's involvement that he was wounded in the skull and taken down from the dressing station by barge to Corbie. After convalescence he returned again to his battalion in France, and found himself once more near High Wood where he recovered his stick which he had left when wounded! Later he was wounded again by a shell splinter and, after sick leave, was given the command of the 8th N. Staffs who went into the line opposite Hébuterne. He later took command of the 12th Brigade, 4th Division, which was involved in the Arras fighting in April 1917 and later in the fight for the Passchendaele Ridge. He was wounded twice more and posted to a Bantam Division. After the Amistice, having been wounded seriously in the war on eight occasions, he was given a brigade of the 38th (Welsh) Division to command.

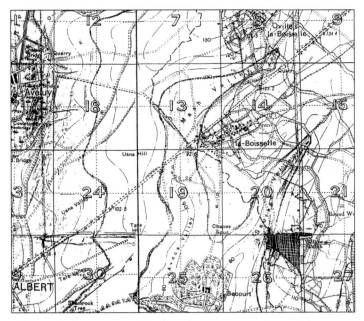

Detail from OS sheet 57D N.E. La Boisselle is in square 14, with Mash Valley to the north and Sausage Valley to the south. The Tara–Usna Ridge runs from north to south on the edge of squares 13 and 19. German trenches are shown as crenellated lines and barbed wire as rows of crosses. The British frontline is shown by dashes (see square 7 for example). (TM 453)

In February 1919 he was sent to join the British Mission in Poland, where he was second-in-command to General Botha before taking over as leader. He was to remain in the country for twenty years, before the coming of the Second World War meant a return to England. Once back home he was given the command of the 61st Division, a Midland territorial formation based in Oxford in which the 7th Glosters were serving. He was sent in command of a force to Norway in April 1940 which was given the impossible task of capturing Trondheim. A year later he was off to Jugoslavia in order to head his third Military Mission. Unfortunately his

Wellington aeroplane suffered loss of engine power and came down off the Libyan coast. Carton de Wiart had to swim for his life and was subsequently captured by the Italians. He was kept captive near Florence and managed to escape but was recaptured. In August 1943 he was set free in order to represent Italy in Lisbon during their surrender negotiations. He then returned to England. In October he went to China as Mr Churchill's personal representative to General Chiang Kai-shek. He was three years in China but while there had a fall which damaged his back and he subsequently spent seven months in hospital.

He was presented with an Honorary MA at Oxford University in December 1947 and a similar award at Aberdeen University. Carton de Wiart's wife died in 1949 and he married Mrs Joan Sutherland in 1951 and went to live in Ireland at the age of 71. He bought Aghinagh House in Killinardrish, County Cork and stayed in Galway while the house was being repaired. His links with Ireland were through his grandmother. In 1950 he published his autobiography called *Happy Odyssey* without the aid of any notes or diaries as they had been left behind in Poland in 1939. He occasionally travelled to London for service reunions and died at home on 5 June 1963 at the age of 83, and was buried in the family plot in the local churchyard. In the following months a Requiem Mass was held in his memory at Westminster Cathedral and three survivors from the fighting at La Boisselle in July 1916 attended the service.

Carton de Wiart was a remarkable man and an incomparable soldier, which is why he would have been a great chum of Winston Churchill who admired action heroes. In the whole of his military career he was probably wounded at least eleven times. No wonder that, apart from the award of the VC and DSO, he was to receive a Knighthood as well as many other decorations. In recent years his name has been commemorated on a plaque at the village church in Thiepval.

In the early 1980s de Wiart's medals and Orders were stolen from the Duke of Wellington's Regimental Museum, but at the present time are in the keeping of the National Army Museum.

T.G. TURRALL

On 2/3 July, apart from the VC awarded to Carton de Wiart of the 8th (Service) Battalion, The Gloucestershire Regiment (Glosters), the decoration was also won by Private Thomas George Turrall of the 10th (Service) Battalion, The Worcestershire Regiment, a battalion also serving with the 57th Brigade, 19th (Western) Division. This battalion, having been withdrawn on 1 July to the Tara–Usna Ridge, took a renewed part in the fighting two days later which was often hand-to-hand.

On 2 July 1916 the 58th Brigade, 19th Division attacked the strongly fortified village of La Boisselle and secured a position on the southern face. As the enemy machine-guns were extremely active it was decided to continue the attack during the night, and the 57th Brigade was given this task. The troops formed up opposite the village where they were forced to endure a heavy bombardment. The order to advance came at 3am and despite the heavy shelling the 10th Worcesters managed to cross the open ground and enter the German defensive positions. However, the enemy had the advantage of numerous dugouts and machine-gun nests and kept appearing, with the result that there was heavy hand-to-hand fighting and the situation became very confused. During the fierce fighting the colonel (G.A. Royston-Piggott), the adjutant and all the rest of the senior battalion officers were either killed or wounded. Control became impossible and the fighting was left to small groups of men. The fighting went on until dawn and by this time most of the enemy strongholds had been cleared.

Before the battle began, Private Turrall had been serving a short sentence in the battalion guardroom; however, his platoon officer

Lieutenant Richard William Jennings decided to allow him to take part in the fighting. The private was a powerfully built man and a noted battalion character. Both he and Lieutenant Jennings had a healthy respect for each other's qualities.

During the fighting, after it began to get light, a small group under Lieutenant Jennings' leadership was suddenly fired upon from a hidden German position. Jennings was severely wounded and had one of his legs shattered by bullets. Turrall took charge of the situation and dragged his officer into the safety of a nearby shell hole, where he then began to dress his wounds and used part of his own puttees as a bandage. While he worked, several bombs were thrown in their direction as the enemy had seen movement in the shell hole. The bombers were concealed behind a hedge and Turrall managed to kill at least one of them with rifle fire, and the enemy withdrew. However, his troubles were not yet over as he could see that there was a mass of Germans attempting to re-take the village in a counter-attack. By then Lieutenant Jennings had fainted and there was no point in firing, so Turrall feigned death and was subsequently prodded with bayonets but survived. Later the enemy counter-attack against the British defences was broken.

Turrall had to remain until dark in his shell hole when he hoisted up his wounded officer, dragging him back towards their own lines. Jennings was a very tall man and his arms were around Turrall's neck, his feet dragged along behind him. The two men were challenged and this was Turrall's worst moment of the day. 'Halt! Hands up!' and Turrall complied, 'That man behind you too. Quick!' However, Turrall's English voice was recognised and the two men were allowed back into their lines.

Although Jennings was able to give a full report on Turrall's bravery, his wounds were to prove fatal and he died a few hours later at Dernancourt field dressing station; some accounts say that he died 48 hours later but this is not so. His body was taken to Méaulte Military Cemetery to the south of Albert where it is buried in Row D, Grave 34. Jennings, who had been Mentioned in Despatches, was the son of a Gloucestershire Parson from Stonehouse. He had been a boxing champion while at Cambridge University and had trained to become a solicitor. He was 27 years old when he died.

The Worcesters were relieved by the 7th South Lancashire Battalion, 56th Brigade and the Worcesters rested in the reserve position known as Ryecroft Avenue. On the 4th they moved up in support at La Boisselle but were relieved after a few hours and retired to the Tara–Usna Line before leaving the battlefield with the rest of the 57th Brigade for billets in Albert. The 10th Worcesters remained in the area for the rest of the month.

Turrall's VC was published in the *London Gazette* of 9 September 1916 and was as follows:

> For most conspicuous bravery and devotion to duty. During a bombing attack by a small party against the enemy, the officer in charge was badly wounded, and the party having penetrated the position to a great depth was compelled eventually to retire.
>
> Private Turrall remained with the wounded officer for three hours, under continuous and very heavy fire from machine-guns and bombs, and, not withstanding that both himself and the officer were at one time completely cut off from our troops, he held to his ground with determination, and finally carried the officer into our lines after our counter-attacks had made this possible.

Turrall, with his parents and his baby daughter, went to Buckingham Palace to receive his award on 30 December 1916.

Thomas George Turrall was the son of Mr and Mrs Turrall of 23 Oakley Road, Small Heath, Birmingham and was born on 5 July 1885. As a child he attended the Dixon Road School and later trained to be a decorator, and many years later in 1932 a local newspaper published a picture of Turrall painting railings. He joined the 10th Worcesters in 1915 when he was in his 30th year. After the award of his VC was announced, 2,000 residents in the region of his home assembled at Small Heath Park to present him with £250 which they had contributed to, together with a gold watch. He was the third Birmingham citizen to gain the VC and received congratulations from the Lord Mayor, Neville Chamberlain. He was also presented with a commissioned portrait of himself.

Turrall attended many regimental functions when he was often the guest of honour. He also attended many of the VC and GC Reunions. He became a well-known and respected local figure in Worcestershire and the Midlands.

On 19 February 1964 he received a visit from two lieutenant colonels from the regiment who found him in 'very good cheer'. Despite this report, however, Turrall died two days later in Selly

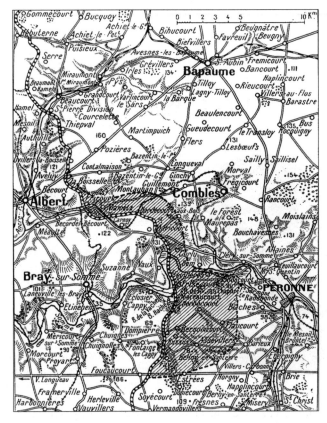

The Somme front, 1–5 July 1916. This map, published in *l'Illustration* magazine in Paris, 7 October 1916, shows the gains of the first few days on the Somme. (HGG)

Oak Hospital. He was 78 years old and was given a full military funeral at the Robin Hood Cemetery, Solihull, Warwickshire which had a large turnout. His coffin was draped in the Union Jack and buglers played the Last Post and Reveille. A pallbearer party of eight men being supplied by the Brigade Depot at Lichfield. The reference for his grave is Section A-4 North, Grave 193, and up to a few years ago his grave was showing signs of being forgotten, but is now kept an eye on by the Worcestershire RH.

After his death his VC and medals were left to his regiment.

T.O.L. WILKINSON

In the early part of July 1916 the 57th Brigade, 19th (Western) Division earned two VCs. On 5 July a member of the 7th (Service) Battalion, The Loyal North (LN) Lancashire Regiment who were part of the 56th Brigade, their sister brigade, was to also earn the nation's highest military honour. The man born in Shropshire of Irish parents, was Thomas Wilkinson.

At the end of June, on the eve of the battle, the 7th LN Lancs were camped at Hénencourt Wood and on the 30th went forward to trenches to the north-east of Albert, the Tara–Usna Line, in support to the 8th Division on 1 July. However, the planned attack on Ovillers had been cancelled and when relieved on the 2nd, they returned to a railway cutting at Albert. At 3am on the 3rd, the battalion was again on the move and resumed support positions in the Tara–Usna Line where the battalion remained until nightfall. The 57th and 58th brigades attacked La Boisselle during the day and the North Lancs were in support of the 7th (Service) Battalion, The King's Own (Royal Lancaster) Regiment, who were occupying a former German frontline trench. On the 4th at 1.00am the LN Lancs were ordered up to a trench line close to the village. This trench was 'very much knocked about and full of dead'. Fighting was renewed at 8am and during the day forty to fifty German prisoners passed through their lines, and at dusk the fighting began to subside. At 2pm on the 5th, the LN Lancs were detailed to help the 7th East Lancs with a bombing attack, although unfortunately the

East Lancs lost ground and fell back to an original British front-line position, and in doing so left behind a machine-gun. The LN Lancs were immediately ordered to recover both the lost ground and the gun which they successfully accomplished. Lieutenant Wilkinson held some Germans up on the left with the machine-gun when they were advancing down a trench. His prompt action prevented a determined rush by the enemy. It was for this deed that he was recommended for a VC by Lieutenant Colonel Sherbrooke, CO of the 1st Sherwood Foresters. Soon after Wilkinson's act of gallantry, however, he was killed when trying to rescue a wounded man who was lying 40 yards in front of the position. The battalion was to remain in the trench line near the now captured La Boisselle until late evening on the 7th, when they were relieved and left for bivouacs to the rear of the Tara–Usna Line.

Wilkinson's posthumous award was gazetted on 26 September 1916 and read as follows:

> For most conspicuous bravery. During an attack, when a party of another unit was retiring without their machine-gun, Lieutenant Wilkinson rushed forward, and, with two of his men, got the gun into action, and held up the enemy until they were relieved.
>
> Later, when the advance was checked during a bombing attack, he forced his way forward and found four or five men of different units stopped by a solid block of earth, over which the enemy were throwing bombs.
>
> With great pluck and promptness he mounted a machine-gun on the top of a parapet and dispersed the enemy bombers. Subsequently he made two most gallant attempts to bring in a wounded man, but at the second attempt he was shot through the heart just before reaching the man.
>
> Throughout the day he set a magnificent example of courage and self-sacrifice.

Thomas Orde Lawder Wilkinson was the second son of Mr Charles Ernest Orde Wilkinson and Edith of Ardanoir, Foynes, County Limerick and was born at The Lodge Farm, Dudmaston, Bridgnorth, Shropshire on 29 June 1891. His father was in Comax, Vancouver at the time of his younger son's birth. In 1908 Thomas attended Wellington College where he was good academically as well as being athletic. In addition he joined the OTC, during which time he became a colour sergeant and later company commander. He left the college in November 1912, after four years, and in the following year visited his parents in Vancouver Island. On 4 August 1914 Wilkinson enlisted as a private in the 16th Battalion, Canadian Scottish. On 30 November he applied for a commission with the 50th (Calgary) Battalion (CEF) and left for England. Once in the country, wasting no time, he got himself transferred to the 7th LN Lancs Regiment and was recommended for a commission in January 1915, and left for France with them as a gunnery officer in 1916. By taking this course he was to see action in France a month before he otherwise would have. Wilkinson's father collected his son's posthumous VC from the King at Buckingham Palace on 29 November 1916.

Wilkinson's body was never found and his name is therefore listed on the Thiepval Memorial to the Missing, Pier 11, Face A, and on the Sandwick War Memorial, British Columbia, Canada. His regiment possesses his wallet, which contains two letters to his parents, and also the original citation written by Lieutenant Colonel Sherbrooke.

Wilkinson's file in the National Archives includes correspondence of 1927 from relatives in Ireland stating that the War Office has still not sent Thomas's war medals to them. At the present time his VC and medals are on loan to the Imperial War Museum.

D.S. BELL

To the south-east of the village of La Boisselle the objective given to the 69th Infantry Brigade, 23rd Division at the end of June 1916 was to capture a position known as Horseshoe Trench, which ran from Lincoln Redoubt to Scot's Redoubt. It was a position that was about 1,500 yards long, on high ground and in a slight curve between La Boisselle and Mametz Wood.

The 69th Brigade consisted of four battalions: the 11th (Service) Battalion, The Princes of Wales's Own (West Yorkshire) Regiment, 10th (Service) Battalion, The Duke of Wellington's Regiment (DWR), West Riding and the 8th and 9th (Service) Battalions, The Princess of Wales's Own (Yorkshire) Regiment. The last two were also known as the Green Howards and it is the last battalion with which we are most concerned with here.

Before the battle began, the 9th Green Howards had been staying in the village of St Sauveur, north-west of Amiens, in the valley of the River Somme. On 1 July the battalion left the village and marched through the night to some woods west of the village of Baizieux, close to Hénencourt, where they bivouacked. By then rumours had filtered through about attempts to capture La Boisselle and of the enormous casualties suffered by the 8th and 34th divisions when doing so.

A day later the Green Howards moved up to billets on the fringe of the battle area outside Albert. They then moved to the Bapaume Road, reaching the Tara–Usna Ridge. The battalion was then to take up positions on the crest of the ridge, which was south-east of La Boisselle, with their headquarters being at Chapes Spur.

On the 4th, bombing attacks were made by the battalion together with the 11th West Yorks, but the enemy responded with great determination. On the 5th an attack was made at dawn by the West Yorks, this time with the 10th DWR, but a German counter-attack nullified any progress and the Yorkshire battalions ended up where they had started from. Another attempt was made by the two battalions in the afternoon and orders were issued for the two Green Howards' battalions to enter the battle. As there had been some progress on the right, only the 9th Battalion was called upon. The time was 6pm and, despite several officers having become casualties, great progress was made and Horseshoe Trench was not only taken but 146 prisoners captured as well as two machine-guns. However, one of the remaining enemy machine-guns began to enfilade the Yorkshire Battalion's position and it was on seeing the damage being inflicted that prompted Second Lieutenant D.S. Bell, supported by Corporal Colwill and Private Batey, to try and destroy the aggressive gun position. The three men crept forward via a communication trench, and then suddenly dashed across the open ground, before Bell shot the gunner with his revolver and the remainder of the gun team were dealt with by bombs. The enemy machine-gun team had clearly not been prepared for such a sudden and brazen frontal attack and was overwhelmed by the speed of it.

On the 6th it was raining hard and the 69th Brigade was relieved in the frontline, but there was little respite for the men for now the village of Contalmaison was the next objective, and sadly Bell was killed during the fighting four days later at a point south-east of the village. At the time he was attached to the 8th Battalion. He was buried where he fell, but in 1920 his body was later transferred a mile away to Gordon Dump Cemetery, IV, A, 8.

The citation for a posthumous VC was published in the *London Gazette* of 9 September and read as follows:

For most conspicuous bravery. During an attack a very heavy enfilade fire was opened on the attacking company by a hostile machine-gun. Second Lieutenant Bell immediately, and on his own initiative, crept up a communication trench, and then, followed by Corporal Colwill and Private Batey, rushed across the open under very heavy fire and attacked the machine-gun, shooting the firer with his revolver, and destroying the gun and personnel with bombs.

This very brave act saved many lives and ensured the success of the attack. Five days later this gallant officer lost his life performing a very similar act of bravery.

Mrs Rhoda Bell, Bell's widow, accompanied by Minnie Bell, her sister-in-law, travelled to London in order to receive Donald's VC from the hands of the King on 13 December.

Donald Simpson Bell was the younger of two sons of Smith Bell, a butcher, and Annie Bell (née Simpson) of Milton Lodge, 87 East Parade, Harrogate and he was born on 3 December 1890. There were also six daughters in the family, one of whom died in infancy. Throughout his short life, Donald was known as 'Donny'. He was educated at St Peter's Church of England School, Harrogate (1905–1908) where he gained a scholarship, where Charles Hull VC had also been a pupil. Bell went on to Harrogate Grammar School, where Archie White, a friend, was also a student. He had a strong physique and by the age of 16 was already 6ft tall and weighed over 14st. Not surprisingly he was very good at all sports and although more the build of a hammer-thrower than a runner, he did possess an amazing turn of speed which was of great use to him when he won his VC. He matriculated in 1908.

While at school he played fullback for Starbeck Football Club near Harrogate and when he began teacher training at a Methodist organisation called Westminster Training College in 1911, he turned out for Crystal Palace for whom he played as an amateur.

On returning north in 1911, Bell became an assistant master at Starbeck Council School and played as an amateur for Newcastle United and Bishop Auckland for two years, but in August 1912 he decided to leave the teaching profession, where his salary never exceeded £2.50 a week, when he joined Bradford Park Avenue professionally. His first match was against Wolves on 13 April 1913.

In November 1914 he was released from his contract and enlisted in the 9th West Yorkshire Regiment as a private becoming the first professional footballer to do so. On 28 October he was promoted to lance corporal. In May 1915, having been promoted to lance sergeant, he applied to join the 6th Yorkshire

Regiment, but in the following month was commissioned into the 9th Yorkshire Regiment instead. He had hoped to join the 6th Battalion because Archie White was serving in it and when training in Belton Park, Grantham the two men had met up again. Bell's battalion arrived in France on 26 August 1915.

Ten months later, on 5 June, he married Rhoda Margaret Bonson in the Wesleyan Chapel in Kirkby Stephen, it proved to be a marriage which was only to last five weeks.

We are very fortunate in that a letter dated 7 July from Bell to his mother has survived. In it he talks about his role in the fighting for the Horseshoe position on 5 July, and the letter 'fleshes out' the standard prose of the official citation.

> ...As I told you, the battalion had been in action and did splendidly capturing a strong German position. I did not go over as I was second in command of the bombers ... a machine-gun was spotted on the left, which could enfilade the whole of the front. When the battalion went over, I with my team, crawled up a communication trench and attacked the gun and the trench and I hit the gun first shot from about 20 yards and knocked it over. We then bombed the dugouts and did in about fifty Bosches. The GOC has been over to congratulate the battalion and he personally thanked me. I must confess that it was the biggest fluke alive and I did nothing. I only chucked one bomb, but it did the trick... I am glad I have been so fortunate, for Pa's sake, for I know he likes his lads to be at the top of the tree. He used to be always on about too much play and too little work, but my altthetics came in handy this trip.... The only thing is I am sore at elbows and knees with crawling over limestone flints etc... believe that God is watching over me and it rests with him whether I pull through or not. I will write again as soon as I get another chance and will send Field PC's every day if possible...

On 16 September, after the VC award had been announced, Brigadier General T.S. Lambert, Commander of the 69th Brigade, wrote a congratulatory letter to Bell's father. Colonel H.G. Holmes and Major H.A.S. Prior also wrote in similar fashion to Bell's widow, who as a registered reader of the *Daily Mail* was given £100 by the newspaper. However, by far the most moving of these letters was one from Bell's batman to Mrs Bell, who had presumably written to him to ask for more personal details about her husband's last days in early July 1916.

The letter was dated 14 November and read as follows:

> ... I sit down and write these few lines in deepest regret, believe me I am most sorry that it should be so. I would wish to God that my later master and friend had still been here with us, or better still, been at home with you.... They (the company) worshipped him in their simple, whole hearted way and so they ought, he saved the lot of us from being completely wiped out, by his heroic act.... I am pleased that his valise arrived to you and that you think it is all right, you would find in it the souvenirs that we got on 5 July in the first great attack, a Prussian helmet, bayonet and pair of boots... I packed them all in it but I cannot quite remember whether his little toilet bag was packed, or he carried it with him at the time of his death... he was called to go to the 8th Battalion of this regiment, that was just on our right, so that we heard nothing of his death until the next day.... The last time we were on the Somme, some of our lads came across Mr Bell's grave and they told me that it was being well cared for, and that there is a cross erected over it,... You ask me if I smoke, yes, but not cigarettes, only a pipe and tobacco so if you will send some, I will be very grateful to you. Believe me, wishing you the best of health and wishes,
>
> Yours in Sympathy, John W. Byers.
> (Private John W. Byers, C. Co. 9th Btn. Yorks Regt., BEF)

Colonel A.C.T. White, VC, MC not only attended the same school as Bell, but was also a sportsman and a member of the Green Howards. Some years later when writing to the *Regimental Magazine* he said this of Bell's deed:

> At Contalmaison the problem was to cross no man's land, badly cut up by shell fire. Probably no one else on the front could have done what he [Bell] did. Laden by steel helmet, haversack, revolver, ammunitions and Mills bombs in their pouches, he was yet able to hurl himself at the German trench at such speed that the enemy would hardly believe what their eyes saw.

Well knowing the risk, he made a similar attempt a few days later, and died. He was a magnificent soldier; and had he lived, with this high intelligence, superb physique, and firm religious principles, he would have risen high in the teaching profession.

On 9 July 2000 a memorial to Bell's memory was unveiled in the pouring rain at Contalmaison on 9 July by Major General Richard Dannatt, then colonel of the regiment and a Green Howards man. The hardy souls who attended the ceremony included twenty members of Donny Bell's family. The memorial was the inspiration of Richard Leake, and contributors for its cost included the Yorkshire Regiment, Friends of the Green Howards and the Professional Footballers Association. Inevitably, the memorial called Bell's Redoubt has been vandalised but repairs have been swiftly carried out.

Apart from his memorial in Contalmaison and his headstone at Gordon Dump, Donald Bell is commemorated at a number of other places, including Starbeck Council School; Starbeck War Memorial; Harrogate High School; St Paul's Parish Church, Harrogate; Harrogate War Memorial and the Wesleyan Methodist Chapel, Harrogate.

Bell's decorations were lent by the Bell family to the Green Howards Museum in Richmond, Yorkshire from 1964, but this arrangement has now ended and in 2010 his VC and trio of war medals were offered for sale and auctioned by Spinks on 25 November 2010, fetching a hammer price of £210,000. The purchaser was the Professional Footballer's Association who plan to exhibit them at their revamped museum in Manchester in 2011.

W.E. BOULTER

After La Boisselle had been captured the main Allied attacks were made against the German Second Line positions of Mametz Wood and Trônes Wood. The latter wood, east of Bernafay Wood, was pear-shaped in outline. It was a position of vital strategic importance to both sides and was only 2 miles from the German station at Combles, which was a very important 'nerve centre'.

By the second week of July Trônes Wood had been captured and then lost by the British several times. The 30th Division, who had been very heavily involved in the fighting, were relieved by the 18th (Eastern) Division on the evening of the 12th. Their orders were that the wood should be taken on the 14th and the attack was part of the plan to take the whole of the German Second Line. The advance was to begin at 3.20am.

The 18th Division had three brigades: the 53rd, 54th and 55th. At first the 55th occupied the frontline trenches and then had to be relieved by the 54th. One of the four battalions in the 54th was the 6th Northamptons and after very fierce hand-to-hand fighting the wood was finally cleared. It was during this part of the fighting that the first 6th Northamptonshire Battalion VC was won by Sergeant William Boulter. His citation was published on 26 October 1916 in the *London Gazette* and reads as follows:

For most conspicuous bravery. When a company and part of another were held up in the attack on a wood [Trônes] by a hostile machine-gun, which was causing heavy casualties,

Sergt Boulter, with utter contempt of danger, and in spite of being severely wounded in the shoulder, advanced alone over the open under heavy fire in front of the gun, and bombed the gun team from their position.

This very gallant act not only saved many casualties, but was of great military value as it materially expedited the operation of clearing the enemy out of the wood, and thus covering the flank of the whole attacking force.

The other battalion who was heavily involved in capturing the wood was the 12th Middlesex and the two battalions were relieved on the 16th. The 6th Northhamptons had suffered 296 casualties. Boulter received his Victoria Cross from the King at Buckingham Palace on 17 March 1917.

William Ewart Boulter, born in Welford Road, Wigston, Leicestershire on 14 October 1892, was the second of four sons of Frederick and Mary Ann Boulter. His father held a managerial position. William was educated at Wigston Council School and became a keen sportsman. After leaving school he worked in the Kettering branch of the Co-operative Store in the haberdashery department. On 4 September, at the age of 21, he joined the 6th Northamptonshire Regiment in Kettering and was promoted to corporal two months later. His rank was made up to sergeant on 26 July 1915 when he was serving in the field. The 6th Northants were formed in Northampton and moved to Colchester where the battalion was attached to the 18th Division, moving to Salisbury Plain where they completed their training before arriving in France on 26 July 1915. The battalion spent their first winter in the trenches at Suzanne and Fricourt, where mining was a constant danger. At the beginning of the battle they were involved in capturing the village of Montauban on the first day. After a short rest the battalion returned to the Somme and were involved in a third success, the capture of Thiepval. Boulter, who was seriously wounded and had gun shot wounds to his left shoulder, on 14 July 1916, was transferred to a hospital in England on the 18th. He was then sent to Ampthill Command Depot in Bedfordshire, which was under the command of the Duke of Bedford. Boulter was convalescent until March 1917 and at this time was recommended for a commission and transferred to 13 Officer Cadet

Battalion (OCB) in Newmarket. After he had been awarded the VC he was presented with a clock by the Co-operative Society at a ceremony at Abingdon Park, Northampton, which 20,000 people attended. The Corporation of Northampton gave him a gold wrist watch and a congratulatory address.

He was discharged to a commission on 26 June 1917 and gazetted as a second lieutenant the next day. In October though, he contracted trench fever and was unable to take any further part in the war, and in February 1918 his service records confirm that he was ill with bronchitis in the United Kingdom. In October 1918 he applied for a job with the Ministry of Labour and was promoted to full lieutenant on 27 December 1918. Finally he was demobilised on 24 April 1919.

After the war he lived in London and was never properly fit and his address in 1927 was the Residential Hotel at Charnwood, Bramley Avenue, Coulsdon, Surrey. Even so, he became a business man, retiring in 1954. In 1955 he became seriously ill when living at 10 Wimbledon Close, The Downs, Wimbledon. He was in hospital for two months before dying on 1 June 1955 at the age of 62. He was cremated at Putney Vale five days later and his ashes scattered in the Garden of Remembrance on the first lawn between two cherry trees and close to a lily pool. He is remembered with a path named after him and the reference is 10939. His widow was Alice Irene Boulter and at one time he had three brothers living at Wigston, his birthplace.

In 1988 Boulter's family attended a Northamptonshire Regimental Reunion when the family-owned VC was presented to the regiment.

W.F. FAULDS

After Trônes Wood and Mametz Wood had been captured by the Allies, the next two woods due to be taken were High Wood to the north-west of Longueval and Delville Wood, part of Longueval. The main attack on 15 July against High Wood failed and the Battle of Delville Wood was begun on same day. Waterlot Farm, north-east of Trônes Wood and south of Longueval village, was captured on the 17th.

On the 15th, 121 officers and 3,022 men of the 1st South African Infantry (SAI) Brigade had entered the wood and fought there for almost a week in appalling conditions. They were pinned down by continuous bombardment and were attacked from three sides. Delville Wood was to become the place that was most associated with the South African forces in the Great War. On the 16th one of their troops, Private W.F. Faulds carried out the first of two outstanding acts of gallantry, thus gaining the first VC for the imperial forces in the Battle of the Somme and also the first VC out of four that were to be awarded for gallantry during this action.

Faulds was a company runner and on the morning of the 16th two companies of the South African Infantry, who had been manning the south-west corner of the wood, were ordered to push out from Princes Street to link up with the 11th (Service) Battalion, The Royal Scots (Lothian) Regiment, 27th Brigade, 9th (Scottish) Division. The plan was to capture an orchard, but the attack failed. Lt Arthur Craig (SAI) led a bombing party against the enemy trenches but came under heavy machine-gun fire. Most of the party were either killed or wounded and Craig himself was severely wounded. In full view of both sides, Private Faulds, together with Privates George Baker and Alexander Estment climbed over the parapet in order to rescue the wounded officer. One of the party was injured but they still managed to carry Craig back to their trench. Later that day the northern part of the wood was vacated in order to allow it to be bombarded by the Allied artillery. On the 18th Private Faulds again risked his life by going out in order to rescue a wounded man, again under intense enemy fire.

Finally, the South Africans, who were in the south-west corner of the wood and almost totally depleted, were relieved in the early evening of the 20th by men of the 76th Infantry Brigade. Their number was 142 survivors, including two wounded officers, and under Colonel Thackeray they left for Happy Valley, a camp close to the town of Bray, on the River Somme to the south.

Faulds' citation was the last such award for making a rescue attempt in saving a wounded man to be rewarded with a VC, and was published on 9 September 1916 and read as follows:

> For most conspicuous bravery and devotion to duty. A bombing party under Lt Craig attempted to rush over 40 yards of ground which lay between the British and enemy trenches. Coming under very heavy rifle and machine-gun fire the officer and the majority of the party were killed or wounded. Unable to move, Lt Craig lay midway between the two lines of trench, the ground being quite open. In full daylight Private Faulds, accompanied by two other men, climbed over the parapet, ran out, picked up the officer, and carried him back, one man being severely wounded in so doing. Two days later Private Faulds again showed most conspicuous bravery in going out alone to bring in a wounded man, and carried him nearly half a mile to a dressing station, subsequently rejoining his platoon. The artillery fire at the time was so intense that stretcher bearers and others considered that any attempt to bring in the wounded men meant certain death. The risk Private Faulds faced unflinchingly, and his bravery was crowned with success.

Lieutenant Craig was transferred to a hospital in England when he wrote to three members of the Faulds family, telling them how Private Faulds had saved his life and that it was a million to one

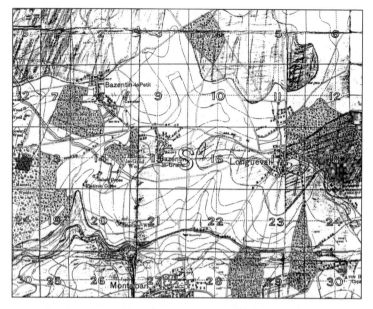

Detail from OS sheet 57D N.E. (for terrain information only). High Wood is at S4, Delville Wood at S12 and 18 with Longueval at S17 and Bazentin le Petit at S8. Mametz Wood is at S13/19 and Trônes Wood S29. (TM 463)

chance that he survived. Craig also wrote to Faulds himself, thanking him, and to his sister and mother. Faulds was awarded his VC by the King at Sandringham on 8 January 1917.

William Frederick Faulds was born at 34 Market Street, Cradock, Cape Province on 19 February 1895. His parents were Alexander and Wilhelmina Faulds. He went to school at Cradock and worked at the Midland Motor Garage, Cradock before joining the Cradock Commando on 19 October 1914 at the age of 19. His mother was a widow with seven children, two of whom were to serve in the SAI. Faulds was always known as Mannie. He served in South-West Africa throughout the campaign until he was discharged on 12 January 1915. On 23 August he enlisted at Potchefstroom, joining the 1st Battalion South African Infantry prior to leaving for France, where he arrived on 16 April 1916.

After news of his VC award had reached Johannesburg, a cable told him that his award 'had sent a thrill of pride throughout the country.'

On 20 August 1916 Faulds was promoted to the rank of lance-corporal, to corporal on 18 October 1916, to sergeant on 12 April 1917, and on 19 May of that year he was commissioned as a second lieutenant. He then served for a short time in the Transport in Egypt before returning to France. During the German breakthrough in March 1918, Faulds was reported as being wounded and in German hands. He was awarded the MC for his work in handling his men during the German attacks at Heudecourt and Marrieres Wood, and this enabled the rest of the battalion to withdraw with only slight losses. He was made temporary lieutenant on 9 November 1918 and repatriated to England ten days later.

After the war he returned to South Africa for demobilisation and was made a full lieutenant on 16 March 1919. Two years later he married Thelma M. Windell in Kimberley and they had two children. He became a mechanic with De Beers and in 1922 he re-enlisted with the Kimberley Regiment. He was promoted to captain and after several years left Kimberley to work in Jagersfontein and then moved to Rhodesia. In 1937 he attended the coronation of King George VI and served for five years in the Second World War, mainly in East Africa. In 1945 he became a government inspector in Rhodesia and died in Salisbury General Hospital at the age of 55 on 16 August 1950. He was buried in the Salisbury Pioneer Cemetery, Remembrance Drive, Harare, on 17 August in a grave without a monument or headstone. However, in 1972 this anonymity was rectified mainly through the efforts of the Cradock branch of the South African Legion.

His VC and medals were originally on display at the South African National Museum of Military History, Johannesburg. He was also commemorated in the South Africa Memorial, Delville Wood. A plaster cast of the Danie de Jager relief displayed at Delville Wood Museum is also on display in the centre, which features a small group of South African survivors from 1st SA Brigade leaving the wood in July 1916.There also other links with the Victoria Cross in Delville Wood Museum Centre.

In November 1995 a new museum was opened within the South African National Museum of Military History in Saxonwold, Johannesburg. It was dedicated to the memory of Captain W.F. Faulds, VC, MC, a South African First World War hero, and provided a new Museum Function Facility and two extra rooms. Faulds' Victoria Cross had been stolen from the main museum the year before and has never been recovered. The original group of Cross and ten medals had previously been purchased for R 80,000.

W. La T. Congreve

Not only were Joseph Davies and Albert Hill to be awarded the VC for their gallantry in Delville Wood on 20 July 1916 but so was William La Touch Congreve, but this time posthumously. Congreve was brigade major of the 76th Brigade, 3rd Division and his brigade consisted of the 8th (Service) Battalion, The King's Own (Royal) Lancaster Regiment, the 2nd Battalion, The Suffolk Regiment, the 10th (Service) Battalion, The Royal Welsh Fusiliers (RWF) and the 1st Battalion Gordon Highlanders.

The long drawn out struggle to capture the village of Longueval and the adjacent Delville Wood was still the main objective on 20 July when two battalions from Congreve's brigade took part in the action: the 2nd Suffolks and the 10th RWF who were meant to meet up in the wood. The Suffolks began their advance from the westerly direction at 3.35am, but the 10th RWF failed to make contact as they had been let down by guides who had lost their way in the prevailing chaotic conditions. Despite this, the now unsupported Suffolks pressed on and as a consequence were decimated. To add to the confusion, when the 10th RWF did finally show up they were mistakenly fired upon by the 11th (Service) Battalion, The Essex Regiment, 18th Brigade, 6th Division. It was these problematic circumstances which Congreve was trying to sort out when, having returned to the area, he was discussing the situation with Major G.C. Stubbs at the Suffolk's HQ alongside Duke Street on the western side of Longueval. Congreve was killed when making notes on the situation by a sniper hidden in stooks of corn, who shot him in the throat as he had climbed down from a disused gun pit and entered the main trench. The time of his death was 10.55am.

The following morning the major's body, accompanied by Major General Haldane's two ADCs, was taken back to Corbie via Carnoy and his father, Lt Gen Sir Walter Congreve of XIII Corps, after attending Fourth Army Conference, left for Corbie in order to attend his son's funeral, but firstly visited his dead son in order to pay his last respects and say his farewells. The major's coffin mounted on a RHA gun carriage was taken for the funeral in Corbie Communal Cemetery in Row F, Grave 35 of Plot 1.

Major William La Touch Congreve was extremely well thought of by the men under his command and one member of the Rifle Brigade had this to say of him:

> He was the most perfect gentleman and the coolest officer in the British Army. He was beloved by all.... Everyone grieved his loss, and none more than his devoted orderly who broke down in tears on news of his master's death.

Congreve was recommended for a VC by Brig Gen R.J. Kentish, commanding officer of the 76th Brigade.

Major General Haldane, commander of the 3rd Division, with whom Congreve had served for twenty months, wrote this of him:

> His loss to me is irreparable, and the Army in him loses one of its very best soldiers and by far the most promising officer I have ever known. Young, almost boyish in appearance, he possessed qualities which are general found only in men of much riper years and of far greater experience. He was unsurpassed in bravery, and was distinguished by the highest standards of duty which guided him. Had he lived but a few months longer he must inevitable have attained command of a brigade. Under his modesty and gentleness he possessed great strength of character. The whole division mourns his loss, for he was beloved by all ranks, and the fine example of duty well done will for long keep him alive in their memories.

In a letter to Congreve's widow, which is quoted in Billy's diary under the title of *Armageddon Road: A VCs Diary 1914–1916*, Haldane also wrote as follows:

I am so upset at what has happened that writing is difficult. Still I must write and say how infinitely sorry I am for you and how deeply sad I feel.... On the 18th, when things were not going too well, and I had been obliged to use the 76th Brigade – which I was preserving for another operation – I went through the ruined village of Montauban into the valley south of Longueval, where the headquarters of the brigade were in a quarry. The enemy was very active, shelling heavily, and Billy had just returned from a dangerous visit to Longueval and gave me a lucid and many account of what was going on there, I mean reassuring under the circumstances. He looked tired, but I knew that if I said he was overworking he would scorn the idea. This was the last time I saw him alive. Cameron, his faithful servant is heartbroken.... I took one look at the dear fellow (Congreve). He looked beautiful in his last sleep, so handsome and noble, and not a trace of pain on his face. He was then half-way to Carnoy and, on my way back there, I met men of my regiment (Gordon Highlanders) carrying wild poppies and cornflowers to lay upon him, for his love for his brigade was amply returned by all ranks.

Major Congreve's VC was published in the *London Gazette* of 26 October 1916 and was awarded for his work over the period from 6–20 July in the region of Montauban, Delville Wood, Longueval and the Bazentin Ridge. The citation read as follows:

For most conspicuous bravery during a period of fourteen days preceding his death in action. This officer constantly performed acts of gallantry and showed the greatest devotion to duty, and by his personal example inspired all around him with confidence at critical periods of the operations. During preliminary preparations for the attack he carried out personal reconnaissances of the enemy lines, taking out parties of officers for over 1,000 yards in front of our line, in order to acquaint them with the ground. All these preparations were made under fire. Later, by night, Major Congreve conducted a battalion to its positions of employment, afterwards returning to it to ascertain the situation after assault. He established himself in an exposed forward position from whence he successfully observed the enemy, and gave orders necessary to drive them from their position. Two days later, when Brigade Headquarters was heavily shelled and many casualties resulted, he went out and assisted the medical officer to remove the wounded to places of safety, although he was himself suffering severely from gas and other shell effects. He again on a subsequent occasion showed supreme courage in tending wounded under heavy shell fire. He finally returned to the frontline to ascertain the situation after an unsuccessful attack, and whilst in the act of writing his report, was shot and killed instantly.

His widow, Pamela Cynthia Congreve, received her husband's decorations from the King at Buckingham Palace on 1 November 1916, which included a DSO and MC as well as the Victoria Cross. Congreve was the first officer in the Great War to earn all three awards.

Four months later, on 21 March 1917 Pamela gave birth to a daughter who was named Mary Gloria. Her father's grave might give a clue to her middle name as it has the inscription of 'In remembrance of my beloved husband and in glorious expectation'. In the following year, on 22 December Pamela re-married a great friend of Billy's, Major the Hon. William Fraser, DSO, MC, the third surviving son of Lord Saltoun, who later became a brigadier having commanded 1st Gordon Highlanders at one point of his career. He had been Billy's best man at his wedding and the marriage took place at St George's, Hanover Square.

William La Touch Congreve was the elder son of Lieutenant General Sir Walter Congreve, VC, KCB, MVO, and Lady Congreve. He was born on 22 March 1891 at Burton Hall, Cheshire, one of the family's two family homes. He was educated at Eton from May 1903 until July 1907. He was then trained by crammers; Mr R.K. Andrew from Sept 1907 until December 1908 and then Messrs Carlisle and Gregson. He entered Sandhurst where he came second for the Sword of Honour award. He was gazetted as a second lieutenant in the Rifle Brigade in March 1911and joined the 3rd Battalion in Tipperary. On 1 February 1913 he was promoted to full lieutenant and left for France with the 3rd Battalion on 12 September 1914. He was appointed ADC to Major General Hubert Hamilton who was commander of the 3rd Division until the general was killed by shrapnel on

13 October. He then became ADC to Hamilton's successor, Major General J.A. Haldane and he continued to serve in the 3rd Division as brigade major to the 76th Brigade.

Congreve was Mentioned in Despatches on four occasions prior to his death in July 1916 and in addition once afterwards. He was also awarded a MC for bravery in 1915 at Hooge. On 24 February 1916 he was also awarded a Legion of Honour and on 6 April recommended for a VC for an exploit in the St Eloi Region of Belgium which was altered to a DSO. He and his orderly had crept up to a huge mine crater which had been sprung on 26 March by the British. By sheer bravado Congreve captured two German officers and seventy-two men from the Prussian Army by simply brandishing his revolver and ordering the enemy garrison to surrender. It was during this period that the Reverend Noel Mellish earned the VC for saving lives of several men over a period of three successive nights.

In June 1916 Congreve was given his Brevet-Majority and on the 1st of the month had married Pamela Maude (1893–1975), an actress and daughter of an actor and theatre manager Cyril Maude, at St Martin's-in-the-Fields, London.

Congreve is commemorated on the panels of the Rifle Brigade Memorial in Winchester Cathedral and at Stow-by-Chartley, Staffordshire. His son also has a plaque to his memory in Stow Church. William also has a plaque to his memory in Corbie Church, designed by Sir Edwin Lutyens.

Two details in his service records in the National Archives (WO 339/7831) reveal that after his death, a garage in Cork asked the War Office for instructions as what to do with a car belonging to Billy, which they had been keeping for five years. And the second item is a copy of an unpaid bill from Burberrys.

On 30 June 1983 Gloria Congreve put her father's decorations, at that time on display at the Royal Green Jackets Museum in Winchester, up for sale as she required money in order to purchase a house in Spain. Not surprisingly this news was not well received and her uncle Christopher was particularly upset. As a consequence an appeal was launched on behalf of the museum who would aim to purchase the VC and medals. The Rifle Brigade had amalgamated with the Royal Green Jackets and with a bid of £26,000 secured the decorations.

J.J. DAVIES

Two days after the South African Private Faulds gained the VC for gallantry in the fighting for Delville Wood, two members of the 10th (Service) Battalion, The Royal Welsh Fusiliers were also to qualify for the British Army's top gallantry award. Their names were Joseph Davies and Albert Hill, and the date of their deeds was 20 July 1916.

The 10th RWF were part of the 76th Brigade, 3rd Division, and the other battalions of the brigade were the 8th (Service) Battalion, The King's Own (Royal Lancaster) Regiment, the 2nd Battalion, The Suffolk Regiment, and the 1st Battalion, The Gordon Highlanders. The division was ordered to try and capture the village of Longueval and the northern section of Delville Wood. The 2nd Suffolks were ordered to attack from the west and the two leading companies, starting off at 3.35am moved forward, but suffered very heavy casualties. The 10th RWF, starting out from the village of Montauban to the south-west, reached the wood at 2.45am and were then to push through the centre of the wood, known as Princes Street, to the north. Due to the presence of so many troops involved within a very small area, the order was given that there should be no firing. The 10th RWF, however, were led astray by their guides and arrived in Princes Street ten minutes behind schedule at 3.45am, having been guided in error to Buchanan Street, a ride to the south-west of Princes Street. Suddenly the whole wood seemed to be full of Germans and the Welsh battalion had great difficulty in finding their way forward.

It was around this time in the centre of the wood and between two enemy attacking lines that Corporal Joseph Davies and Private Albert Hill were both to earn the VC. Davies had become separated from his company (D), which was the leading company, and together with eight men had become surrounded. The group took cover in a shell hole and by bombing the enemy and using rapid fire they managed to repulse their attackers. Davies then followed up a retreating party of the enemy and bayoneted several of them. Then all went quiet and his group deployed for another attack, but as all the company officers had become casualties, Davies took charge and led the men forward under heavy fire from all directions. He then returned for another group and led them into a further attack. The enemy was only 50 yards distant and the firing so intense that his party had to retire after 150 yards. However, the gallant corporal kept a tight control on the reserves in the trenches before they were finally relieved. Owing to the very confusing state of the position, the RWF were mistakenly fired upon by the 11th Essex and they suffered further casualties. The total casualties of the RWF were 180, including 50 missing, and they were relieved on the following day and spent four days at Breslau Trench before marching back to camp at Bois des Tailles. The 10th RWF remained in the Somme area until 23 August.

Davies' citation was published in the *London Gazette* of 26 September 1916, and read as follows:

> For most conspicuous bravery. Prior to an attack on the enemy in a wood, he became separated with eight men from the rest of his company. When the enemy delivered their second counter-attack his party was completely surrounded, but he got them into a shell hole, and by throwing bombs and opening rapid fire, succeeded in routing them. Not content with this, he followed them up in their retreat, and bayoneted several of them.
>
> Corporal Davies set a magnificent example of pluck and determination. He had done very gallant work, and was badly wounded in the 'Second Battle of Ypres'.

Four days after his VC was gazetted, he was presented with the VC ribbon at Enquin-les-Mines by the commanding officer of the 76th Brigade, Brigadier R.J. Kentish. A week later he was given the decoration itself by the King at Buckingham Palace on 7 October. As Davies had been badly wounded in the shoulder in Delville Wood, the King had to pin the medal on his sling.

Joseph John Davies was the son of John and Annie Davies and born on April 1889 at Tipton, Staffordshire. He was one of seven children, three sons and four daughters. The family lived at 48 Cross Street, Wednesbury, which no longer exists as the site has been redeveloped. He attended Great Bridge Council School, Tipton and later became a colliery worker. He then decided to join the Army and enlisted in the 1st Welsh Regiment on 19 August 1909 at the age of 20. He served in Egypt from 18 January 1910 until 27 January 1914 and spent a year of this time with the Camel Corps. He served in India between 28 January and 17 November 1914. His father was also in the Army serving with the 7th Royal Fusiliers.

After the war began, the 1st Welsh returned from India and were involved in fighting at Ypres in 1915, when Davies was wounded for the first time. In July he was wounded a second time when the knuckles of both hands were smashed by German bayonets. In August 1915 he was posted to the 1st Garrison Battalion, RWF and served with them in Gibralter for a short period. In May 1916 he appears to have been transferred and then served with the 3rd Battalion during which time he was promoted to corporal and then sergeant, but when serving in Delville Wood he was a member of the 10th Battalion. In the Spring of 1918 Davies was briefly made up to staff sergeant before reverting to sergeant. He then returned to the 3rd RWF. In May 1917 he was transferred to the Military Provost Staff, as his wounds made him unfit for active duty. In the same year he married Elsie Thomas of Presteigne, Herefordshire (Powys), and they were to have two daughters. He left the RWF on 14 December 1918 and in 1920 enlisted with the Herefordshire Regiment and served with them until November 1922. At this period his home was at 8 Bath Street, Hereford. Due to the severe injuries that he sustained during the Great War he was unable to return to his former job at the colliery, and was employed for a time as a commissionaire by Birmingham Corporation Gasworks. He then moved to Poole, Dorset where he worked at the Holton Heath Cordite Factory. During the Second World War he served as a regimental sergeant major with Poole Cadet Force and at the same time was chief warden at Oakdale in

Poole. He lived at 11 North Road, Parkstone, Poole before moving to Milne Road, Waterloo, Poole. His last address was 2 Trinidad House, Parkstone, Poole.

Davies died in Bournemouth Hospital, Hampshire on 16 February 1976 at the age of 86. He was cremated in Bournemouth on 25 February without a service and his ashes were scattered at Evening Hill in Poole overlooking the harbour. The cremation reference was 87514.

Apart from his war wounds, he had also suffered from severe arthritis for many years. His decorations included the DCM and the Russian Cross of St George (1st Class) awarded to him in Manchester in 1917 by General Campbell. His name was once commemorated at Great Bridge School, Tipton and at Davies Court, Hightown, Wrexham in North Wales. His VC and medals are in the possession of the RWF Museum at Caernarfon Castle, Caernarfon.

As with his chum Joseph Davies, Hill's name is commemorated by the name of a residential Court in Hightown, Wrexham. The two are also commemorated in Delville Wood with a memorial provided for by the RWF which can be found at the main entrance walk at the back of the museum.

A. HILL

At the time that Corporal Davies was winning a VC while fighting with D Company of the 10th (Service) Battalion, The Royal Welsh Fusiliers, Albert Hill was fighting with C Company of the same battalion and was also to be awarded the VC. The citation for Hill's gallantry on 20 July was published on 26 September in the *London Gazette* as follows:

For most conspicuous bravery. When the battalion had deployed under very heavy fire for an attack on the enemy in a wood he dashed forward when the order to charge was given, and, meeting two of the enemy suddenly, bayoneted them both. He was sent later by his platoon sergeant to get into touch with the company and, finding himself cut off and almost surrounded by some twenty of the enemy, attacked them with bombs, killing and wounding many and scattering the remainder.

He then joined a sergeant of his company, and helped him find the way back to the lines. When he got back, hearing that his company officer and a scout were lying out wounded, he went out and assisted to bring in the wounded officer, two other men bringing in the scout.

Finally, he himself captured and brought in as prisoners two of the enemy. His conduct throughout was magnificent.

He had been recommended the VC by his sergeant, Hugh Green and his commanding officer Captain Scales. He was presented with his VC ribbon at the same time as Corporal J. Davies at

Enquin-les-Mines by Brigadier General R.J. Kentish, DSO on 30 September 1916, which was the day that Kentish left the 76th Brigade. Of the ceremony Lieutenant C.J. Hupfield (2nd Suffolks) wrote to Canon W.M. Lummis:

> I arrived at Enquin-les-Mines in pitch darkness (29 Sept). Next day there was a battalion parade and later the whole brigade was drawn up to bid good-bye to its General Kentish, who had led it through the Somme fighting. Many medals, including two VCs were given on the field. It was a glorious day; all units had their field kitchens out and we lunched in the open, marching past the general afterwards.

Lummis, who was a lieutenant with the 2nd Suffolks at the time, was on leave. He was also on leave when his battalion were involved in the Delville Wood fighting, which may have saved his life.

The King presented Hill with his VC at Buckingham Palace on 18 November 1916.

In March 1918 Albert Hill was briefly Lummis' orderly when the latter was acting quartermaster with the 2nd Suffolks.

Albert Hill was the son of Harry and Elizabeth Hill and born in Hulme, Manchester on 24 May 1895. He was one of ten children, six boys and four girls. His family moved to 7 Peacock Street, Denton (near Manchester) in 1907 but his father, who worked in the colliery at Ashton Moss, died soon after and the family moved to a cottage at 45 High Street, Denton. Albert attended Trinity Wesleyan School, Denton and after he left school he began work at the Alpha Mill. He then became apprenticed to a very large local firm of hat makers called Joseph Wilson and Sons, where he was a member of the planking department.

Hill enlisted with the RWF on 3 August 1914 at the age of 19 and served in France and Flanders from 27 September 1915, although as he was both small and slight his family thought that he would be rejected for active service. Two of his brothers also enlisted. On 11 October 1916 after he had been presented with his VC ribbon but before the King had presented him with the decoration itself, Hill arrived back at Denton where he was given a huge local welcome. Thousands of people turned out to greet their 'local hero' and the huge crowd sang songs and hymns including 'See the Conquering Hero Comes'. Hill was received by the mayor and presented with an Illuminated Address and then carried shoulder high to his widowed mother's house in the High Street. She waited for him with tears in her eyes. At the door of the cottage was a crowd of children and Hill swooped down on one of his nieces and carried her into the cottage where she sat on his knee while he talked to his friends. At the time he had the reputation of being one of the youngest and as the smallest VC holder. He was also known as Denton's VC and the Hatters' VC. He was demobilised in February 1919 and married Doris May Wilson of Hyde, Cheshire a year later on 14 February 1920. He had made his own hat as part of the bridal trousseau. After their marriage the couple lived at 3 Perrin Street, Hyde.

Hill had resumed work at Wilsons but in 1923 he and his wife decided to emigrate to the United States. He lived in Central Falls before moving to Pawtucket, Rhode Island where he worked as a building labourer with a construction company until he retired. The Hills lived at 41 Thornley Street, 117 Maryland Avenue and finally at 175 Broad Street, Pawtucket. By now the family consisted of one son and three daughters as well as seven grandchildren. On the outbreak of the Second World War he had travelled to Canada in order to re-enlist, but had been told that his work as a construction worker would be of more use to the war effort. As with other Great War VC holders who were alive in 1937 or 1953, Hill was eligible for the Coronation Medals. For the latter he was invited to England for the coronation celebrations. The couple had good seats for the coronation procession itself on 2 June 1953 and also spent a week in Hyde and Denton seeing relatives and being received by the mayor of Denton. When at Hyde town hall Mr and Mrs Hill were officially welcomed by the mayor and Hill was presented with a special tie pin with the local coat of arms on it, as the mayor of Hyde had also been a Hatter. At Denton the couple were also officially welcomed and were shown a book of press cuttings about Hill's life.

In 1956 Hill and his wife attended the VC centenary celebrations in London and met the Queen. Albert Hill died eighteen years later at the Memorial Hospital on 17 February 1971 at the age of 75 and was buried three days later at Highland Memorial Park, Johnston, Rhode Island. The Reference is 10075, 'Buttonwood' Division, Section K, Lot 196, Grave 1. Hill is commemorated with a plaque on the gates of the Memorial Gardens in Stockport Road, Denton, Manchester which was unveiled by a local councillor in

March 1996. The plaque notes that Hill resided in Denton between 1907 and 1923. Hill's name is also included on a plaque unveiled in 1995 outside the Ashton Town Hall, Manchester, and he was one of eight holders of the VC who had local connections. As with his great friend, Joseph Davies, Hill's name is commemorated by the name of a residential Court in Hilltown, Wrexham. The two are also commemorated in Delville Wood with a memorial provided for by the RWF which can be found at the main entrance walk at the rear of the museum.

T.W.H. VEALE

The 8th (Service) Battalion, The Devonshire Regiment had already seen heavy fighting for the village of Mametz on 1 July 1916 as well as being involved in the capture of the German Second Line, when they were called upon to help with the capture of High Wood on the 14th and again on the 20th. Their initial position was to the south-west of the wood itself and their role was to attack towards Delville Wood in an easterly direction. At the time heavy fire was coming from the Switch Lane at the northern edge of High Wood and also from the northern edge of Delville Wood.

The 8th Devons were part of the 20th Brigade of the 7th Division and they attacked with their sister battalion, the 2nd Gordons on their left.

The immediate target of the two battalions was a track called Wood Lane, a route that ran along the eastern side of High Wood and then in a south-easterly direction. It was strongly defended and it was clear that the task of the 20th Brigade was bound to be a hopeless one until the whole of High Wood had been cleared. During the fighting, Private Theodore Veale had gone up to the front in order to assist the stretcher bearers and on hearing from a company corporal that someone was waving his hand to come in, he snatched up a rifle and bomb and went out for about 50 yards when several shots went by him. In his own words when writing to his mother about the incident he wrote:

> I flopped down on the ground, but got up again and ran on
> till I got to the spot where the man had been waving. To my

surprise it was one of our wounded officers (Lt Eric Savill later Sir Eric) I laid down and did all I could for him, and I was well fired at whilst I was there. He (Lt Eric Savill, C Company Commander) had been so close to the Germans, I pulled him back about 15 yards, for I found to my surprise that I was only about 10 yards from the Germans. I pulled him back, thinking they were going to pull him in. I went back to get some water, and I took it to him. They fired at me again, and it was surprising how it was that I was not hit. But I meant to save him at all costs, so off I crawled back again, because it was all open, and I got two more men and a corporal to come with a waterproof sheet, which we put him on.

We tried to pull him back. We got about 80 yards back, and then had to rest, for you know how one's back aches after stooping. Well, the corporal stood up like on his knees, and we saw five Germans pop up out of the grass about 100 yards away. We had to go over a bit of a bridge, and they shot the corporal (Cpl Allen) through the head. That made the other two with me nervous, and they wanted to get back. So I said, 'Get back, and I'll manage.' So they went, and I pulled the wounded officer into a hole, and left him comfortable, and went back. Then I sent a team out to cover any of them that might try to fire at him, and tracked out to him myself with water.

Later, Veale went out with the chaplain who was also acting as a stretcher bearer, Lieutenant Duff and Sergeant Smith. They reached Savill just before dark and just when they were going to get him home they spotted another group of Germans creeping up. Duff covered the Germans with his revolver while Veale risked his life and ran back 150 yards for his gun, and then raced back. At this fifth attempt Veale was able to drag Savill in with Lt Duff's assistance.

The citation for Veale's VC was published in the *London Gazette* of 9 September 1916, and read as follows:

For most conspicuous bravery. Hearing that a wounded officer was lying out in front, Private Veale went out in search, and found him lying amidst growing corn within 50 yards of the enemy. He dragged the officer to a shell hole, returned for water and took it out. Finding that he could not single-handed carry in the officer, he returned for assistance, and took out two volunteers. One of the party was killed when carrying the officer, and heavy fire necessitated leaving the officer in a shell hole.

At dusk Private Veale went out again with volunteers to bring in the officer. Whilst doing this an enemy patrol was observed approaching.

Private Veale at once went back and procured a Lewis gun, and with the fire of the gun he covered the party, and the officer was finally carried to safety.

The courage and determination displayed was of the highest order.

The first that Veale knew of his award was when he read about it in newspapers in the trenches, and he didn't receive it from the King until he attended an investiture at Buckingham Palace on 5 February 1917. A direct result of Veale's bravery was his promotion to the rank of corporal with immediate effect.

Theodore William Henry Veale was born in either 30 or 34 Clarence Street, Dartmouth, Devon on 11 November 1890. He was the eldest son of Henry Veale, a local builder and Ada Veale who was a professional concert pianist. The family address was 12 Mansard Terrace, Dartmouth.

Veale was educated at Dartmouth Council Schools and was a successful and gifted athlete. At the beginning of the war when he was still only 20 years of age, Veale was so impressed by the recruiting rallies that he became the first man in Dartmouth to volunteer. He joined the 8th Devons on 4 September 1914 and one of the men that he trained with at athletics was Lt Eric Savill.

After the award of the VC to Veale was announced, there was considerable interest and excitement in the Devonshire town where Veale was a popular figure.

When Veale returned to Dartmouth he was given a very enthusiastic reception, which began as soon as he got out of the train when it arrived at Kingswear Station. He was then ferried across the River Dart and at some point a local Salvation Army Band played the French National Anthem 'The Marseillaise'. Once in the town itself Veale was shouldered aloft by six men of the Devonshire Regiment and taken to the Guildhall where he was greeted by the mayor and given a public reception. Veale was presented with an Illuminated Address and an inscribed silver coffee pot and salver. He was then taken by carriage to his family home at 12 Mansard Terrace where the residents had laid on a 'welcome home' by decorating their homes with bunting. Eric Savill met up with Veale a few days later, having travelled from Torquay, and he presented him with a gold watch and chain.

One of the many letters of congratulations that Veale received was from Edwin Savill in which he thanked Veale for saving his son's life. Lt Savill was to work for the Royal Family at Windsor Great Park after the war was over.

Veale was discharged from the army on 15 March 1919 and at the time was suffering from chest troubles probably caused by his exposure to poison gas. In 1921 Veale was introduced to the then Prince of Wales who was photographed signing Veale's autograph book. Veale is apparently still in the army as he is in uniform with his corporal's stripes.

In 1966 Veale was one of a group of VC holders who were invited by the Ministry of Defence to take part in the 50th anniversary commemoration of the Battle of the Somme.

Two years later Veale was employed as a commissionaire at the *Daily Mail* Ideal Home Exhibition but later became so hard up that he had to put his VC and medals up for sale. They appeared in a shop window near Trafalgar Square in 1973 when Veale was living in Park Road, Balham, South London. Fortunately the Devonshire Regiment was informed of what was happening and the asking price of £2,100 was raised and the decorations are on display in the Devonshire and Dorset Regimental Museum in Dorchester, Dorset. On 25 April 1980, with the aid of a walking frame, the 87-year-old Theodore Veale reviewed a Passing Out Parade of Territorial Army recruits of the Royal Engineers at Inglis Barracks, Mill Hill. Seven months later Veale died on 6 November 1980 at his daughter's home in Ware Road, Hoddesdon, Hertfordshire, when he was five days short of his 89th birthday. He was cremated at Enfield Crematorium on 12 November after a full military funeral, reference 138457, and his ashes scattered in area M3-D8. He had been one of the oldest surviving VC holders.

It is a curious and also humorous coincidence that three Great War VC holders born in the county of Devon included Veale, Sage and Onions! Sage served with the Somerset Light Infantry and the other two served with the Devonshire Regiment.

Sir Eric Savill, the man who Veale rescued east of High Wood, died in April 1980 a few months before his rescuer. He had become well known in the 1930s for the creation of a 35-acre ornamental garden in Windsor Great Park which became a popular tourist attraction.

At the instigation of the *Dartmouth Chronicle* and its owner, Sir Ray Tindle, a fund was set up for a memorial to Theodore Veale which was unveiled on 10 November 2002 on what turned out to be a wet and blustery day. It was erected in the Royal Avenue Gardens, Dartmouth and was unveiled by Veale's daughter, Mrs Theodora Grindell. She wore her father's medals which had been lent by the Devonshire & Dorset Regimental Museum in Dorchester. In addition her daughter laid a wreath and relatives of Sir Eric Savill also attended the ceremony. There followed a march past by the Devonshire & Dorsetshire Regiment with band and a Remembrance Service at St Saviour's Church. On the following day at Kingswear, across the River Dart, a service was held to commemorate the life of Lt Col H. Jones who had won a VC in May 1982 during the Falklands campaign.

J. LEAK

Despite the Allied failure to capture Longueval, Delville Wood and High Wood, the second phase of the Battle of the Somme was still planned to continue. By now the village of Pozières was the main immediate Allied objective, but owing to its dominant geographical position, any attempt to wrench it from enemy hands was bound to lead to very fierce fighting and its subsequent casualties. As had occurred on the Gallipoli Peninsula the year before, the struggle for the possession of the village of Pozières was to become one of the sacrificial periods which later contributed to the Australian nation 'coming of age'.

On 23 July as if to underline the Australian contribution, two members of the 1st Australian Division were to win the VC on the same day. Their names were Private John Leak of the 9th (Queensland), Australian Infantry Battalion (3rd Brigade) and Second Lieutenant Arthur Blackburn of the 10th (South Australia) Australian Infantry Battalion. British troops had reached the German advanced position in front of Pozières and the enemy lines ran in a south-easterly direction from the direction of Mouquet Farm, which in reality was just a ruined set of buildings. Before the Australian Division was called upon there had been three attempts to take the village all of which had failed.

The main defence lines were a double trench system known as OG1 and OG2 (Old German), and on 20 July the 9th (Queensland) Battalion led the Australians into the area and an extremely fierce fight developed early on the 22nd. On the 23rd another attack was made with the 1st Australian Brigade on the left and the 3rd Brigade on the right. The 9th (Queensland) Battalion covered

450 yards on the extreme right and under the shelter of a very heavy artillery barrage the troops made some progress. However, at a point where OG1 met another trench, Pozières Trench, there was fierce enemy resistance and two machine-guns held up the Australians. The German bombs 'outranged' the Australian ones and it was at this point that Leak, without being given any instructions, suddenly leapt out of his trench and ran forward and destroyed the enemy strong point, bayoneting the three survivors. When his comrades caught up with him they found him calmly wiping the German blood from his bayonet using his felt hat. The time was 12.59am. Most of Pozières Trench was now taken but the 9th had nearly run out of bombs and later in the engagement were driven back with Leak always the last to withdraw at each stage, covering his comrades' retreat. The post was retaken after reinforcements arrived. The fighting for possession of Pozières raged for four more days and the 9th Battalion who had gone into battle with 1,016 men emerged with 623.

On 21 August Leak was wounded in the fighting at Mouquet Farm, close to the village of Thiepval and 1,500 yards north-west of Pozières. His VC was gazetted on 9 September 1916 and read as follows:

> For most conspicuous bravery. He was one of a party who finally captured an enemy strong point. At one assault, when the enemy's bombs were outranging ours, Private Leak rushed out of the trench, ran forward under heavy machine-gun fire at close range, and threw bombs into the enemy's bombing post. He then jumped into the post and bayoneted three unwounded enemy bombers.
>
> Later, when the enemy in overwhelming numbers was driving his party back, he was always the last to withdraw at each stage, and kept on throwing bombs. His courage and energy had such an effect on the enemy that, on arrival of reinforcements, the whole trench was recaptured.

Leak was presented with his decoration by the King at Buckingham Palace on 4 November 1916.

John Leak was born in Portsmouth, England in 1896 and was half Welsh and half Australian; his father was James and he had a brother, also called James. John Leak migrated to Australia prior to the war and became a teamster in the road haulage business in Rockhampton, Queensland. On 28 January 1915 he enlisted with the AIF and embarked on a troopship with the 5th Reinforcements prior to joining the 9th (Queensland) Battalion in Gallipoli on 22 June 1915. He was wounded on 21 August and on 2 September was admitted to 1st Field Ambulance and later moved to the 1st Australian CCC in Malta suffering with colitis. He was then transferred to the 5th Southern General Hospital in Portsmouth on 8 October.

After the withdrawal from the Gallipoli Peninsula in January 1916, the 1st Australian Division left for Egypt and later sailed to France to take part in the Battle of the Somme. Leak rejoined his battalion when they were still in Egypt on 4 March 1916 and who arrived in Marseilles on 3 April. A month after his VC action and having been being badly wounded by gunshot wounds at Mouquet Farm on 23 August, Leak was out of action for fourteen months until he was declared fit enough to rejoin the 9th Battalion on 15 October 1917. In early November Leak got into trouble with the authorities and was accused of desertion when he was absent from the line and was subsequently court-martialled on the 23rd. However, his sentence was suspended and he returned to the line a month later. Three months later he was severely gassed at Hollebeke, Belgium on 7 March 1918 and was unable to resume army duties until 26 June. He was out of action yet again, this time with bronchitis, and rejoined the 9th Battalion on 14 Oct 1918. As for his court-martial sentence, it was reviewed on three occasions and after the Armistice in November it was finally remitted on Christmas Day.

After the war was over, Leak married Beatrice May Chapman at St John's Baptist Church, Cardiff, South Wales on 30 December 1918. The couple embarked for Australia on 9 February 1919 and he was finally discharged in Queensland on 31 May 1919. They then remained in Queensland for two and a half years before moving to New South Wales. By now the marriage appears to have broken down and Leak moved again to South Australia and then moved westwards to Esperance in Western Australia where he became a mechanic and garage owner. On 12 January 1927 he married again, this time to Ada Victoria Bood-Smith and the couple were to have four sons and three daughters. When he retired he went to live at Crafers in South Australia. In later years he suffered from bronchitis and emphysema which had been brought on by his war service and was unable to attend the Victoria Cross Centenary Celebrations in London in 1956. In 1966 a duplicate of Leak's VC turned up at an antique shop in Carlton, Victoria that the dealer said he had purchased 'years ago'. Mr Leak said at the time that his VC had always been kept under lock and key but fakes were made of the medals from time to time. The Ministry of Defence thought it unlikely that two medals would have been struck for the same award.

At the age of 80 John Leak died in Adelaide after a heart attack at Redwood Park, Crafers, South Australia on 20 October 1972. He was buried in Stirling District Cemetery, Adelaide, Block 14-A and is commemorated at the Australian War Memorial in Canberra and his name is also one of ninety-six holders of the VC commemorated at the Victoria Cross Park in the same city. He is also commemorated on the VC Memorial in the Queen Victoria Building, Sydney. His VC and medals remain in private hands.

A.S. BLACKBURN

On 23 July 1916, the day that John Leak earned the VC for gallantry in Pozières Trench, a second member of the AIF, Lieutenant A.S. Blackburn gained his decoration not far from Pozières Trench when his battalion the 10th (South Australia) Australian Infantry Battalion, 3rd Australian Brigade, 1st Australian Division was presented with a similar situation a few hours after Leak's action, having been asked for assistance by the 9th Battalion.

Within two hours of Pozières Trench being captured, the division encountered very stiff resistance at the lines OG1 and OG2 which ran from Mouquet Farm in a south-easterly direction and across the main Albert–Bapaume Road to the south of Pozières Mill. The fighting resulted in the line being bent back at right angles. Less than a couple of hundred metres from the trench that had held up Private Leak's platoon, Lt Blackburn's battalion was presented with a similar problem.

During the 9th Battalion's attempt to destroy a German machine-gun post in OG1, their commanding officer, Lt Col W.F.J. McCann was seriously wounded in the head and their adjutant Lt C.H. Ruddle was killed. The source of bombs had dried up and the Australian attackers were driven down OG1 Trench to a point where they set up a barricade 120 yards short of Pozières Trench. Reserve companies of the 10th Battalion under Major F.G. Giles then arrived from the south-east (Black Watch Alley) in OG1. At 5.30am, assessing the situation Giles instructed Blackburn to take a party of fifty men along with two teams of bombers, in order to continue the fight. At the barricade he found the exhausted remains of McCann's party. Blackburn, with a small group from his own company together with a few bombers, leapt over the barricade and rushed the enemy to bomb them out of their positions. Bay after bay was captured this way despite machine-gun fire from OG2 and from the direction of Munster Alley which ran back at right angles from the German Second Line. With a party of four men, Blackburn then set off in order to destroy a troublesome enemy machine-gun but, in exposing themselves to German fire, every man was killed. Blackburn then returned for assistance and asked Colonel Robertson to arrange for artillery cover and also for trench mortar support. He then took another group of bombers and this time gained a further 30 yards of ground.

The situation became very confused and enemy resistance stiffened. Blackburn crawled forward with Sgt R.M. Inwood and searched for the link between his 10th and 9th battalions. They discovered that there was a strong German position at a cross trench which cut OG1 at right angles. During a rush on this enemy post, Inwood was killed and Blackburn's party was in danger of being cut off. They were saved by the finding of a tunnel which ran under the Pozières–Bazentin Road and which by chance led to a group of men from the 9th Battalion in what was part of the eastern end of Pozières Trench. Blackburn was sent out no fewer than four more times, which meant eight times in all, and Howitzer protection was abandoned as it proved to be too unreliable. Blackburn had the assistance of seventy men, of whom forty became casualties. He was finally relieved by a platoon under a Lt Partridge, who in turn was relieved and the attack towards the OG positions stopped 600 yards short of its goal. However, Lt Blackburn had been instrumental in providing the link-up between the two battalions, the line was in fact broken but the two units had the gap covered. In this early fighting for the village of Pozières the casualties were at their heaviest and the enemy at its most resolute.

It was hardly surprising that along with Pte Leak, Lt Blackburn was to be awarded the VC for all his hard work on this day and it was a miracle that he survived. The award was gazetted on 9 September 1916 and read as follows:

> For most conspicuous bravery, he was directed with fifty men to drive the enemy from a strong point. By dogged determination, he eventually captured their trench, after

personally leading four separate parties of bombers against it, many of whom became casualties.

In face of fierce opposition he captured 250 yards of trench. Then, after crawling forward with a sergeant to reconnoitre, he returned, attacked and seized another 120 yards of trench, establishing communications with the battalion on his left.

He received the decoration from the King at Buckingham Palace on 4 October 1916. He was the first man from South Australia to win the award.

Arthur Seaforth Blackburn was born at Woodville, Hyde Park, Adelaide, South Australia on 25 November 1892. His father was Canon T. Blackburn, rector of St Margarets, Woodville for twenty years. His mother was Margaret Stewart, formerly Brown, and was the Canon's second wife. Arthur was educated at Pulteney Grammar School, St Peter's College and the University of Adelaide where he studied law. Graduating in 1913 he was called to the Bar in December. He then lived at Hyde Park where he was a practising solicitor having been articled to C.B. Hardy.

Fifteen days after the war began, Blackburn was one of the first to enlist, which he did at Morphettville with the 10th AIF. He became a member of A Company and, after training, his battalion was to be part of the Australian Force to capture the Gallipoli Peninsula from Turkish Forces and they left for Egypt in October 1914. The battalion took part in the Australian landings on 25 April when with a colleague, Pte P. Robin, the two men distinguished themselves by reaching the furthest point after circling the east side of Scrubby Knoll, about 2,000 yards from Anzac Cove. Robin was killed shortly afterwards. Their instructions had been 'Go like Hell for Third Ridge'. Blackburn had been promoted to lance corporal in May 1915 and was commissioned as a second lieutenant on 4 August, and in November the unit left the Peninsula for the port of Lemnos and later Egypt, where he was made full lieutenant on 26 February 1916 and in the same month embarked for France. Prior to the Somme battle, he was transferred to D Company as platoon commander and on 23 July the 10th Battalion was in reserve after the 9th Battalion had attacked and called for assistance. At the end of 1916 he was not fit enough to continue as an

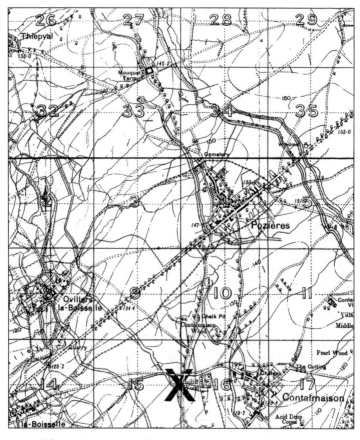

Detail from OS map area of Martinpuich, part of 57D S.E. and 57C S.W., corrected to 6 July 1916. The railway ran diagonally across square X3, north of Pozières and across square 5. The windmill is in square 35 and Mouquet Farm in square 33. (TM 8291)

active soldier and returned to Adelaide in December. He married Rose Ada Kelly, daughter of J.H. Kelly of Walkerville on 22 March 1917 in his former college chapel, and in time they were to have two sons and two daughters. He was discharged from the AIF on 10 April 1917. He returned to the legal profession, becoming a member of the South Australian House of Assembly between 1918 and 1921 as Nationalist member for Sturt. The speeches which he made in the Assembly Chamber were usually concerned with the welfare of returning servicemen. Blackburn also became a founding member of the Returned Sailors', Soldiers' and Airmen's Imperial League and was president of the State Branch from 1917 to 1921.

Four years later he entered into a law partnership with Lt Col W.F.J. McCann who had been with him at Pozières and who had also been at the same award ceremony at Buckingham Palace on 4 October 1916.Their practice was in Adelaide.

Blackburn had been appointed to the Reserve of Officers and served on various committees, his militia service began on 31 October 1925 when he was given the rank of lieutenant and he became a member of the 43rd Battalion. He was promoted to captain in 1927 and on 1 July transferred to a light horse regiment. He became city coroner in 1933 and in 1935 moved to 5 Salisbury Terrace, Collinswood.

On 15 January 1937 Blackburn was promoted to major. By 1939 he had served all told as a militia officer for fifteen years and was promoted to lieutenant colonel and took command of a motorised cavalry regiment, the 18th Light Horse (Machine-Gun) Regiment on 1 July 1939. In 1940 he gave up the law and joined the 2nd/3rd Australian Machine-Gun Battalion, AIF, which fought under his command in Syria in 1941 where as the most senior officer present he accepted the surrender of Damascus on 21 June. He and his group were later transferred to South East Asia and by now he had been promoted to the rank of temporary brigadier general with the 7th Australian Division. After three weeks of fighting together with a small Dutch group, they were forced to surrender by the Japanese. He was a prisoner in Singapore, Moji in South Japan, Pusan in Korea and finally Mukden, Manchuria where he was liberated in September 1945. On his return to Adelaide he was greeted by three VC holders: Thomas Caldwell, Philip Davey and Reg Inwood. Blackburn's health was poor but by now his spirit hadn't been broken by being a prisoner of the Japanese. In 1946 he was made a CBE (Military).

Between 1947 and 1955 he served as Commissioner in the Commonwealth Court of Conciliation and Arbitration and took on various directorships. He had again been chairman of trustees of the Services Canteen Trust from 1955 to 1960. In 1955 he became a member of the Australian National Airlines Commission. It was for all these community duties that he was made a CMG in 1955 and in 1956 he travelled to London for the VC Centenary.

Arthur Blackburn died suddenly of a burst aneurism at Crafers, Adelaide on 24 November 1960, one day short of his 68th birthday. He was buried with full military honours at West Terrace, AIF Cemetery, Light Ova Section Grave 4-C-North. He was survived by his widow and the couple's four children. He is commemorated at the Australian War Memorial in Canberra where his decorations and war medals are also held. His name is also remembered in the VC Memorial Park in Canberra and in the VC memorial in Queen Victoria building, Sydney.

T. COOKE

The third member of the Australian forces to gain the VC for gallantry at Pozières in July 1916 was Pte T. Cooke of the 8th (Victoria) Australian Infantry Battalion, 2nd Australian Brigade, 1st Australian Division. It was awarded for action during the period 24/25 July and not 28 July as several reference books state.

The Allies were still trying to complete their capture of Pozières but had not yet succeeded in clearing the enemy out of the OG positions. To quote the historian C.E.W. Bean: 'The right front company of the 8th, in pushing through Pozières, met with heavy fire and the loss of three officers, but reached the post already held in the orchard, where a party of the 1st Pioneers at once began to dig a redoubt... but the intended positions between the village and the OG lines had not yet been occupied... At 8.15, while the bombardment continued, large numbers of the enemy were seen advancing southwards on the crest near Pozières windmill. This movement was observed from many parts of the Australian front, and was interpreted as an attempt to counter-attack.' It was met by a heavy artillery barrage. Cooke had been ordered with his gun-team to a dangerous point, where he held out under heavy fire until all his comrades had been killed. When assistance was eventually sent he was found dead beside his gun at Orchard Post. He was subsequently awarded the VC posthumously. His award was gazetted on 9 September 1916 and read as follows:

For most conspicuous bravery. After a Lewis gun had been disabled, he was ordered to take his gun and gun-team to a dangerous part of the line. Here he did fine work, but came under very heavy fire, with the result that finally he was the only man left. He still stuck to his post, and continued to fire his gun. When assistance came he was found dead beside his gun. He set a splendid example of determination and devotion to duty.

The Battalion War Diary described the situation in the following way:

At 3.30 under cover of artillery fire the attack was launched, the battalion attacking on a frontage of two companies (C and D companys) right and left respectively with B Company in support. The attack proceeded vigorously through the village, and each trench and strong point being quickly cleared of the enemy. The left company D with an irresistible advance reached its objective by 5am and proceeded to establish itself 50 yards north of the cemetery. Our right company C met with strong opposition, but fighting with great determination speedily overcame it, and shortly after 5am, reached their objective NE of the village and at once dug in. Bombing parties of the 4th Battalion working up German Trench cooperated splendidly, driving the enemy towards positions occupied by our left company, where they were either killed or made prisoner.

When the battalion was relieved two days later their total casualties were 347, with sixteen reported missing.

Thomas Cooke was the son of Tom and Caroline Anne Cook (née Cooper) and was born in Kaikoura, Marlborough, New Zealand on 5 July 1881. His English-born father was a carpenter by trade. Thomas attended Kaikoura Demonstration High School and later moved to Wellington with his family where he married Maud Elizabeth Elliott on 4 June 1902. Like his father, Thomas was a builder's carpenter by trade and the family moved to Richmond, a suburb of Melbourne in 1912 and in time the Cookes had three children, two girls and a boy. Tom's favourite recreation was playing the first cornet in a band.

At the age of 33 he enlisted with the AIF in Melbourne on 16 February 1915 and was allotted to the 24th Battalion as reinforcement. He trained at Broadmeadows and embarked for Egypt in November on the troopship *Commonwealth* and on arrival was transferred to the 8th (Victoria) Australian Infantry Battalion, 2nd Australian Brigade, 1st Australian Division at Serapeum in the Suez Canal Zone. His battalion left for France on 26 March 1916 and from April to July served in the Fleurbaix and Messines sections of the Western Front. In mid-July his battalion moved southwards to the Somme. He was acting corporal from 25 November 1915 until 24 February 1916 when a member of the 7th Battalion, but then relinquished his stripe when he transferred to the 8th Battalion. After news of his posthumous award was published in New Zealand, the inhabitants of his birthplace and in Wellington were delighted and an attempt to honour his memory was made, although I have not found out what form it took.

Cooke, whose widow remarried, is commemorated with a street named after him in Canberra, ACT and is one of nintey-six VC holders remembered in Victoria Cross Memorial Park, also in Canberra. In addition his name is one of the same group who are remembered in the Victoria Cross Memorial in the Queen Victoria Building in Sydney. His VC and medals are displayed at the National Army Museum at Waiouru, New Zealand.

A. Gill

By 25 July the British had abandoned their series of attacks to capture High Wood, which they were not to achieve until mid-September. However, the next day brought them the prize of the capture of Pozières village, which the enemy had been so loathe to let go.

On the 28th the British were to finally capture the village of Longueval and the adjacent Delville Wood. This was not achieved without heavy fighting and the gaining of another posthumous award of the VC this time by Sergeant Albert Gill. His battalion was the 1st Battalion, The King's Royal Rifle Corps (KRRC), 99th Brigade, 2nd Division. The other three battalions in this brigade were the 1st Battalion, Prince Charlotte of Wales's Royal Berkshire Regiment and two units of the Royal Fusiliers: the 22nd (Service) Battalion (Kensington), The Royal Fusiliers (City of London) Regiment and 23rd (Service) Battalion (1st Sportsman's), The Royal Fusiliers (City of London) Regiment.

At 7am on the 27th, the 99th Brigade made what was to be the final assault to clear the enemy from Delville Wood. The 1st Royal Berkshires, the 1st KRRC and the 23rd Royal Fusiliers led the attack and drove the enemy to the fringe of the wood. However, there then followed a strong German counter-attack and it was during this period of fighting that Sgt Gill won his VC. The citation was published on 26 October1916 and read as follows:

> For most conspicuous bravery. The enemy made a very strong counter-attack on the right flank of the battalion, and rushed the bombing post, after killing all the company bombers.

Sgt Gill rallied the remnants of his platoon, none of whom were skilled bombers, and reorganised his defences, a most difficult and dangerous task, the trench being very shallow and much damaged. Soon afterwards the enemy nearly surrounded his men by creeping up through the thick undergrowth, and commenced sniping at about 20 yards' range. Although it was almost certain death, Sgt Gill stood boldly up in order to direct the fire of his men. He was killed almost at once, but not before he had shown his men where the enemy were, and thus enabled them to hold up their advance.

By his supreme devotion to duty and self-sacrifice he saved a very dangerous situation.

Delville Wood was finally cleared of the enemy by the 2nd Division, on 28 July, the following day.

His widow received her husband's award from the King at Buckingham Palace on 29 Nov 1916.

Albert Gill, known by his comrades as 'Gilly', was the son of Henry and Sophia Gill and was born on 8 September 1879 at Hospital Street, Birmingham. The family later lived in Dugdale Street which has since been redeveloped, and later Gill himself was to live at 2 Back of Cope Street, Spring Hill, Birmingham. Before joining up, he worked for the Post Office for seventeen years and was about 35 years of age when the Great War began. In 1912 he and his family visited Australia and two of his three children were later to die early while he was serving in France.

Three weeks after Gill had been killed, his company commander wrote to Mrs Rosetta Gill in a letter dated 16 August 1916:

> The Adjutant has handed me your letter of 8 August, as I was your late husband's company commander. I am afraid that it is quite true that your husband was killed in action on 27 July. He was shot through the head, and must have died at once. He could have known nothing about it. I would have written to you before had I known your address, as your husband was one of the most valued men in my company and a man who anyone would be proud to call friend. He was killed when rallying his men under terrible fire, and

had he lived he would certainly have got the DCM. I was quite close to him, despite the very trying circumstances. The battalion had just taken a wood [Delville], and the Germans were counter-attacking heavily. I am glad to say we drove them back, and we have since received the thanks of everyone, from Sir Douglas Haig down. It was entirely owing to the heroic example and self-sacrifice of men like your husband that we did so well. He was loved by his platoon, of which I am sorry to say only four or five men remain. That day's work will always remain fixed in my memory as the one in which I lost so many gallant comrades. I lost all the officers and sergeants in my own company, and very many of the men. You should be justly proud of your husband in his life and death. He had one of the finest natures I have ever known. No words of mine can express my sympathy with you in your terrible sorrow. May the memory of his heroic end support you.

Mrs Gill was presented with her husband's VC by the King at Buckingham Palace on 29 November 1916.

Albert Gill was buried at Delville Wood cemetery, Row IV, C, 3 and was the fourth man to gain the VC for the fight for Delville Wood. His decorations were sold at Sothebys on 19 July 1965 for £800 and were sold again at auction on 29 March 2000 for the hammer price of £60,000 by Dix Noonan Webb.

C.C. CASTLETON

The main part of the village of Pozières had been captured by 26 July 1916, but the struggle for the Pozières Heights was not finally resolved by the Allies until 4 August.

It was on 29 July when the fourth member of the Australian Force was to win a VC and, as with Pte T. Cooke four days before him, Sgt Castleton of the 5th Australian Machine Gun Company, was to lose his life in doing so. His unit, and the 5th (New South Wales) Brigade, was part of the 2nd Australian Division which had replaced the 1st Australian Division between 25 and 27 July. There were four New South Wales Battalions in the Brigade: the 17th, 18th, 19th and 20th. The plan was to make an assault on the Pozières Heights.

Before midnight on 28/29 July the enemy had seen leading troops of the 20th Battalion moving into assembly positions to the south of the Albert–Bapaume Road, and had fired on the second wave of troops with machine-guns. This fire was accompanied by flares and a barrage, and the Australian attackers were forced to lie out for three hours until the machine-gun fire had subsided. Just before dawn the troops began to withdraw. It had been the 'makeshift' jumping off arrangements which had led to the failure of this attack. The leading wave of the 17th Battalion had been detected by the enemy when the Australians were seen to be climbing out of their trenches in order to bomb up the OG2 position. The bombing attack was called off because there was no sign of the 20th's attack and when the battalion withdrew, Castleton, who was stationed at the sandbag block of OG1, went out into no man's land in order to rescue some of the wounded whom he had seen lying there. It was in the same vicinity where Lt A.S. Blackburn and Pte J. Leak had also won the VC. Castleton brought in two men and was struck by a bullet and killed when bringing in a third casualty. His citation was published on 26 September 1916 and read as follows:

> For most conspicuous bravery. During an attack on the enemy trenches the infantry was temporarily driven back by the intense machine-gun fire opened by the enemy. Many wounded were left in 'No Man's Land' lying in shell holes.
>
> Sergeant Castleton went out twice in face of this intense fire and each time brought in a wounded man on his back.
>
> He went out a third time and was bringing in another wounded man when he was himself hit in the back and killed instantly.
>
> He set a splendid example of courage and self-sacrifice.

The 5th Brigade had lost 146 men, including six officers, mostly from the 20th Battalion. Castleton's body was eventually brought from its original burial site between Pozières and the Bazentin villages and laid to rest in Pozières British Cemetery, Row IV, L, 43 and his posthumous VC, which was recommended by the brigadier general commanding the 5th Australian Brigade, was presented to his father by the King at Buckingham Palace on 29 November 1916.

Claude Charles Castleton was the son of Thomas Charles Castleton and his wife Edith Lucy Payne and was born in Morton Road, Kirkley, South Lowestoft, Suffolk on 12 April 1893. He attended Morton Road School and later the local Grammar School. He was a very practical and adventurous boy and during the school holidays used to take himself off camping and sailing on the Norfolk Broads. Later he became a pupil teacher at Morton Road School where he had himself gone as a child and had won a scholarship. His father was a builder and the family house was at 18 Wilson Road which is adjacent to Morton Road.

At the age of 19 Castleton decided to emigrate to Australia with the idea of seeing as much of the world as he could, before settling down in England again. He reached Melbourne in the autumn of 1912 and worked on a sheep farm and tried his hand at prospecting gold. He moved on to Tasmania and then travelled extensively throughout the states of Victoria, New South Wales and Queensland. When war broke out in August 1914 he was in Port Moresby, Papua New Guinea. He offered his services and together with one other white man was in charge of a large number of Aborigines who carried out coastal defence duties. He also worked at a cable and wireless station before returning to Sydney where he enlisted in March 1915. He stated his occupation as prospector.

His 18th Battalion, part of 2nd Brigade, sailed for Egypt in June 1915 and reached Gallipoli in early August. During the action at Anzac Cove he was to show qualities of leadership and courage when, on losing an officer and a sergeant, the fellow members of his company turned to him as their natural leader. Castleton was evacuated from the Peninsula with dysentery on 15 September and was promoted to the rank of corporal on 7 December, returning to the Peninsula on 8 December, but only for a short time as the Anzac Force was soon evacuated. On 20 February while serving in Egypt he was made a temporary sergeant and on 8 March was transferred to the 5th Machine Gun Company. His new rank was confirmed on the 16th and his brigade arrived in France a week later.

After Castleton was killed on 29 July 1916 a comrade wrote to his father saying:

> We were helping to hold a first line of trenches, when our infantrymen made an attack on the enemy. As may be expected, we had some casualties, Claude, knowing some of our wounded men to be out in no man's land, could not resist going to their assistance. Amidst shrapnel and heavy machine-gun fire and gas, he leaped out, and recovered two wounded men, and was in the act of bringing in a third, when to our sorrow, he was either hit by rifle or machine-gun fire. First aid men went to his assistance immediately, but could do no good; he had done his last. We gave him a decent burial behind our frontline, erecting a small cross with his name, number etc, over his grave. His name will stand forever amongst the officers and men of his company, and also with the infantrymen and officers to whom we were attached....

After the war Castleton's parents paid for a plaque to be put up in South Cliff United Reform Church, Morton Road which is where the family worshipped and is still in existence. The church itself is only about 108 years old. Castleton's name is also listed on a panel of 711 names in St Margaret's Parish Church, Lowestoft of local men and women who died during the Great War, many of whom would have been employed in the fishing industry. At one time a portrait of him hung in the town hall and his VC was still in the possession of his family in 1968 but has since been acquired by the Australian War Memorial in Canberra. Claude's brother Frank became town clerk of Folkestone, Kent and the small terraced house where the family lived, number 18 Wilson Street, South Lowestoft, still exists, although it has been 'modernised'.

Since the first edition of the present book was published in 1991 a commemorative plaque has been erected on the front of the house. The small green circular plaque commemorates Castleton's links with the house prior to his leaving for Australia in 1912. In addition the house has also been repainted and is now a holiday let called 'Sea Breezes'.

In 1961 the South Cliff Congregational Church became the United Reform Church, but eventually congregation numbers became so low that the church had to be closed and remained unused until 1995 when it was taken over as a Roman Catholic Church and re-named as St Nicholas, Pakefield in South Lowestoft.

Two more links with Castleton's memory can be found in Lowestoft as there exists a small close of fifteen houses called Castleton Close as well as Castleton Avenue, which is part of the B1384 road in the town. His name is also one of ninety-six Australian VCs won in the Great War, commemorated in Victoria Cross Park Memorial in Canberra and dedicated in July 2000, a hundred years after Australia received its first VC. The same ninety-six names are also commemorated in the Victoria Cross Memorial in the Queen Victoria Building, Sydney. Finally there is also a crescent named after Castleton in Canberra, ACT.

W.J.G. EVANS

The 30th Division consisted of the 21st, 89th and 90th brigades. In the last named brigade were three battalions of the Manchester Regiment, the 16th, 17th and 18th (Service) battalions, The Manchester Regiment, as well as the 2nd Battalion, The Royal Scots Fusiliers.

Earlier in July 1916 the division had been involved in the capture of Montauban and Trônes Wood. It was later withdrawn in order to be made ready for an attack on the very strongly-held village of Guillemont. The 21st Brigade made an attempt on the 23rd but was let down by a lack of artillery support. A second attempt to capture the village was planned to be made on 30 July, a day which began as very misty and then became very hot with temperatures in the 80s. The 30th Division was to attack through the lines of the 35th Division and the 89th Brigade was to reach the southern end of the village while the 5th Brigade, 2nd Division was to capture Guillemont Station and the enemy trenches beyond it. Zero hour was fixed at 4.45am and Maltz Horn Farm was quickly taken and the advance continued downhill in an easterly direction. The 18th Manchesters had left their assembly trenches at Brick Lane for the 3-mile walk to Guillemont via Trônes Wood and the enemy, sensing an attack, bombarded their route and used gas shells as well. Although men wore gas helmets, they soon became stifled by them and lost all sense of direction. In addition, Trônes Wood was a nightmare of unburied bodies and smashed trees. The battalion emerged finally on the east side of the wood at 4.30am and was due at their assembly positions at 5.00am. The attack was carried out in a heavy ground mist and the 89th Brigade advanced on the right with the 90th on the left. The two leading battalions of the latter brigade, the 18th Manchesters and the 2nd Royal Scots reached their positions in the western part of the village but without artillery back-up. Worse was to follow in that the enemy artillery was so accurate that any support was cut off by it. The Royal Scots were virtually annihilated and the 18th and two companies of the 17th Manchesters were taken prisoner. It was during this chaos that Company Sergeant Major George Evans of B Company (18th Manchesters) was to gain the VC and his citation, which was published on 30 January 1920 read as follows:

> For most conspicuous bravery and devotion to duty during the attack on Guillemont on 30 July, 1916, when under heavy rifle and machine-gun fire he volunteered to take back an important message after five runners had been killed in attempting to do so. He had to cover about 700 yards, the whole of which was under observation from the enemy.
>
> Company Sergeant Major Evans, however, succeeded in delivering the message, and although wounded, rejoined his company, although advised to go to the dressing station.
>
> The return journey to the company again meant a journey of 700 yards under severe rifle and machine-gun fire, but by dodging from shell hole to shell hole he was able to do so, and was taken prisoner some hours later.
>
> On previous occasions at Montauban and Trônes Wood this gallant warrant officer displayed great bravery and devotion to duty, and has always been a splendid example to his men.

B Company had been almost entirely made up of recruits from Lloyd's Packing House in Manchester, and the total number of casualties of the 18th Manchesters for the attack against Guillemont was 476 including killed, wounded and missing. This figure included sixteen officers. Evans' battalion withdrew to Citadel Camp and later moved to Mansell Copse before leaving the Somme area.

Evans' VC was to be the last one gazetted in the Great War, the last of 634 to be awarded. He was presented with it on 12 March 1920 and the reason for the delay was that he had been made a prisoner of war and probably those who recommended him for the award were also POWs.

George Evans was born on 16 February 1876 in Kensington, West London. His parents were Daniel Jones Evans and Georgina Evans. His mother died in 1876, six weeks after George was born, and his father died in 1889.

George attended several schools and as a consequence became very self-reliant. He grew up to be a burly 6ft tall man with a friendly presence. On 4 March 1894, at the age of 18 he enlisted in the Scots Guards and served in the South African War between 1899 and 1902 with the 1st Battalion. He saw action at Belmont and Modder River. Evans spent six months in Orange Free State and during the war became a member of the Imperial Representative Corps which accompanied the Duke and Duchess of York, later King George V and Queen Mary, when they visited Australia for the Commonwealth Celebrations. He returned to South Africa and then served in the final part of the Boer War. He subsequently became an Instructor for the Scots Guards, but after eight years was discharged in August 1902. He served for five years with the Derby Borough Police Force and later in Manchester he began a successful career with the Children's Society, the NSPCC, as an inspector. However, a few months after war began in August 1914 Evans rejoined the Army on 4 January 1915. He did not join the Guards but the Manchester Regiment (3rd City Pals), two months later he was promoted second class warrant officer, company sergeant major on 15 March and left for France on 8 November 1915. He was wounded in the arm during the Somme fighting before being taken prisoner on 11 September 1916.

Evans was later to say that as a prisoner of war he was treated like a criminal and spent the two years in various German camps. He existed on parcels from home and lost six stone in weight. Finally he was exchanged and arrived in Holland on 6 June 1918, but it was not until 19 November 1918 that he was sent back to England and demobilised on 20 February 1919.

George Evans married Clara Bates at St Mark's, Cheetham Hill, Manchester and they had four children, two boys and two girls. The couples first home was either at 36 Cheetham Hill or at 62 Woodlands Road, Manchester. His wife deputised for her husband in the NSPCC while he was absent for five years. In 1920 Evans was presented with a wallet containing the proceeds collected from a public fund at the Higher Crump Constitutional Club, Manchester.

Evans, who through his work with the NSPCC became known as the 'Children's VC', returned to live and work in London, first stationed in Hackney and then in Sydenham, where he died suddenly at his home on 5 Tremaine Road, Annerly, South London, on 28 September 1937 at the age of 61. He was buried with full military honours close to his home at Elmers End Cemetery, Beckenham. A bearer party from the Scots Guards was in attendance and the Last Post and Reveille were played at the graveside. George Evans' VC and medals were born on a cushion at the ceremony and Masonic Funeral Rites were observed. His funeral was a pretty grand affair and many local dignatories attended as well as colleagues from the Scots Guards, the Manchester Regiment, the NSPCC and the Police Force. A memorial service to his memory was also held in Manchester Cathedral. Evans' grave has the reference Row 1, T-8, 16239 and was originally cared for by the local Scots Guards, but over the years has fallen into a poor state. This situation was rectified by members of the Evans family who supervised the task of restoring it in 2009. His name was inscribed in the memorial in the Guards Chapel in Birdcage Walk, London as well as being listed in the memorial books of the Manchester and King's Regiments in Manchester Cathedral. His name is also remembered as one of eight names of the holders of the VC in Lewisham Civic Centre. His VC and medals are in private hands.

J. MILLER

On 30 July 1916 the principal III Corps operation was to try and capture the Intermediate Trench to the north of Bazentin le Petit and due west of High Wood. The division to be involved was the 19th (Western) and the brigade the 57th. This brigade consisted of 10th (Service) Battalion, the Royal Warwickshire Regiment, 8th (Service) Battalion, The Royal Gloucestershire Regiment, 10th (Service) Battalion, The Worcestershire Regiment and the 8th (Service) Battalion, The Prince of Wales' (North Staffordshire) Regiment. The 7th (Service) Battalion, The King's Own (Royal Lancaster) Regiment were also to be involved and they were attached from the 56th Brigade. Initially the British concentrated artillery fire on the northwest part of High Wood and the Switch Line north of the wood, and the King's Own and the 10th R. Warwicks closed right up to the barrage. The Intermediate Trench and the Germans in it were rushed, but owing to the slow progress of the Worcesters and the Glosters in arriving, ground was lost as the enemy machine-guns had recovered from the swiftness of the sudden attack. However, a section of the Intermediate Trench was retained with the assistance of the 5th (Service) Battalion Pioneers, The South Wales Borderers and the 81st Field Company RE. German shell fire made movement difficult and communication with the frontline well nigh impossible. It was in this situation that Pte John Miller was to win a posthumous VC.

Miller was ordered to take a message during a break in communications and his citation, which was published on 9 September, tells the story as follows:

For most conspicuous bravery. His battalion was consolidating a position after its capture by assault and Private Miller was ordered to take an important message under heavy shell and rifle fire, and to bring back a reply at all costs.

He was compelled to cross the open, and on leaving the trench was shot almost immediately in the back, the bullet coming out through his abdomen. In spite of this, with heroic courage and self-sacrifice, he compressed with his hand the gaping wound in his abdomen, delivered his message, staggered back with the answer, and fell at the feet of the officer to whom he delivered it.

He gave his life with a supreme devotion to duty.

He was buried at Dartmoor Cemetery near Bécordel, Plot 1, Row C, Grave 64, and his decoration was presented to his father by the King at Buckingham Palace on 29 November 1916.

James Miller, son of George and Mary Miller, was born at Taylor's Farm, Hoghton, near Preston on 13 March 1890. The family later moved to 1 Ollerton Terrace, Withnell near Chorley. Miller attended Abbey Village Primary School and later went to work at a Wiggins Teape papermill at Withnell Fold. He became a popular local footballer.

On the outbreak of war when Miller was 24 years old he enlisted with the 7th King's Own Royal Lancaster Regiment, one of the New Army units. The battalion was formed at Bowerham Barracks and left for France on 18 July 1915. Six of his brothers also joined the Colours, and two of them didn't survive the war. Miller saw action at Lens and Loos in Autumn 1915 and his battalion moved to the Somme in April 1916. They were also in action at La Boisselle between 3 and 7 July, consolidating positions at Mametz Wood and then Bazentin le Petit.

In 1917 a memorial, raised by public subscription, was unveiled at Withnell by Lt Col Thorne of the King's Own on 14 July 1917. It took the form of a Celtic Cross and was erected on the edge of the village churchyard at St Paul's, Withnell. A commemorative stone was also placed near to Miller's place of work at the Wiggins Teape papermill.

The secretary of the King's Own Old Comrades' Association wrote a poem that tells the story of Miller's gallantry which is called 'The Message'.

E.N.F. Bell, Thiepval, 1 July 1916

G. S. Cather   P. Hansen   D. Cather

Hazelwood School. G.S. Cather, P. Hansen and D. Cather

J.L. Green, Fonquevillers, 1 July 1916

S.W. Loudoun-Shand, Fricourt,
1 July 1916

W.F. McFadzean, near Thiepval Wood, 1 July 1916

R. Quigg, Hamel, 1 July 1916

A galaxy of Ulster heroes in 1954. R. Quigg is second from the left (*Belfast Tel.*)

J.Y. Turnbull, Leipzig Salient, 1 July 1916

G. Sanders, near Thiepval, 1 July 1916

A. Carton de Wiart, La Boisselle, 3 July 1916

T.G. Turrall, La Boisselle, 3 July 1916

T.G. Turrall at Buckingham Palace with his daughter

W.E. Boutler at Buckingham Palace on 17 March 1917

W.E. Boulter, Trônes Wood, 14 July 1916

W.F. Faulds, Delville Wood, 18 July 1916

J.J. Davies, Delville Wood, 20 July 1916

J. Leak, Pozières, 23rd July 1916

T. Cooke, Pozières, 24/25 July 1916

T.W.H. Veale with the Prince of Wales in 1921 (*Dartmouth Illustrated*)

Thiepval Memorial, 1 July 1966. Lef to right: Reverend A. Proctor, R.E. Ryder, F.J. Edwards, A.C.T. White, T. Adlam and T. Veale (*Soldier*)

A. Gill, Delville Wood, 27 July 1916

C.C. Castleton, Pozières, 28 July 1916

W.J.G. Evans with his family at
Buckingham Palace in 1920 (*TMB*)

J. Miller, Bazentin le Petit, 31 July 1916

W.H. Short, Munster Alley, 6 August 1916

F.J. Edwards with his great friend R.E. Ryder at Horse Guards, Whitehall in 1963

R.B. Bradford, Eaucourt L'Abbaye, 1 October 1916

Pte. John Cunningham, V.C., East York Regt. (portrait left) in a communication-trench beyond a captured line went forward alone, and meeting ten of the enemy killed them with bombs and cleared the trench up to the next line.

J. Cunningham, opposite Hébuterne, 13 November 1916

Pozières British Cemetery (*CWGC*)

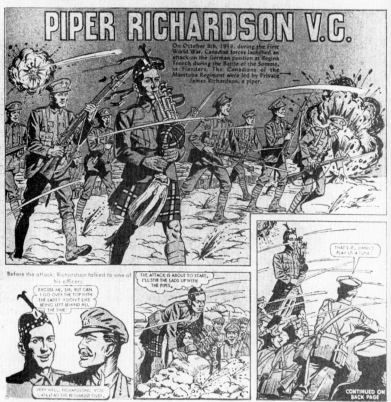

The Victor, 4 September 1965

In 1988 it was decided to clean and restore the memorial at the church and an appeal was launched by the vicar on behalf of James Arnold, a nephew of James Miller. Mr Arnold was overwhelmed with offers of help from the Royal British Legion and others, and the memorial was restored and made ready for rededication in August 1988. Miller's VC, which is normally kept in a bank vault, was included in the memorial procession when it was worn by Mr Arnold. The procession was organised by the Chorley branch of the Royal British Legion and there was a good turnout for the parade and service, during which wreaths were laid. Mr Arnold owns his late uncle's shaving mirror which was twisted by the impact of a bullet and the VC decoration itself is now in the hands of the King's Own Regimental Museum in the City Museum in Lancaster.

Miller's name is also included on his mother's headstone in St Paul's Churchyard, and included on the Regimental Memorial in The Priory, Lancaster.

W.H. SHORT

Of the fifty-one VCs to be awarded for gallantry during the Battle of the Somme, twenty-six were gained in July – a fact that reflects that most such awards are given for the period covering the beginning of a battle. Conversely only four were to be awarded in connection with the fighting during the month of August, which in turn suggests that it was the quietest month of the campaign. The first of these four was to be won in Munster Alley, a continuation of Pozières Trench going in a north-easterly direction. At this time it was part of the German Trench system known as OG2 and continuing on from Pozières Trench on the south-east side of the Albert–Bapaume Road, running back at right angles towards the village of Martinpuich. The Pozières Trench, the Allied equivalent, was opposite it running in a south-westerly direction.

In the week since Private Miller won his posthumous award at Bazentin le Petit, the Somme battle had mainly raged in and around the village of Pozières.

By now the German Second Line on a front of 2,000 yards to the north of the village had been taken, as had ground to the west and also to the east towards Martinpuich. The enemy had tried to retake Delville Wood to the south-east but had failed and the struggle for Guillemont also continued.

The 23rd Division contained three infantry brigades: the 68th, 69th and 70th. The 69th included the 8th and 9th (Service) battalions of The Princess of Wales's Own (Yorkshire) Regiment who arrived in Contalmaison on 25 July. The other two battalions were the 11th (Service) Battalion, The Prince of Wales's Own (West

Yorkshire) Regiment and the 10th (Service) Battalion, The Duke of Wellington's (West Riding) Regiment, who secured 60 yards of Munster Alley but was unable to make progress over open ground to a position called Torr Trench.

However in the afternoon of the 6th, the 8th Yorkshire Regiment did manage to bomb the enemy out of 150 yards of Munster Alley and also gain part of the eastern end of Torr Trench. Although two Lewis guns had been brought up to cover Munster Alley and Torr Trench, it was the divisional artillery who really did the work as the shelling virtually blew Torr Trench out of existence. The ground became unrecognisable and defences totally destroyed and the German dead lay all around. It was during this engagement that Private William Short of the Yorkshire Regiment was to gain a posthumous VC. He was a company bomber and had been seriously wounded in the foot but had refused to go for treatment. Later when his leg was shattered he still refused to withdraw and lay in the trench adjusting detonators and straightening pins for his bomber colleagues. Short's battalion was relieved at 9pm by part of the 11th W. Yorks after they had been bombing and attacking for five hours.

William Short was the third member of the Yorkshire Regiment to win the VC in the Battle of the Somme but died of his wounds at the age of 31 the following day, 7 August. He was buried in Contalmaison Château Cemetery, reference Plot II, Row B, Grave 16. His battalion was also relieved that day prior to moving to Scots Redoubt. They remained in the Somme area until early October.

Short's citation was published in the *London Gazette* on 9 September 1916 and read as follows:

For most conspicuous bravery. He was foremost in the attack, bombing the enemy with great gallantry when he was severely wounded in the foot. He was urged to go back, but refused and continued to throw bombs.

Later his leg was shattered by a shell, and he was unable to stand, so he lay in the trench adjusting detonators, and straightening the pins of bombs for his comrades.

He died before he could be carried out of the trench. For the last eleven months he had always volunteered for dangerous enterprises, and has always set a magnificent example of bravery and devotion to duty.

Readers will notice that the citation states that Short died before he was carried out of the trench instead of dying the next day. His decoration was presented to his father on 29 November 1916 at Buckingham Palace.

William Short was the son of Mr James Short and Mrs Annie Short and was born at 11 William Street, Eston, Middlesbrough, Yorkshire on 4 February 1885. Some records say that he was born in 1901 but this was the date of his baptism. As a boy he continued to live in Eston but as a young man he lived at 35 Vaughan Street, Grangetown, Yorkshire. He was a popular local footballer and became known as 'Twiggie' Short. He played for Grangetown Albion, Saltburn and Lazenby United Clubs. The only photograph of him that seems to exist is one of him taken in football kit. He had two brothers, Harry and Enoch, and one sister.

As a young man before the war, Short worked as a craneman at the steelworks at Eston called Bolckow, Vaughan & Co. He enlisted on 2 September 1915 and left for France on 26 August 1915 with C Company of the 8th Yorkshire Regiment. Shortly before his death he was given ten days special furlough as a reward for gallantry in the field. Apparently, when on leave he was in a very nervous state and according to his mother was 'weary and gaunt'.

After the war a memorial in the form of an obelisk was built in Grangetown to Short's memory, which was unveiled by Councillor W.G. Grace on 26 July 1919. Short's commanding officer who had lost an arm during the war, Lt Col B.C.M. Western was one of the official guests at the unveiling. The obelisk, built of Cleveland ironstone, was unveiled in the Town Square at Grangetown but later moved to Eston Cemetery. It was vandalised in the 1990s. Short's name is also included on the Grangetown War Memorial.

Short's mother died after the Second World War and his father, sister and brother lived on at 18 Leighton Road, Grangetown for a number of years.

The last of the Short brothers sold William's VC and medals to the Green Howards (formerly the Yorkshire Regiment) in 1979 and they are on display in the Regimental Museum in Richmond, Yorkshire. His helmet is in the collection of the Imperial War Museum.

G.G. COURY

The German-held village of Guillemont had been attacked at the end of July and a new British plan was drawn up to attack it again on 7 August. It was on the boundary of the XIII Corps and it was the 55th (West Lancashire) Division (TF) which was to bear the brunt of the fighting. On the right was the French Sixth Army, which was to attack at the same time.

The 55th Division consisted of three brigades: the 164th (North Lancashire), 165th (Liverpool) and the 166th (South Lancashire) and the attack against the positions in front of Guillemont began at 4.20am the following morning. On the right, the 165th Brigade made a little progress before being stopped by fire to the south of the village. On the left of the 165th Brigade was the 164th and two of their battalions, the 1/8th (Irish) Battalion (TF), The King's (Liverpool) Regiment and the 1/4th Battalion (TF), The King's Own (Royal Lancaster) Regiment, who were checked in front of the wire to the south-west of Guillemont, and after trying to dig in beyond bombing distance of the Germans were forced to retreat to their assembly trenches. The 1/8th King's, also of the 164th Brigade, broke through into the village but the 1/4th Battalion (TF), The Loyal North Lancashire Regiment, who were sent forward to hold the captured line were bombed out of it during an enemy counter-attack.

Second Lieutenant G.G. Coury of the 3rd Battalion, attached to the 1/4th Battalion, The Prince of Wales's Volunteers (South Lancashire) Regiment was in charge of a Pioneer half-company which was ordered to dig a forward communication trench, and he also attempted to rally the retreating troops when they came under very heavy fire. At the same time he was able to rescue, at great personal risk to himself, Major J.L. Swainson, CO of the 1/4th King's Own, 164th Brigade, who unfortunately died of wounds soon afterwards. Swainson, originally of the Duke of Cornwall's Regiment, was a holder of the DSO and Coury was to be awarded the VC for his action at Arrow Head Copse, very close to the German frontline to the south-west of Guillemont. Not only did he bring in Major Swainson under intense fire but he also re-organised his positions and subsequently defeated further enemy counter-attacks; later the Pioneers constructed shelters around Chimpanzee Trench. The battalion was to be in the region for three whole weeks before being relieved and sent to Aigneville for rest. Three days before he gained the VC, Coury had quelled a panic in his company lines when he managed to have a trench fire extinguished. His citation was published on 26 October 1916 and read as follows:

> For most conspicuous bravery. During an advance he was in command of two platoons ordered to dig a communication trench from the old firing line to the position won. By his fine example and utter contempt of danger he kept up his task under intense fire.
>
> Later, after his battalion had suffered severe casualties and the commanding officer had been wounded, he went out in front of the advanced position in broad daylight and in full view of the enemy found his commanding officer, and brought him back to the new advanced trench over ground swept by machine-gun fire.
>
> He not only carried out his original task and saved his commanding officer, but also assisted in rallying the attacking troops when they were shaken and in leading them forward.

Coury was back in Liverpool on 14 November where he was welcomed home. Four days later he received his VC from the King in the forecourt of Buckingham Palace.

Gabriel George Coury was the second of four sons born to Raphael Coury, who was an Armenian and Marie Dagher who was born in Lebanon. The family was completed with two daughters. Gabriel was born on 13 June 1896 at 16 Croxteth

Grove, which is off Sefton Park Road, a salubrious area which then boasted substantial houses. He attended St Francis Xavier's School, Salisbury, Liverpool and then Stonyhurst College where he won many prizes for sport, and developed long and powerful arms and was well able to defend himself! While at Stonyhurst he served as a rifleman with the college OTC for four and a half years. He acquired a good command of the French language from Marie Coury, his mother.

His father had business connections with the cotton trade and Gabriel became an apprentice to the cotton firm of Reynolds and Gibsons (Brokers and Merchants) in 1913. In the following year he enlisted in August at the age of 18 with the 2/6th (Service) Battalion, The King's (Liverpool) Regiment (TF), and after he applied was appointed to a commission in January 1915 and in April he was transferred to the 1/3rd The Prince of Wales's Volunteers (South Lancashire) Regiment commission. He carried out his training in Blackpool, Canterbury and Margate and transferred to the 1/4th (South Lancs) serving in the Ypres Sector. In October 1915 this battalion had become a Pioneer Battalion and in January 1916 Coury joined the Pioneers of the 55th (West Lancashire) Division (TF). This division played no part in the early stages of the Somme battle but at the end of July was heavily involved fighting in the Guillemont region.

A corporal of the South Lancashire Regiment, who was witness to Coury's gallantry, told of how he had won the VC in the *Liverpool Post* on 30 October 1916:

> He was the bravest officer I ever served under.... The task given to the men under him was no soft one. To dig a new trench in the thick of a battle is a thing that requires some nerve, and a better officer than Lt Coury could not have been chosen to direct the operation. He showed absolute contempt for death, and made us all feel that a dozen deaths were as nothing compared with the necessity of completing the task given to us. It was when we got into the captured position that Lt Coury showed what he was capable of. We had gone through a hellish ordeal. We had suffered severely, and a lot of our officers and men lay out there in the open, wounded. It blew hurricanes of fire across the open, and it seemed to invite certain death to go out there. Word was brought that our commanding officer was among the wounded. Lt Coury

determined to go out to him. He started out under fiendish
fire. The enemy's snipers were after him from the first, but he
ran on regardless of the hail of bullets flying around him. He
reached the spot where our commander lay, and after resting for a while started back again, carrying the commander.
The journey back was one of the most thrilling sights I have
ever seen. The enemy redoubled their efforts to pick off the
brave officer as he toiled painfully towards out trench. Both
he and his burden disappeared out of view for a short time,
and we thought he was done for. After a time he appeared
again, making his way amidst a storm of bullets and burst-
ing shells. There was intense excitement, and we waited with
baited breath, praying that he might be spared, but fearing
the worst. The brave officer toiled slowly forward. Several
times he stumbled, and we gave him up for lost. Once he fell.
We thought he would never rise again; but rise he did, and
resumed the terrible journey. Before he got back the enemy's
machine guns were turned on full-blast and it was nothing
short of a miracle that the lieutenant was able to make his
way through it all. At last he got within a few yards of our
trench. We rushed out to meet him. He stumbled again, but
regained his footing and continued straight on. Then there
was another furious gust of fire. Down he went again. Would
he ever rise, ... Under heavy fire all the time, rescuer and
rescued were helped into the trench, which was now being
subjected to very severe artillery fire. Then the enemy tried a
counter-attack, and it was the duty of Lt Coury to organise
the defence. That he did with wonderful skill. He got together
the men of different units and thoroughly organised the position. When the enemy tried to attack they were thrown back
in confusion, and the counter-attack was pressed home. The
men were very enthusiastic over the capable way the situation had been handled when it was most difficult, and all
were loud in their praise of our lieutenant. Undoubtedly he
saved the day at its most critical stage.

On 8 August Coury was made a full lieutenant, but he had
decided to transfer to the RFC and on 28 August joined No. 13
Squadron at Savy Aubigny, north-west of Arras. While there he
trained as an observer and qualified on 10 November. Carrying
out mainly photographic reconnaissance, he flew as an observer

in a De Havilland BE-2. When he attended his investiture in November 1916 he was in the uniform of the RFC and shortly afterwards returned to Liverpool where he was given a very enthusiastic welcome. He was received by the Lord Mayor and given the Freedom of the Cotton Exchange, the highest honour in the trade. In December he was also welcomed at St Francis Xavier's School when he returned there. Two months later in February 1917 he was given two weeks leave during which time he revisited Stonyhurst where he was given a great reception. He was one of seven members of Stonyhurst to be awarded a VC and the college OTC provided a Guard of Honour.

Coury rejoined his squadron on 4 March and managed to survive 'Bloody April' and was back in England on 18 May in order to train for his pilot's licence. He qualified four months later and on 20 September 1917 was eligible to begin his work as a ferry pilot when based at Kenley.

He was never to return to France as on 22 November he had a serious flying accident near Croydon when taking an aircraft abroad which crashed before reaching the channel. His aircraft caught fire and he was severely injured and badly burned. However he partially recovered in hospital in Woolwich between October and December 1917.

On 7 January 1918 Coury married Katherine Mary Lovell at St Mary's Roman Catholic Church in Clapham which was close to his bride's home. Eight months later he was promoted to the rank of captain and at the end of the year his wife gave birth to a daughter, the first of three girls.

Despite his injuries, Coury returned to flying but crashed again in June and by this time he had lost confidence in his flying capabilities. Later his health declined and he was seriously ill with influenza and other medical problems. He was admitted to the RAF Hospital in Hillingdon Hall, Hampstead on 1 March 1919. After his recovery he resigned his commission and was demobilised. His home address in April 1919 was 43 Canning Street, Liverpool and in 1920 he attended the Garden Party for holders of the VC held at Buckingham Palace. In the same year he badgered the War Office about the possibility of receiving a disability pension to compensate for his injuries. For good measure he threw in neurasthenia as well. The War Office were not at all sympathetic to his pleas and his injuries were 'deemed not of a very severe nature'.

He regularly visited Stonyhurst and the college decided to commission a portrait of him by Thomas Baines. In 1929 he attended the House of Lords VC celebrations.

As far as employment was concerned, after the war Coury returned to work at Reynolds & Gibson where he remained until 1926. His family address was then at 2 Merton Grove, Bootle but in the following year the family moved to 38 Brooke Road, Waterloo. Also in the same year he and his wife travelled to Alexandria, Egypt where he was a cotton shipper and agent, and the couple returned in 1932.

On the outbreak of the Second World War he was living at 50 Queen's Road, Southport and soon after Coury applied to the War Office on 27 February 1940 for permission to join the 4th Anti-Aircraft RASC and duly passed the medical. In June 1944 he took part in the Normandy landings. He remained with the advancing Allies as they moved through France, Holland, Belgium and finally into Germany. He was demobilised in August 1945 by which time he had added to the number of his medals with the 1939–45 Star and three other Second World War medals. He then moved the family from Southport back to Liverpool. However back in the city he realised that the cotton trade had virtually collapsed and that subsequently he was without a job. He then made the bold decision to open a fish and chip shop and the premises were at 113 Brunswick Road, Liverpool. It was called 'The Frying Pan' and, encouraged by its success, he decided to open a branch.

In 1954 the Liverpool Cotton Exchange reopened and Coury took a job with George. H. Way as a manager and senior sales-man. At the same time he left his other business interests to his wife to manage.

In 1955 Coury's health broke down and he was admitted to Walton Hospital where he very nearly died and even received last sacraments. However, he later appeared to have recovered and was discharged from hospital only to die at home on 23 February at the early age of 59.

His funeral took place at St Peter and St Paul's, Great Crosby, Liverpool on 26 February when he was given full military honours. Three hundred people attended the service including a Boer War VC veteran, Lt Col Donald Farmer. The South Lancashire Regiment sent a bearer party of National Servicemen and the RAF was also represented.

On 12 November 1962 Coury's widow presented her husband's decoration and medals to the Regiment at Warrington. In 1982 a replica of the VC, which was on display in the Regimental Museum, was stolen, but the real VC and medals are on display at the Lancashire County and Regimental Museum in Preston.

N.G. CHAVASSE

On 8 August British plans were to attack the German-held village of Guillemont, but owing in part to the British trenches to the forward of Trônes Wood, Guillemont Road becoming very congested, any attack had become impossible to properly organise. Despite this failure though, XIII Corps HQ insisted that a further attempt should be made the following day with zero hour set for 4.20am.

However, there was no British artillery barrage during the night which allowed the enemy to safely repair his defences and prepare for the expected attack. The supporting barrage, when it did start was very hurried as it only began five minutes before zero hour. On the left of the 55th (West Lancashire) Division (TF), the 166th (South Lancashire) Brigade had replaced the 164th (North Lancashire) Brigade which led to further confusion. The 1/10th (Scottish) Battalion (TF), The King's (Liverpool) Regiment of the latter brigade kept close up to the barrage but suffered heavy casualties when getting near to enemy wire. Casualties included many officers who were hit during what became four separate charges and it was during this period that Captain Noel Chavasse of the RAMC, who was attached to The King's, began his sterling work in saving the lives of his comrades. His efforts would earn him two Victoria Crosses and his decoration would be the second of five such awards to be gained in connection with the struggle to capture Guillemont. At the end of the day the battalion's casualties totalled 280 out of a total of 600 men which the battalion had started out with, and the survivors withdrew to support trenches and the Great Bear.

The citation for Chavasse's VC was published in the *London Gazette* of 26 October and tells the story of his gallantry as follows:

> For most conspicuous bravery and devotion to duty. During an attack he attended the wounded in the open all day, under heavy fire, frequently in view of the enemy. During the ensuing night he searched for wounded on the ground in front of the enemy's lines for four hours. Next day he took one stretcher bearer to the advanced trenches, and under heavy shell fire carried an urgent case for 500 yards into safety, being wounded in the side by a shell splinter during the journey. The same night he took up a party of twenty volunteers, rescued three wounded men from a shell hole 25 yards from the enemy's trench, buried the bodies of two officers, and collected many identity discs, although fired on by bombs and machine-guns. Altogether he saved the lives of some twenty badly wounded men, besides the ordinary cases which passed through his hands. His courage and self-sacrifice were beyond praise.

Chavasse was presented with his VC by the King at Buckingham Palace on 5 February 1917.

By October, two months after the events at Guillemont in August, the 10th King's Battalion numbers had been made up to strength and had returned to the Ypres Sector. During this next period spent in the Salient the men carried on with routine trench duties, being in and out of the line for eight-day periods. In the following year, on 20 July 1917, the battalion took over trenches close to Wieltje, to the north-east of Ypres and St Jean. This was at the point when preparations were being made for what was to be the Third Battle of Ypres, an attempt to capture the Passchendaele Ridge.

On 31 July, the opening day of this battle, the battalion, still part of 166th Brigade moved forward in support of the 55th Division's advance and for once weather conditions were dry and fair. Some progress was made into German-held territory and a few support trenches were captured. Chavasse set up an RAP in a captured German dugout in an area which was soon under intense artillery fire, but he remained there while caring for a stream of wounded. Despite being wounded in the skull, he carried on with this work and after his own wound was dressed he continued to treat the wounded for the rest of the day. Very little food was available and to make matters worse it began to rain, which quickly turned the ground into a muddy swamp. Despite these adverse conditions he then set out to gather up more wounded from shell holes in the open ground. To add even more to his woes the enemy used mustard gas as a counter-barrage, which the King's were poorly protected against.

In the early hours of 2 August, while Chavasse was resting, he was wounded again when a shell struck the dugout which killed or wounded everyone in it. Finally persuaded to take some rest, Chavasse, having received several additional wounds including abdominal ones, thought it unlikely that any help would be quickly forthcoming and despite his wounds he set off for assistance and crawled half a mile back to seek aid. He was then taken through Ypres to the 46th Field Ambulance at Brandhoek where he was examined by an American doctor, Dr J.A.C. Colston who sent him to No. 32 CCS which was also at Brandhoek. By this time his face was unrecognisable as it had been blackened by the shell burst. His abdomen was operated on and his other wounds dressed; however, his life couldn't be saved and after receiving Holy Communion he died at about 2pm on 4 August.

Chavasse's battalion had come out of the line on the 3rd, with their ranks once more severely depleted. They too moved to Brandhoek, and despite their exhaustion the men insisted on attending their medical officer's funeral prior to getting any rest.

As he was dying Chavasse managed to dictate a letter to his fiancée Gladys Chavasse, who was a cousin. They had become engaged in April 1916 and her home was in Bromsgrove, Worcestershire. Some accounts state that she was in the Salient at this time with a special marriage licence which would have allowed the couple to marry anywhere, but this story seems to be hardly credible. Of course she was unaware that Chavasse was seriously wounded and her fiancée's letter explained what had happened to him and why he had carried on with his work in the field despite having a fractured skull. Of his impending death he remarked to her 'that duty called and duty must be obeyed'.

It would appear from Chavasse's efforts to look after the underprivileged in much of his work prior to the war, coupled with his often self-sacrificing attempts in saving life during the war and his concern for the welfare of his army colleagues, that he was responsible to a sort of higher being. He appears to have been fulfilling some sort of special divine mission during the short time which he spent on earth. He certainly seems to be an exceptional human being.

For his work in the Salient, Chavasse was awarded a Bar to his VC, which of course was awarded posthumously, this was the only occasion during the Great War when two such awards were made to one man and it was presented to his family in 1917 by the GOC Western Command, Lt Gen Sir W.P. Campbell.

The citation for this second award was published in the *London Gazette* on 14 September and read as follows:

> For most conspicuous gallantry and undaunted devotion to duty in action in front of Wieltje between 31 July and 2 August 1917. Early in the action he was severely wounded in the head while carrying a wounded man to his dressing station. He refused to leave his post and for two days not only continued to attend to the cases brought to his first air post, but repeatedly and under heavy fire went out to the firing line with stretcher parties to search for wounded and dressed those lying out. During these searches he found a number of badly wounded men in the open and assisted to carry them in over heavy and difficult ground. He was practically without food during this period, worn with fatigue and faint with his wounds. By his extraordinary energy and inspiring example he was instrumental in succouring many men who must otherwise have succumbed under the bad weather conditions. On the morning of 2 August he was again wounded seriously by a shell and died in hospital on 4 August...

Noel Chavasse died only a few weeks after his brother Aidan, who had been reported missing, and at the same time Noel's twin brother Christopher was still serving as an army chaplain.

A memorial service was held on 29 August 1917 to the memory of the men who had lost their lives when serving with the King's (Liverpool) Regiment at St Nicholas' Church, Liverpool and the large congregation was made up of local dignitaries, members of the regiment and of relatives of the members of the regiment. The north side of the church was occupied by the wives and relatives of dead soldiers. The Bishop of Liverpool officiated as well as the Lord Mayor. The address was given by Canon J.B. Lancelot who alluded to Noel Chavasse and said 'It was no wonder that the King felt that the whole Army would mourn the death of so brave and distinguished a brother...'.

Gladys Chavasse, who had already been under pressure from her father not to marry Noel, was naturally heartbroken by his death and was bitter that Noel had gone on caring for the wounded knowing that his own life would be threatened by the subsequent exhaustion.

On 8 October 1917 Noel's kit arrived at his parent's home in Liverpool and, as a footnote, was destroyed twenty years later in the Liverpool blitz. In his will Noel had left his brother Christopher £750 and Christopher used some of this money to commission a portrait of his twin to present to his father as a birthday present. Noel also left £700 in shares and war loans as well as a watch. When the cemetery at Brandhoek was laid out after the war the original wooden cross on Chavasse's grave was sent back home, and was subsequently deposited by Christopher Chavasse in The Chapel of St Peter's College, Oxford.

Noel Godfrey Chavasse and his twin brother Christopher Maude were born on 9 November 1884 at 36 New Inn Hall Street, Oxford. Their father was the Reverend Francis Chavasse and their mother Edith Jane Maude, a daughter of Canon Maude, Rector of Chirk. There were five other children in the family. Noel was educated at Magdalen College School, Oxford between the ages of 12 and 16 and the school later named a school house after their famous student and there is also a memorial board there.

When Noel's father was appointed Lord Bishop of Liverpool in 1900 the family moved up to Lancashire and lived in the Bishop's Palace, 19 Abercromby Square, close to the city centre; the square later became part of Liverpool University. An English Heritage plaque which marks the family connection was unveiled on the house by Edgar Chavasse, a nephew, on 13 November 2001.

Noel continued his studies at Liverpool College (1900–1904) until he left for Trinity College, Oxford where he studied from 1904 to 1908. His twin brother also attended the same college but only graduated at his second attempt. Noel though gained a 1st Class Degree in Physiology and also won his Blue in two sports. Both he and his twin brother were very good athletes, representing their country at the 1908 Olympic Games. Noel was able to turn in a time of 10½ seconds for the 100 yards in 1907 when taking part in inter-varsity athletics. In addition he joined the OTC.

Noel's future was always to be in medicine and he began training for a medical career, continuing his clinical studies back in Liverpool. At the time he was living at home, and carried out 'muscular christian' work in such places as clubs and reform schools for boys. He had links with the Grafton Street Industrial School, a school for boys in need of education and correction.

In 1910 at the second attempt, he was awarded a Fellowship of the Royal College of Surgeons and in January 1912 had completed his medical examinations; six months later was registered as a doctor by the General Medical Council. Also in 1912 Noel spent some time in Dublin where he worked at the Rotunda Hospital. After he had graduated he spent a year at the Radcliffe Infirmary, researching blood plasma, and later took up a post at the Royal Southern Hospital, Liverpool where he became house surgeon. He was there for a year and by now had become interested in orthopaedics under the tutelage of the famous surgeon, Robert Jones. The Liverpool Royal Southern Hospital was a Free Hospital which catered especially for the Liverpool poor.

All this medical experience was to stand him in good stead a year later when he joined the Royal Army Medical Corps in 1913 and was attached to the 10th King's. Christopher, having trained for the Ministry, beat his brother to France when he was appointed as the chaplain to No. 10 General Hospital at St Nazaire. Noel served with the 10th King's in France and Belgium, having arrived in France in November 1914. Their first positions were in trenches in the Salient during the First Battle of Ypres. In June of the following year the battalion saw action at Hooge near Ypres. This was where Chavasse first came to the notice of the military authorities when he personally went out into no man's land for almost forty-eight hours until satisfied that no more wounded men were needing to be brought in. For this work he was awarded the MC. The battalion was severely depleted after the action but numbers gradually made up with the arrival of reserves from England. Chavasse asked one of his sisters to arrange and send out a thousand pairs of socks and other comforts at his own expense for the use of the men in his battalion.

However, it does appear that Chavasse's name also became known to the authorities for different reasons than bravery as he became a severe critic of the way that military hygiene was dealt with and in particular he felt that not enough was being done to curb the ever increasing cases of venereal diseases in the army. To cap it all he also appeared to sympathise with the plight of men who deliberately mutilated themselves in order to avoid frontline service.

It should be also noted that during the war Chavasse became interested in tetanus, a disease which was potentially rife in the conditions of the Western Front. No antidote was available until a vaccine was found in the 1930s, but he became a prime mover in using an anti-tetanus serum on men who had been wounded on the battlefield. This treatment was a success and helped to keep numbers of cases down, saving many lives.

Christopher and Noel were not the only set of twins in the Chavasse family as they had twin sisters as well and in addition there were three other children. Of these seven, five served in the Great War, and three won the MC, and May, one of the twin sisters who served as a nurse in Etaples, was Mentioned in Despatches. Dr Bernard Chavasse, one of the brothers and a surgeon was killed in a car accident in 1942. Strangely, Gladys, Noel's fiancée, who re-married in Bromsgrove in December 1919, was also killed as a result of a motor accident, this time in France in 1962, and her body was brought back to Bromsgrove for burial. In 1942, following a boating accident Christopher had a leg amputated and suffered from the resulting pain for the rest of his life. Having been a joint founder with his father of St Peter's College, he became its first Master and Bishop of Rochester, a post he occupied for twenty-one years. He died in 1963.

The Chavasse VC and medals which had been donated by Christopher in the 1930s were originally displayed on the staircase at St Peter's College, Oxford, but the insurers became nervous and replicas were made to replace the originals which were then locked away in a bank vault for about fifteen years. In 1979 the medal group were allowed out of Oxford for a short while, for display at the dedication of a memorial plaque at the headquarters of the Territorial Army Company of the Liverpool Scottish at Forbes House, Score Lane, Liverpool. Noel's name is also included on a memorial board in the college.

Later the college and the Chavasse family decided that it might be a better idea to present the VC and medals on permanent loan to the Imperial War Museum, which they did on 22 February 1990 in the presence of Queen Elizabeth, the Queen Mother. Other Chavasse family medals, which had belonged to Bernard, were lent but not given to the Imperial War Museum, as was another group which had belonged to May, who not only served as a Red Cross nurse in the Great War but also in the Second World War as a Queen Alexandra Nurse. She and her sister Marjorie celebrated their 100th birthday in 1986. As a footnote, The Liverpool Scottish Museum had always hoped that they would be presented with Noel's VC and medals as the family was so very well known in Liverpool for much of the twentieth century.

Noel Chavasse has been commemorated with more memorials than any other holder of the Victoria Cross and as he was son of a Lord Bishop his name is included on the House of Lords Memorial in Westminster. Liverpool College School has a school house named after him and the school chapel has as its altar a memorial dedicated to his memory and also a wooden cross to Old Liverpudlians. A tablet to his memory is also in the College Library.

In 1975 Noel's headstone in Brandhoek New Military Cemetery in Belgium, made of Portland stone, was replaced by one of Botticino stone, which also contained the wrong information, but by April 1981 it had been corrected in order to reflect that Chavasse was the winner of a VC and Bar, the only man to achieve this honour during the Great War. In 1998 a Chavasse VC Memorial was set up outside the local church at Brandhoek, which was unveiled by Edgar Chavasse. It had been arranged by the Flambertus History Society of Vlamertinghe.

A plaque to Noel's memory, formerly in the RAMC HQ, Wellington Barracks, Liverpool, was re-erected in the TA Centre and unveiled in October 1979 when Mr Sam Moulton, Noel's former groom, was present. In 1988 their new HQ in Merseyside was called Chavasse House.

Other memorials are at Trinity College, Oxford, Liverpool School, Liverpool Cathedral (Roll of Honour) in the War Memorial Chapel and memorial window where there is also a bust of him, Liverpool Town Hall (Roll of Honour), Liverpool Cricket Club has a Chavasse room and Wavertree Royal British Legion Club has a Chavasse Bar. A brass plaque had been fixed on a wall in the Royal Southern Hospital but it disappeared when the hospital closed in the 1970s.

A sword, portrait and plaque were kept at the Liverpool Scottish barracks at Forbes House, Childwall, Liverpool which had originally been dedicated by Christopher, and are now in the safe keeping of the Liverpool Scottish Museum Trust. In 2006 a new 64p postage stamp featuring Chavasse was issued by the Isle of Man Post Office, and Liverpool Moat House Hotel (now demolished) had a Chavasse suite. Chavasse Park in the former dock area of Liverpool is an open space forming part of the new Liverpool One shopping complex.

In 2005 an appeal was launched in Liverpool for a memorial sculpture to sixteen men who had won a Victoria Cross and had connections with the city. The sum required was £112,000 and Tom Murphy, a local artist was commissioned to design a bronze sculpture. It was unveiled on 17 August 2008, close to the former Chavasse family home in the precincts of Liverpool University by the Lord Mayor of Liverpool, in the presence of a thousand people including relatives of the VC holders.

It is difficult to work out as to just why the college felt it had the right to actually sell Noel Chavasse's decorations, especially when they were already in a safe place in the Imperial War Museum on permanent loan. But sell them they did and in November 2009 Lord Ashcroft paid them a handsome million and a half pounds in a private transaction. They therefore remain on display in the Imperial War Museum but are now part of a special gallery built to house the peer's extensive collection of Victoria Crosses and other decorations, which was opened in November 2010.

M. O'MEARA

By 9/10 August, in the struggles to capture the Pozières Heights, the Allied line had reached and occupied a line known as Park Lane and the 4th Australian Brigade, 4th Australian Division took over the front of the British 12th Division on the night of the 10th as far as the Pozières–Thiepval Road. On the 10th, General Gough, in command of the Reserve Army, gave orders for the Australian objective to be the enemy's frontal positions which ran across the OG lines and on southwards to a quarry off the Pozières–Thiepval Road. The 12th Division was ordered to capture Skyline Trench. This plan was later slightly modified and the task for II Corps west of Skyline Trench would now only consist of delivering 'holding attacks'.

With the approval of the Corps and Reserve Army, Major General H.V. Cox, in command of the 4th Australian Division, had requested permission to see what progress his troops could make. At 1am on the morning of the 11th, after a preliminary bombardment, two battalions of the 4th Australian Brigade, 4th Australian Division: the 13th (New South Wales) Australian Infantry Battalion and the 16th (Western Australia and Southern Australia) Australian Infantry Battalion, moved forward from Park Lane. The 13th Battalion established a frontal post to the south-east of Mouquet Farm. The farm was north-west of Pozières and situated roughly between Thiepval and Courcelette. At dawn an enemy bombing attack was checked and to the left the 16th Battalion established positions facing a quarry on the opposite slope. During the next twenty-four hours the enemy attacked from Mouquet Farm and their artillery took a very heavy toll on the

Australian forward positions. It was during this period that the gallantry of Private O'Meara of the 16th Battalion was to earn him a Victoria Cross.

The 16th Battalion had suffered very heavily during the fighting and bombardment and it became very difficult to reach men in the forward positions as they were totally exposed. However, due to the heroism of Private Martin O'Meara, the essential carrying of supplies of water, food and ammunition continued. He passed through artillery barrages on no fewer than four occasions and once he took a party of men with him in order to bring in the wounded. O'Meara didn't rest until he was absolutely sure that all the wounded had been brought in. Of his exploits, the 16th Battalion War Diary noted of these forward positions that '...the trench as a trench had ceased to exist...' O'Meara was said to have rescued more than twenty-five men lying out in no man's land in conditions which were indescribable. In total the battalion suffered 406 casualties over a four-day period. Later in the day the weary 16th Battalion was relieved by the 50th (Southern Australian) Australian Infantry Battalion of the 13th Australian Brigade.

The citation for O'Meara's VC was published in the *London Gazette* of 9 September and read as follows:

> For most conspicuous bravery. During four days of very heavy fighting he repeatedly went out and brought in wounded officers and men from 'No Man's Land' under intense artillery and machine-gun fire.
>
> He also volunteered and carried up ammunition and bombs through a heavy barrage to a portion of the trenches which was being heavily shelled at the time.
>
> He showed throughout an utter contempt of danger, and undoubtedly saved many lives.

O'Meara was presented with his decoration by the King on 21 July 1917.

Martin O'Meara was the son of a labourer Michael O'Meara and of Margaret O'Meara (formerly Connor), and was born on 6 November 1885. His place of birth was Lorrha, Rathcabbin, near Birr, County Tipperary, Ireland and as a young man he decided to emigrate and worked his passage to Australia as a ship's stoker.

O'Meara lived initially in South Australia before moving to Western Australia where he enlisted with the AIF in Perth on 19 August 1915 when he was nearly 30 years of age. He was 5ft 7in and gave his occupation as a sleeper-hewer on the railways. Like so many Australian soldiers in the Great War he carried out his early training at Blackboy Camp, near Northam. He left from Fremantle, Australia on 22 December 1915 for training in Egypt prior to leaving for France and the Western Front as one of a party of reinforcements for the 16th (Western Australia and Southern Australia) Australian Infantry Battalion.

Two years after his exploits between 9 and 12 August 1916, he was first promoted corporal on 13 August 1918 and then sergeant on 30 August 1918. By this time he had been wounded on three occasions: on 13 June 1916, 9 April 1917 and 18 August 1917. Also in 1917, when he had been allocated a short leave, he managed to fit in a visit to his native home in Ireland and money was collected in the Lorrha region as a testimonial for the former resident. In his will dated 1917 he left the money collected for him to be spent on the restoration of Lorrha Abbey, but it was not sufficient and instead the money was used for repairing the original parish church. O'Meara was a Roman Catholic, and had a sister in Ireland.

He served with the 16th Battalion for the rest of the war, left France for Australia on 15 September 1918 and was demobilised from the AIF in Perth on 30 November 1919. The rest of his life was spent in tragic circumstances as the experiences that he had in the war led to a complete collapse of his health. As a result he had to spend his remaining years in Military Hospitals. His illness was described as 'chronic mania'. He died seventeen years after the war ended at Claremont Mental Hospital, Perth on 20 December 1935. He never married. His occupation listed on his death certificate was given as 'returned soldier' and he was buried in the Karrakatta Catholic Cemetery in Perth with full military honours. The grave reference is HA, Plot 93. His funeral was attended by three other holders of the VC. His name is commemorated in the Australian War Memorial in Canberra and in the city suburbs, and is one of ninety-six names remembered in the Victoria Cross Memorial Park. In Sydney his name is one of ninety-six holders of the VC commemorated on the Victoria Cross Memorial in Queen Victoria Building. His name is also listed on his family grave at Lorrha Abbey.

As O'Meara had no living relative in the country, his VC and medals were presented to the 16th Battalion, who in turn presented them to the Western Australian Army Museum, Perth in 1986.

W.B. ALLEN

No VCs were awarded for gallantry during the Battle of the Somme between 12 August and 3 September 1916, a fact which in turn reflects the lack of Allied progress in that three-week period. Much of the military action during this time had taken place in the areas close to Thiepval, Pozières, High Wood and Guillemont.

By early September Munster Alley near Pozières had been taken and the Allied advance north-west of Pozières had continued. Nevertheless, to the south-west the German stronghold village of Guillemont was now about to fall into Allied hands. But before returning to the events at Guillemont where three VCs were gained on 3 September, it is the deeds of a medical officer at the other end of the British frontline, north of Mesnil, west of Thiepval and south-west of Hamel which we are concerned with here. The heroic deed took place during an attack across the River Ancre, which the reference books describe as 'The Ancre Attack'. The 49th (West Riding) Division (TF) on the right and the 39th Division on the left were ordered to attack the enemy-held ground from in front of the Redan Ridge south-eastwards to the front of Schwaben Redoubt. The British artillery carried out a frontal bombardment, but the two divisions were unable to get a real foothold in the German positions. Indeed the enemy was able to enfilade any trenches that he had lost temporarily, from the direction of St Pierre Divion. The Schwaben Redoubt, too, was virtually an impossible objective to take.

A howitzer battery of the CCXLVI Brigade of the RFA (49th Division) was one of the artillery batteries in action to the south-west of Hamel, close to Mesnil, and was shelled, resulting in many casualties. Captain W.B. Allen of the RAMC, attached to the 1/3rd West Riding (No. 21) Field Ambulance, 246th (West Riding) Brigade (TF) of the RFA, attended to the wounded with no regard to his own safety and was wounded several times in the process. A citation announcing the award of a VC to this brave man was published on 26 October and read as follows:

> For most conspicuous bravery and devotion to duty. When gun detachments were unloading high explosive ammunition from wagons which had just come up, the enemy suddenly began to shell the battery position. The first shell fell on one of the limbers, exploded the ammunition and caused several casualties.
>
> Captain Allen saw the occurrence and at once, with utter disregard of danger, ran straight across the open, under heavy shell fire, commenced dressing the wounded, and undoubtedly by his promptness saved many of them from bleeding to death.
>
> He was himself hit four times during the first hour by pieces of shells, one of which fractured two of his ribs, but he never even mentioned this at the time, and coolly went on with his work till the last man was dressed and safely removed.
>
> He then went over to another battery and tended a wounded officer. It was only when this was done that he returned to his dug-out and reported his own injury.

Allen was decorated by the King at Hyde Park on 2 June 1917.

William Barnsley Allen was the son of Percy E. Allen and Edith Barnsley Allen and was born in Sheffield on 8 June 1892. The family home, however, was in Scarborough at 6 Victoria Avenue. William's father was a salesman and he sent his son to school at St Cuthbert's College, Worksop, Nottinghamshire. From there he went onto Sheffield University in 1908 to study at the Sheffield Medical School. While at the university he became a member of the OTC.

Allen was a first class student and gained the Kaye Scholarship, the University Gold Medal for Pathology as well as three other prizes. He graduated with an MB and ChB with Second Class Honours, and having qualified he joined the medical staff at the Royal Hospital in Sheffield in June 1914 as house physician.

A brilliant medical career lay ahead of him but the outbreak of war in August 1914 put a stop to all that.

Allen enlisted on 8 August in the RAMC and was attached to the West Riding Field Ambulance and had been commissioned as a lieutenant. He left for France on 1 April 1915 and was made captain in the same month. In May 1916 he got married in Gainsborough to Mollie Young, daughter of W.Y. Mercer. Three months later he gained his first medal, a Military Cross.

In September he won the VC near Mesnil, as we have seen, and having been wounded was invalided to England on 22 July 1917, where he remained for several months. He was actually blind during this period and took six months to recover his sight. On 4 January 1918 his rank was made up to acting major. Three weeks before the Armistice, after being gassed and wounded, he was wounded for the third time and sent home sick to England. By now he had won a Bar to his MC and was then awarded the DSO which was gazetted on 2 April 1919. He had also been Mentioned in Despatches in September and October 1916. During the war he had been bayoneted in the side when assisting enemy wounded and on other occasions received severe chest wounds, as well as being gassed and blinded.

Allen was transferred to the Regular RAMC and his rank reverted to captain. He left for India and was appointed to the staff of the Prince of Wales and the Duke of Connaught. However he was still very weak as a result of his war wounds and to make matters worse, while in India, contracted malaria and dysentery. He returned to England with his health completely broken. He retired from the Army in 1923 and took up a medical practice in Hounslow. He then decided to move to the south coast in order to help his health and lived in Bracklesham Bay, near Chichester. His house was in Stocks Lane and called Perley's Marsh. He resumed his medical career and also set up a Riding School in the village, the Bracklesham Bay Riding School. Riding was one of his favourite pastimes. He used to ride along the beach for gallops of up to 5 miles as there were no groynes on the beach at that time.

Sadly he was still suffering as a result of his war wounds and he took to drink and drugs, as this was the only way that he could obtain any sort of relief. In addition he was now suffering from encephalitis lethargica, called sleepy sickness, which was treated but without success.

In 1932 he crashed his car in Bracklesham and was examined at his home by a police surgeon who found him to be under the influence of drink. Allen's solicitor told the court at Chichester of Allen's war record and said 'he has been a physical wreck, nerves gone, and not being able to sleep, had taken to drugs and whisky'. Allen had his licence suspended for five years and was fined a nominal £1.

On 27 August 1933 Allen was found seriously ill by a member of the staff of his riding stables (Allen's wife was ill herself at the time and in a nursing home) who called for Doctor C.R. Sadler at 6.41am; however, when the doctor arrived at 7.15am, it was too late to save Allen's life. At the subsequent inquest in Chichester the doctor testified that Allen had been taking lumino, opium and morphia in unknown quantities, and when questioned he considered that Allen was suffering from opium poisoning. The verdict on Allen's death was one of 'misadventure' rather than suicide. Nearly fifteen years after the Great War ended it had claimed yet another victim.

Allen was given a 'hero's funeral' and was buried in Earnley Cemetery near Bracklesham. He is still remembered today according to the local press as 'a slim clever man who was a very good doctor. He was a good and generous man and well liked locally'.

After Allen's marriage to Mary Mercer ended, he later married Gertrude, who died in 1955. Allen had two children, a daughter and a son, who was born in 1923.

Allen's VC and medals are in the collection of the RAMC in Aldershot and his name is listed on the Memorial Board at the RAMC College, Millbank, London. A replica VC is displayed on a wall of the Faculty Room at the Sheffield Medical School and finally at the Somme Barracks in West Street, Sheffield, former home of the OTC, there is an ante-room named after him together with a small display of artefacts.

T. HUGHES

On 3 September 1916 the British plan to finally capture Guillemont, the shambles that had once been a village, was for an advance to be made in three stages. The British began their bombardment at 8.15am in order to pave the way for an attack, and at 8.33am a special barrage was directed towards the north-east of the village. On the extreme left of the 59th Brigade, 20th (Light) Division, the 10th (Service) Battalion, The King's Royal Rifle Corps pressed forward and was able to surprise the enemy. The 6th (Service) Battalion, The Connaught Rangers of the 47th Brigade, 16th (Irish) Division were keen to get into the action and followed the KRRC, taking part in an attack on the northern side of Mount Street (This 'street' was the former high street that ran through the centre of the village). From Rim Trench the Connaught Rangers had moved through a quarry, which was to the left of Mount Street as they entered the village, before proceeding to capture all their objectives.

Private Thomas Hughes of the 6th Connaught Rangers won a VC during this advance and later described what happened in his own words:

> On the 3rd of September we went over the top. After being in four different places, I noticed a machine-gun firing in the German lines. So I rushed up, shot both the chaps on the gun and brought it back. I remember no more until I found

myself down in the dressing station. P.S. I forgot to mention I brought four German prisoners with the gun.

His citation was published on 26 October 1916 and read as follows:

For most conspicuous bravery and determination. He was wounded in an attack, but returned at once to the firing line after having his wounds dressed.

Later, seeing a hostile machine-gun he dashed out in front of his company, shot the gunner, and single-handed captured the gun. Though again wounded he brought back three or four prisoners.

When relieved, the battalion returned to Carnoy on 5 September and later left the Somme region on 21 September 1916.

In his book *War Letters to a Wife*, Rowland Feilding of the Connaughts wrote on 29 October 1916:

We have our tails up to-day because we have just heard that Private Hughes, of this battalion, has been awarded the VC for his behaviour at Guillemont. It is something to have a V.C. belonging to your battalion!

Hughes was awarded his VC by the King at a special ceremony on 2 June 1917 at Hyde Park, when he had to use two sticks to help him walk.

Thomas Hughes was the son of Mr and Mrs Hughes of County Monaghan and was born at Coravoo, near Castleblaney on 10 November 1885. After the war, it is unlikely that he was able to work because of his wounds, and became increasingly dependent on drink. Indeed in 1924 he was fined for being in the possession of illegal liquor.

He was found dead at his home Fincairn, Broomfield near Carrickmaross, County Monaghan on 4 January 1942. He was 56 years of age, and was thought of as County Monaghan's own 'Sergeant York'. He was buried four days later in Broomfield Old Cemetery attached to St Patrick's RC Church in Castleblaney. His headstone was arranged for by his family and by comrades of the British Legion.

Hughes left his VC to his sister and in the late 1950s she found herself in reduced circumstances and took steps to sell her brother's decorations, which included the 1914–15 Star and the 1937 King George VI Coronation Medal. The set was purchased by a London dealer for £420 and as a result of a subscription by former members of the Connaught Rangers, who bought it for £500 and presented to the Sandhurst Military Museum, the Rangers having been disbanded in 1922. Then later it was passed to the National Army Museum in Chelsea.

On 3 September 2009 a memorial plaque at Guillemont Church to the Guillemont VCs was unveiled to the memory of Hughes, John Vincent Holland and David Jones. A service to the memory of the 16th (Irish) Division was also held and it was all arranged by the Somme Association of Belfast.

J.V. HOLLAND

On 3 September we have seen that the 59th Brigade and battalions of the 60th Brigade, both of the 20th (Light) Division, had the southern part of the village of Guillemont as their objective. On the left of this division were battalions of the 47th Brigade of the 16th (Irish) Division who were to relieve the 60th Brigade. By 12.30pm it was already known that the first objective along the whole front had been captured.

Lt J.V. Holland of the 7th (Service) Battalion, The Prince of Wales's (Leinster) Regiment (Royal Canadians), 47th Brigade, though his work as officer in charge of the battalion bombers earned himself a VC, was on attachment from the 3rd Leinsters. His battalion's attack from the left flank, delivered south-eastwards from trenches beyond Guillemont station, proved so successful that it virtually carried the day. In the entry of the battalion history, F.E. Whitton wrote: 'the 7th Leinsters had bombed, captured, bayoneted or brained with the butts of their rifles all the Germans in the first trench... a short breathing space was allowed and then the Battalion pushed onto Green Street with similar success.' Over 300 Germans were taken prisoner by the brigade and their casualties were 1,147 out of 2,400 attackers. The Leinsters' contribution was the capture of fifty of the enemy but they suffered badly with twelve officer casualties and 219 other ranks. In effect, they were reduced to one lieutenant and five men.

Lieutenant J.V. Holland was awarded a VC for his gallantry when leading his party through Guillemont, and two days later the Leinsters were relieved and left for Carnoy. The citation for his VC was published in the *London Gazette* of 26 October as follows:

For most conspicuous bravery during a heavy engagement when, not content with bombing hostile dug-outs within the objective, he fearlessly led his bombers through our own artillery barrage and cleared a part of the village in front. He started out with 26 bombers and finished with only five, after capturing some 50 prisoners. By this very gallant action he undoubtedly broke the spirit of the enemy, and saved us many casualties when the battalion made a further advance. He was far from well at the time, and later had to go to hospital.

He was presented with his VC by the King at Buckingham Palace on 5 February 1917.

John Vincent Holland was the son of John Holland, a veterinary surgeon, and Katherine (formerly Peppard) of the Model Farm, Athy, County Kildare, Ireland. He was born on 19 July 1889, one of eight children. He attended Clongowes Wood College, at Naas, County Kildare and then continued his studies at Liverpool University. He was a veterinary student, but gave up his studies and his father paid for him to travel extensively in South America where he was involved with ranching, railway engineering and hunting. At the age of 25 he returned to England and enlisted as a trooper in the 2nd Life Guards on 2 September 1914. He trained at Cumbermere Barracks, Windsor. Captain F.C. Hitchcock in his book *Stand To* states that Holland was nicknamed 'Tin-Belly' as a result of his service with the Life Guards. Holland was granted a commission with the 3rd Leinsters in February 1915 and was attached to the 2nd Royal Dublin Fusiliers and was wounded on the night of 26 June in the Second Battle of Ypres. He returned to England and Ireland in order to recover and when he went back to France he was attached to the 7th Leinsters, with whom he fought as battalion bombing officer at Loos, Hulluch and the Somme in 1916. He had been made a full lieutenant in July 1916. After the action at Guillemont he was promoted to the rank of captain. Later he was Mentioned in Despatches, and awarded 'The Parchment Certificate of the Irish Division'. After his award was announced Major General W.B. Hickie, in command of the 16th (Irish) Division, wrote a congratulatory letter to Holland's father and Brigadier General E.M. Pereira of the 47th Brigade wrote to Holland himself:

My Dear Holland,... I did not expect an answer to my telegram which I sent to show how much the Brigade appreciated the honour you had reflected on them by your gallant action at Guillemont, I am very glad that the bombers are also included – I think that two got the DCM and six more the Military Medal – so you will be able to rejoice that the gallant men who went with you were not forgotten. We were all very sorry that you yourself were not present when the Battalion celebrated the event, and that could not hear the cheers that were raised for you. I am sorry that you have been so seedy, but I hope that you are now picking up, but I hope that you will live long to wear the proudest distinction that can be awarded to a soldier.

One of Holland's bombers, Pte A. Lee also wrote to him and quotes a few words that Holland had said on 3 September 1916 at Guillemont: 'Boys, a Victoria Cross is to be won'.

John Holland was married at the cathedral in Queenstown on 15 January 1917 to Frances Grogan, daughter of Joseph Grogan, JP of the Manor House, Queenstown, Rossleague. Grogan's business interests included the servicing of Royal Navy vessels at Queenstown where the navy had a base during the war. The military wedding was a 'brilliant and impressive one . . . and the bridegroom's Regiment paid every military honour and courtesy to their first and only VC and his newly-wedded bride.' Holland was then made staff instructor, number 16, Officer Cadet Battalion, Kinnel Park, Rhyl.

After the war Holland joined the 9th Lancers in India where he was able to carry on with his favourite pursuits of horseriding and hunting. He was appointed major and was transferred to Kenya for a period of colonial service. By this time there were two sons in the family and their English home was at 34 Elm Road, Seaforth, Merseyside. Holland returned from Kenya in 1936 and the family then moved setting home in Colwyn Bay, Wales. He was employed in various civil service occupations, and in 1940 after the outbreak of the Second World War, he returned to the Army in India but was invalided out in 1941. He then took up a position with the Ministry of Food. In the 1950s he and his wife emigrated to Tasmania where Frances died in 1960.

Holland was a tall, aristocratic looking man and never really settled down to civilian life, and was probably at his happiest when serving with the army abroad. He visited London in 1956 with the Australian contingent for the Victoria Cross Review held before the Queen in Hyde Park. He died in St John's Park Hospital, Hobart, Tasmania at the age of 85 on 27 February 1975. He was buried at Cornelian Bay Cemetery, Hobart in the RC section, N-D, Lot 63, next to his wife, on 1 March after a service of Requiem Mass at St Mary's Cathedral. He was given a full military funeral.

On 3 September 2009 a memorial plaque at Guillemont Church to the Guillemont VCs was unveiled to the memory of John Holland, Thomas Hughes and David Jones. A service to the memory of the 16th (Irish) Division was also held and it was all arranged by the Somme Association of Belfast.

Holland's decorations are in private hands.

D. Jones

Having served in the Ypres Salient close to Hooge in June 1916, the 12th (Service) Battalion, The King's (Liverpool) Regiment, with the rest of the 20th (Light) Division, took part in the Somme battle from 22 August and nearly two weeks later on 3 September, together with the 16th (Irish) Division and supported by the 7th Division, they began attempts to capture the extremely well-defended village of Guillemont. The plan was for the 20th Division to capture the village and to establish a line 500 yards to the east of the village. The 12th King's, part of the 61st Brigade, was to be prominent during this fighting and one of their sergeants, David Jones was to win a posthumous VC.

In the late afternoon of the 3rd it was known that the 7th Division had entered Ginchy, to the north-east of Guillemont. Measures were taken to protect the flank of the corps by positioning troops astride the Guillemont–Ginchy Road, an initiative that according to the *Official History* 'owed much to a company commander of the 12th King's, 61st Brigade. His battalion had been sent up to reinforce the 47th Brigade, 16th Irish Divsion.' Sergeant D. Jones, at 5.30pm and again at 6.30pm, helped to fight off two German counter-attacks by rifle and Lewis gun fire. His platoon, which belonged to C Company of the 12th King's, was well forward on the southern side of Ginchy and was to beat off several more attacks before being relieved on 5 September.

His citation was published on 26 October 1916 and read as follows:

For most conspicuous bravery, devotion to duty, and ability displayed in the handling of his platoon.

The platoon to which he belonged was ordered to a forward position, and during the advance came under heavy machine-gun fire, the officer being killed and the platoon suffering heavy losses.

Sergeant Jones led forward the remainder, occupied the position, and held it for two days and two nights without food or water, until relieved. On the second day he drove back three counter-attacks, inflicting heavy losses. His coolness was most praiseworthy. It was due entirely to his resource and example that his men retained confidence and held their post.

The Battalion War Diary noted that upon relief (completed by 5.30am) 'Sergeant D. Jones with two Lewis gun teams remained in the line, the incoming battalion (the Borders) having brought no Lewis guns. With most of his party killed, Sergeant Jones held his position against several strong attacks until relieved the next morning, arriving at Sandpit Camp at 9.10am. The battalion then moved to Méricourt l'Abbé and remained in the Somme area for the rest of the Somme battle.'

On 7 October, the first day of the battle for the Transloy Ridges, the 20th (Light) Division were again in action and their 60th and 61st brigades had their jumping off points on the road that ran in a south-easterly direction from Guedecourt towards Le Transloy. The fighting began at 1.45pm and the 61st Brigade, with the 7th (Service) Battalion, The King's Own Yorkshire Light Infantry and the 12th King's to the fore, made progress of about 500 yards and enter the western section of Rainbow Trench. David Jones was in number 10 platoon of the latter battalion and was killed during the fighting. At one point a number of Germans gave themselves up and those who retired towards Beaulencourt became easy targets. The two battalions even reached as far as a section of Cloudy Trench, a stretch of about 300 yards. However, part of Rainbow Trench to their south-east was still in enemy hands and so there was a danger in advancing too quickly. The 7th (Service) Battalion, (Prince Albert's) Somerset Light Infantry relieved the 12th King's later in the day. Jones' body was buried to the east of Bapaume at Bancourt British Cemetery, Plot V, Row F, Grave 20.

Jones' VC was presented to his widow by the King at Buckingham Palace on 31 March 1917. The King asked Mrs Jones to wear the medal on the right breast, which she did, although she was slightly embarrassed when soldiers saluted her!

David Jones was the son of David and Jessie Jones, formerly Ginochio. He was the youngest of six children and was born on 10 January 1891 at 3 Hutchinson Street, then in the West Derby District of Liverpool, but now part of Merseyside.

His father was employed as a cotton porter and later became a carrier with a grocery firm, Cooper & Co., although he had been trained as an iron moulder. The family later moved from Hutchison Street to 25 Elmore Terrace, close to Everton Terrace. David Jones attended school at Heyworth Street School, Everton and later joined Blake's Motor company, Lord Street, Liverpool as a trainee motor mechanic. In 1909 he also joined the Territorial Force serving with the 9th King's (Liverpool) Regiment and was discharged on 7 June 1913 when at the end of his engagement.

Jones re-enlisted as a private on 29 August 1914, joining the 12th (Service) Battalion which became part of the 20th (Light) Division and assembled in Aldershot. In January 1915 the 12th Battalion was transferred to the 61st Brigade. Prior to going overseas, Jones was granted a fortnight's leave during which time he got married on 27 May. His bride was Elizabeth Dorothea Doyle and their home was 87 Heyworth Street.

After this leave and not knowing that he was never to see his new wife again, Jones left for France.

In June 1915 his division was inspected by the King and on 24 June the battalion left for France. It took part in the Battle of Loos and the battalion's first experience of being under fire was when supporting the Meerut Division at Petrie on 25 September. Jones had been promoted from the rank of private and at the time of his death he was a sergeant.

Six months after his death two memorial tablets as well as a photographic portrait were unveiled on 3 April 1917 at Heyworth Street School. One of the tablets, a brass one, was fixed by the pupils on a wall inside the school, and a polished granite tablet was erected at the front of the school facing Heyworth Street. The ceremonies were attended by the Lord Mayor of Liverpool. Those present included Jones' widow and other members of his family. The band of the 3rd Battalion Royal Welsh Fusiliers led the singing of two hymns and also played the Last Post. A contingent from the King's Regiment was also in attendance.

After the war was over Mrs Jones married a William J. Woosey, who was a plumber. When the King's Regiment merged with the Manchester Regiment, she was not happy with the arrangement and presented David Jones' VC to his former employer, Blake's Motor Company. Each year a member of the firm used to travel to London and present a wreath at the Cenotaph in Whitehall on Remembrance Sunday. In the 1970s the brass plaque in Heyworth School was moved to a position in Everton Catholic Primary School and was later moved into the keeping of the King's Regimental Museum. At the time of writing the granite tablet remains in a disused library building at St Doming Road, Everton and will hopefully be retrieved.

There is also a memorial tablet in St Nathaniel's, Edge Hill, Liverpool and on 3 September 2009 a memorial plaque at Guillemont Church to the Guillemont VCs was unveiled to the memory of Jones, John Vincent Holland and Thomas Hughes. A service to the memory of the 16th (Irish) Division was also held and it was all arranged by the Somme Association of Belfast.

Jones' VC, but not his medals, were later in the collection of the King's Regimental Museum but J. Blake & Son Trustees donated it to the Museum of Liverpool on the city's Pierhead in October 2009.

L. CLARKE

In the six days between 3 and 9 September 1916, Pozières Ridge had finally been taken by the Allies and there had been continuous fighting towards High Wood. Most of Leuze Wood towards Combles had also been taken, as had Faffemont Farm. Finally on 9 September the village of Ginchy was to fall into Allied hands after extremely hard fighting.

Back on the western side of the Somme battlefield the Australian and Canadian troops were trying to move towards Mouquet Farm as part of the plan to occupy the German stronghold of Thiepval. The position to the north-west of the Pozières OG Trench lines was called Fabeck Graben, a section of which had been lost by the enemy in early September. Although Sir Douglas Haig wanted the Canadian Army to be allowed to 'settle in' before they were committed to the fray, there was little chance as the enemy were not going to give up their positions in front of Mouquet Farm without a considerable fight.

In addition to relieving the Australians on the Mouquet Farm front, the Canadian Army, in the form of the 2nd (East Ontario) Canadian Infantry Battalion, were also ordered to attack on the south side of the Albert–Bapaume Road. Their objective was the German front trench astride the railway leading to Martinpuich. The fighting continued on a front of 500 yards and more than sixty German prisoners were taken. However, the line was continuously bombarded by the enemy artillery and several German counter-attacks were fought off. It was during this time that Corporal L. Clarke of the 2nd Canadian Battalion won his VC. He attacked a party of the enemy virtually on his own and routed them, and took one prisoner despite being seriously wounded in the leg by a German bayonet. The attack had begun at 4.45pm and three out of the four companies in the battalion made the assault. When they reached the enemy line they found that the Allied barrage had not been very successful, and there were many Germans waiting for them.

Corporal Clarke was ordered by Lieutenant Hoey to take part of a bombing section and clear out some of the enemy on the left flank. He was then to join up with Sergeant W.H. Nicholls at a block that the latter was to build. Clarke was the first to enter what turned out to be a strongly fortified position and he and the rest of his group bombed the Germans out. At this time a party of Germans had already seen enough of Clarke's methods and had to be urged to the attack. Clarke took them all on, firstly with the use of his revolver, and then seizing a German rifle he used that as well. The senior of the two German officers lunged at Clarke and wounded him severely just below the knee with his bayonet. It was the officer's last act as Clarke then shot him. The remaining five Germans turned and fled, and even then Clarke pursued them hard. One of the German soldiers, who spoke excellent English, surrendered and Clarke turned him over to Sergeant Nicholls who had managed to finish building the trench. Lieutenant Hoey had to order Clarke to have his wounds attended to; nevertheless, Clarke returned to his platoon in their billets the next day.

Despite his wounds, Clarke continued to take part in the fighting and on 11 October his battalion was instructed to secure the recently captured Regina Trench, which was still coming under heavy enemy artillery fire. When crouching down in the rear of a trench a shell exploded and the trench collapsed, burying him. He was trapped but his brother managed to dig him out and he was taken to Number One General Hospital near Le Havre, but died there on the 19th. He was buried at Etretat Churchyard, Plot II, Row C, Grave 3A. The citation for his VC was published on 26 October and read as follows:

For most conspicuous bravery. He was detailed with his section of bombers to clear the continuation of a newly-captured trench and cover the construction of a 'block'. After most of his party had become casualties, he was building a 'block' when about twenty of the enemy with two officers counter-attacked. He boldly advanced against them, emptied his revolver into them, and afterwards two enemy rifles, which he picked up in the trench.

One of the officers then attacked him with the bayonet, wounding him in the leg, but he shot him dead. The enemy then ran away, pursued by Acting Corporal Clarke, who shot four more and captured a fifth.

Later he was ordered to the dressing station, but returned next day to duty.

Clarke's father, Mr H.T. Clarke received his son's posthumous VC at a ceremony in Winnipeg in 1917 from the hands of the Governor-General of Canada, the 9th Duke of Devonshire, in front of a crowd of 30,000 people.

Lionel Beaumaurice (Leo) Clarke was born on 1 December 1892 in Waterdown, Hamilton, Ontario. He was the son of Henry Trevelyan Clarke and Rossetta Caroline Nona Clarke, of 785 Pine Street, Winnipeg, Manitoba. His early years were spent in England but his parents returned to Winnipeg in the period 1903–1905. After leaving school, Leo Clarke held a number of jobs and when war broke out in August 1914 was working on the survey in the Canadian north. He returned to Winnipeg, Manitoba and enlisted as a private with the 27th Battalion CEF on 25 February 1915. He left with them to sail to England in June and then to France in September. He transferred to the 2nd Canadian Battalion in order to be near his brother who was serving with the unit. Clarke was wounded for the first time at the end of 1915.

On 6 August 1916 he was made an acting corporal and with his unit moved south to the Somme battlefield at the beginning of September. The immediate goals were Mouquet Farm and the village of Courcelette, a mile behind the German frontline trenches.

At 2pm on Sunday 19 September 1971 a historical plaque to the memory of Corporal Leo Clarke was unveiled in front of the Royal Canadian Legion Building, Hamilton Street, Waterdown, Ontario. Relatives of the Clarke family attended the ceremony. Other VC holders who lived in Pine Street included Frederick Hall and Robert Shankland. The street, renamed Valour Road in 1925, has a bronze plaque commemorating this fact attached to a street lamp at the corner of the street with Portage Avenue. Clarke's decorations are in private hands.

D.F. BROWN

 In between 9 September when Corporal L. Clarke won his posthumous VC and 15 September when three VCs were awarded, the Allies were making preparations for the third phase of the Battle of the Somme. The 15th was to be a day of great progress and advances were made to the depth of 2,000–3,000 yards on parts of the 16-mile front. With the support of the first ever appearance of the 'Tank' in battle the villages of Flers, Martinpuich and Courcelette were taken. Even High Wood, which was meant to have been captured in mid-July, fell to the British after two months of bitter struggle.

The New Zealand Division was given the task of capturing the series of trenches on the sloping ground between Delville Wood and High Wood. The 2nd Battalion, The Auckland Regiment and the 2nd Battalion, The Otago Regiment of the 2nd New Zealand Brigade advanced and the former battalion captured Coffee Trench easily, but the Ortagos met with considerable enemy resistance at a position called Crest Trench. One German machine-gun was giving great trouble in particular. Sergeants D.F. Brown and J. Rodgers crawled forward to within 30 yards of the machine-gun before rushing forward and killing the crew. The attackers then moved quickly on towards the Switch Trench, virtually ignoring the Allied barrage which they were catching up with. Sergeant Brown and his company destroyed another German machine-gun position and with the aid of bombs and bayonets the Switch Trench was captured. They next moved onto the Flers Line where they remained for five hours and Brown's company eventually came out of the line, still with their two Sergeants, but with only forty-nine men.

Brown was awarded the VC for his heroism, but was killed sixteen days later near Eaucourt l'Abbaye, on 1 October. As before, Brown was in the thick of the fighting. The Otagos attacked Circus Trench which led to the Abbey Road in front of Eaucourt l'Abbaye. The artillery had pounded the enemy positions since early morning and at one minute before zero hour, which was 3.15pm, about sixty oil mortars were fired which set the German trenches alight and created a black oily smoke. The New Zealanders then charged the enemy on a front of 1,800 yards. The 2nd Brigade penetrated to a depth of 800 yards. As on 15 September Brown took on a German machine-gun crew and bayoneted them. However, his luck finally ran out when he was wounded by a machine-gun and died of his wounds. The citation for his VC was not published in the *London Gazette* until 14 June and read as follows:

For most conspicuous bravery and determination in attack when the company to which he belonged suffered very heavy casualties in officers and men from machine-gun fire.

At great personal risk this NCO advanced with a comrade and succeeded in reaching a point within 30 yards of the enemy guns. Four of the gun crew were killed and the gun captured.

The advance of the company was continued till it was again held up by machine-gun fire. Again Sergeant Brown and his comrade with great gallantry rushed the gun and killed the crew. After this second position had been won, the company came under very heavy shell fire, and the utter contempt for danger and coolness under fire of this non-commissioned officer did much to keep up the spirit of his men. On a subsequent occasion in attack Sergeant Brown showed most conspicuous gallantry. He attacked single-handed a machine-gun which was holding up the attack, killed the gun crew and captured the gun. Later, whilst sniping the retreating enemy, this very gallant soldier was killed.

Brown was buried at Warlencourt British Cemetery near the Abbaye on the Bapaume Road, Plot III, Row F, Grave 11. Robert Brown, Sergeant Brown's father was presented with his son's VC by His Excellency the Right Honourable The Earl of Liverpool, Governor-General of New Zealand, at Oamaru on 30 August 1917.

Donald Forrester Brown was born in Dunedin, New Zealand on 23 February 1890, the son of Robert and Jessie Brown. Robert was a draper and his son Donald attended the South School in Oamaru and then Waitaki Boys' school in the same town, and he later took up farming in Totara. Selling his farm he enlisted at the age of 25 with the New Zealand Expeditionary Force on 19 October 1915 and after training embarked for Egypt with the 9th Reinforcements in January 1916. In April they left for France. His was the first VC to be won by a member of the New Zealand Forces in France, who arrived in May, and his other decorations included the British War Medal and the Victory Medal. He is commemorated at the HQ of the Royal New Zealand Returned and Services' Association (RSA) in Dunedin. His VC and medals are in private hands.

F. McNess

The Guards Division was based at Ginchy on 15 September from where they were to launch an attack towards Les Boeufs. At 6.20am, when the creeping barrage began, the Guards moved forward, keeping 30 yards behind it. As they advanced towards a strong point known as The Triangle to the north-east, they were caught by terrific fire from the right where the Germans still held The Quadrilateral; at this point they were opposite the British 6th Division. Despite this fire, all four battalions of the 2nd Guards Brigade reached The Triangle, including the 1st Scots Guards. However, casualties were high even though the battle had been going for barely an hour. It was during this fighting that Lance Sergeant Fred McNess earned his VC, but in doing so was seriously wounded in the head and in other parts of his body.

McNess described the event in a letter home that was printed in the local papers in Leeds a few weeks later:

> ... after getting through a small opening in the barbed wire in front of the German Trench, I took a party up the communication trench, and for an hour and a half a corporal and I slowly but surely drove the enemy back. The remainder of the boys passed the bombs to us, we being the only two who could use them. Then we ran short, but finding large quantities of German bombs we experimented with them until we found out how to use them. Then we fought them with their own bombs. It was a case of hand-to-hand fighting all the way up. Then I got wounded. It was like this. One of the men in my platoon was shot through the lungs.

... I was just preparing another bomb when a German threw a bomb which burst right in front of my dial... (McNess had the left side of his neck and part of his jaw, his lower teeth and some of his upper teeth blown away by the German bomb) I had to walk 2 miles to the first field dressing station. Here I received a rough dressing, then German prisoners carried me 3 miles to the ambulance. (At one stage he was treated by Noel Chavasse). I underwent an operation at the first hospital I came to then another one at Rouen (9th General Hospital), one on the day I arrived here, and I have another coming off tomorrow, it is just a case of straightening up old repairs.

The battalion was relieved the next day and returned to the Citadel Camp near Fricourt. Their casualties had been 288 and the brigade remained in the Somme region for the rest of the battle.

The 'official version' of McNess' heroism was published in a citation dated 26 October 1916 and read as follows:

For most conspicuous bravery. During a severe engagement he led his men on with the greatest dash in the face of heavy shell and machine-gun fire. When the first line of enemy trenches was reached, it was found that the left flank was exposed, and that the enemy was bombing down the trench.

Sergeant McNess thereupon organised a counter-attack and led it in person. He was very severely wounded in the neck and jaw, but went on passing through the barrage of hostile bombs in order to bring up fresh supplies to his own men.

Finally he established a 'block', and continued encouraging his men and throwing bombs till utterly exhausted by loss of blood.

McNess later went under the knife at King George's Hospital, Stamford Street, London where the surgeons used part of his rib to reconstruct his jaw. At this time he was summoned to receive his VC and was driven from the hospital to Buckingham Palace on 9 December 1916. He was accompanied by a sergeant of the RAMC. At the palace and was greeted by Colonel Fludyer, till recently commander of the Scots Guards, who conducted McNess to the royal presence. An observer noted that McNess 'appeared to be in a very sorry plight, though exceedingly cheerful. He was badly wounded in the neck, arm, shoulder and side. McNess was with the King for about twenty minutes while the story of what had happened was read out. The King talked to him and expressed concern about his wounds. McNess was decorated after the generals and he was the only VC holder to be presented on that day.'

Fred McNess was born in Bramley, Leeds on 22 January 1892. He was the son of John McNess of Perth who served at one time with the Royal Engineers and of Mary McNess. There were three sons and one daughter in the family. Fred attended Bramley National School and grew up to be a strapping young man of 5ft 9in. He was also a great walker and nature lover and used to ramble through the Wharfedale valleys at weekends. He was a carter's assistant to a carrier called Joseph Harry Boan before the war and enlisted with the 3rd (Reserve) Battalion of the Scots Guards in London on 10 January1915. He was appointed unpaid corporal on 7 February 1916 and left for France to join the 1st Battalion on 6 April 1916. He was made corporal on 25 August 1916, later lance sergeant.

After he was presented with the VC in December 1916 he was sent for a time to convalesce at Welbeck Abbey but soon returned to King George's Hospital where he was to remain for eighteen months. In mid-July 1917 McNess received an official welcome at Leeds and in his home town of Bramley and crowds of people turned out to greet him. In the evening a brass band led a parade through the streets of the town. In October 1917 McNess was presented with a massive clock and sidepieces in bronze by Colonel J.W. Smith-Neill, Commander of the Scots Guards at Wellington Barracks. On 14 June 1918 he finally left King George's when he was discharged from the army with a pension as not being physically fit enough for army duties. In early January 1920 he was again fêted by his home town as were other members of the returned forces. However McNess was presented with an Illuminated Address and the sum of £400 which allowed him to start up a shoe repair business at 95 Woodhouse Lane, Leeds. Arrangements had also been made for him to be trained for this profession. His widowed mother lived at the family home at 35 Eightlands Lane, Bramley, Leeds.

On 16 November 1929 McNess was one of eight Leeds VCs who acted as pallbearers at the funeral of John Raynes VC at Harehills Cemetery, Leeds.

Until he retired McNess lived at 6 Springbank Crescent, Headingly, Leeds and latterly worked on the staff of the Leeds City Engineers Department as a filing clerk. In 1939 he wrote to the Scots Guards enquiring about the possibility of a recall and was thanked but politely turned down because the injuries he had received in the Great War made him medically unfit for service. On retirement at the age of 64 he and his wife who he had first met when she was nursing him, decided to move to the south coast and bought a bungalow at 37 Petersfield Road, Boscombe, Hants in January 1956.

On 4 May 1958, while his wife Dorothy was out of the house, he took his own life. Although no one can know McNess' actual state of mind at the time, I think that it can be assumed that he was in a period of deep depression; a depression which must have had its roots in his very severe war wounds suffered nearly forty years before. In addition his move to the south of England may have had an unsettling effect on him as well. At the inquest Mrs McNess gave evidence that 'her husband was badly wounded in the First World War and had suffered depression and headaches'. The coroner's verdict was 'that he took his life while the balance of his mind was disturbed'. McNess' funeral took place at Bournemouth on 8 May and his decorations were displayed on the coffin. Later his body was cremated.

Unfortunately his suicide was not only a tragedy in itself, but the Ministry of Pensions and National Insurance chose to ignore the root cause of it and immediately suspended Mrs McNess' right to her late husband's pension. Their reason for doing this was the manner of McNess' death, and the lack of real proof that McNess' wounds were the sole cause of his death. Mrs McNess was faced with living on her widow's pension of just £2 per week. However, there is a redeeming element in all this and that is the role that McNess' regiment played. Dorothy McNess wrote to them for assistance at the outset of her problems from an address at 11 Cecil Court, Charmiston Road, Bournemouth. As a result she was paid £10 per month out of Regimental Funds.

Mrs McNess was invited to appeal, which she did. The Scots Guards also took a hand and wrote directly to John Boyd-Carpenter, an ex-Guardsman who was the minister responsible.

McNess' former doctor from Leeds wasn't much help as 'he felt that he could not relate the war injury directly to his suicide partly as McNess never spoke of the war.' Before he died McNess had prostate trouble and an ulcer on his face and died shortly after moving to his new house. Several witnesses of McNess' shyness and unwillingness to talk about the war mention this fact in reports of his death. The negotiations that Mrs McNess had with the Ministry continued for about a year and at the same time she was also trying to sell her new home. Unfortunately nobody wished to buy the property owing to its unfortunate associations. At one point contracts had actually been exchanged, but at the last minute the wife of the man buying the propertly suddenly died and the sale fell through.

This story, however, does have a happy ending and Boyd-Carpenter was able to write to the Scots Guards telling them that the appeal had been successful (18 June 1957). The pension was backdated to McNess' death a year before and in time the bunga-low was sold and Mrs McNess went to live with her family. She was naturally overjoyed about the outcome of her appeal and she received her new pension book on 15 July 1957 and wrote off immediately to the regiment.

In 1956 Mrs McNess had also mentioned to the regiment that her late husband had always expressed the wish that they should have his decorations after his death and they were duly presented. Apart from the VC, he had been awarded the British War Medal, Victory Medal, Kings Certificate No 843, War Badge and Cetificate 925. The regiment were very grateful to receive the decorations and promised to look after them. At the end of 1956 McNess' VC was part of an exhibition of Yorkshire VCs held in Leeds. This would have been part of the centenary of the founding of the Victoria Cross.

A painting of McNess' VC action near Ginchy on 15 September 1916 is on display at the Regimental HQ, Wellington Barracks, Birdcage Walk, London. In the Victoria Gardens in Leeds, on The Headrow side of Cookridge Street are various memorials includ-ing one to the Victoria Cross holders who were born or buried in Leeds. Unveiled in November 1992, it is outside the Henry Moore Institute and McNess is one of seventeen names inscribed on it. The Leeds War Memorial had been moved to this site in 1937 from a site in the City Square.

The grandchildren of McNess have kept the memory of their relative very much alive and have McNess' portraits on display in their homes, and Michael Morris had a copy of an Illuminated Address. Christine Williams in her recollections of her grandfather remembers him with affection and that he had only one good hand and 'was a tall, stooped man with a thin face that moved only on one side when he talked or smiled. He walked with a limp and his voice was quiet.' McNess had died when she was 11 years old.

J. V. CAMPBELL

Three VCs were to be awarded on 15 September; to Donald Brown of the New Zealand Division in the struggle for the trenches between Delville Wood and High Wood, to Fred McNess of the 1st Scots Guards, 2nd Guards Brigade for bombing the Germans out of their positions north-east of Ginchy, and to Lieutenant Colonel J.V. Campbell of the 3rd Coldstream Guards, 1st Guards Brigade for taking personal command of a third line of his battalion when the first two waves had been decimated.

The Guards Division were occupying the village of Ginchy on 15 September and the overall Fourth Army Plan in this part of the Somme battlefield was to capture the enemy defences between Morval and Le Sars. The southern limit of the Guards Division attack was 500 yards south of the Ginchy–Les Boeufs Road. The plan was that the 2nd and 3rd Coldstream Guards of the 1st Guards Brigade were to advance and occupy the first three objectives, then the 1st Irish Guards of the same brigade were to pass through the captured lines and reach the fourth line which was named the Red Line. Opposition was expected from the left flank and the 2nd Grenadier Guards were ordered to form a defensive flank on this left side of the attack.

The infantry of the 1st Brigade went forward at zero hour, 6.20am, and was in trouble from the start as the first waves of the Coldstreams were literally mown down. The enemy was positioned with machine-guns in the Flers–Ginchy Sunken Road and inflicted great damage on one of the British Army's crack units. Major Vaughan, second-in-command of the 3rd Coldstreams was killed as was their adjutant. They had not even covered 100 yards of ground. The infantry tried to deal with the attackers in the Sunken Road, although tanks had been assigned to this task but had failed to show up.

Lieutenant Colonel Campbell, in charge of the 3rd Coldstreams, realised that there would be no progress until the Sunken Road was cleared and the attack on the left flank pressed home. He had with him his hunting horn from his time with the Shropshire Harriers and blew just one note on it, which was sufficient to rally the wavering troops who then moved forward in an irresistible rush. The Guardsmen carried the Sunken Road and went down the slope of one valley and up the slope of another. Finally they reached as far as the German Third Line. The position had been captured at 7.15am and the infantry were not to attack further until their right flank had been protected. However, it was discovered that they were not after all in the German Third Line but in fact in the enemy First Line, meaning that it was important to press on and the Coldstreams were ordered to move forward in the direction of the church at Les Boeufs, which was then visible. The troops advanced but were almost immediately checked by intense enemy fire and for a second time that morning Campbell sounded his hunting horn.

This time the German Third Line was really reached and Campbell wanted to press on and capture Les Boeufs and sent a message back for reinforcements to be sent up. However, General Feilding, in charge of the attack, would not allow this as the 6th Division on the left flank had not made progress and any forward thrust by the Guards would leave them dangerously exposed to a serious counter-attack. Instead the positions known as the Blue Line were to be consolidated. When they were relieved they returned to Citadel Camp having suffered 361 casualties.

Not surprisingly Campbell was awarded the VC for taking command of the situation and in saving the day for the Guards. Despite their success in terms of ground covered, it was at a huge cost of human life. His award was published on 26 October 1916 and read as follows:

For most conspicuous bravery and able leading in an attack.

Seeing that the first two waves of his battalion had been decimated by machine-gun and rifle fire, he took personal command of the third line, rallied his men with the utmost gallantry, and led them against the enemy machine-guns, capturing the guns and killing the personnel.

Later in the day, after consultation with other unit commanders, he again rallied the survivors of his battalion, and at a critical moment led them through a very heavy hostile fire barrage against the objective. He was one of the first to enter the enemy trench.

His personal gallantry and initiative at a very critical moment turned the fortunes of the day and enabled the division to press on and capture objectives of the highest tactical importance.

On 14 November Campbell was presented with his VC by the King at Buckingham Palace and on the 16th he was transferred and became CO of the 3rd Coldstream Guards, 137th Brigade, 46th North Midland Territorial Division, a position he held until 7 November 1918.

John Vaughan Campbell was born into a military family on 31 October 1876 in London. His father was the Hon. Ronald Campbell and his mother formerly Katherine Claughton, daughter of Bishop Claughton of St Albans. John was also the grandson of the 2nd Earl of Cawdor.

Ronald Campbell was killed in the Zulu War and John was sent to Eton and then Sandhurst. He joined the Coldstream Guards on 5 September 1896 when he was nearly 21 years of age. He was made a lieutenant on 6 April 1898 and adjutant to the regiment on 29 December 1900 until 13 July 1903.

He served in the South African War 1899–1902 as acting assistant provost-marshal and later station staff officer and took part in the advance on Kimberley in addition to other engagements.

He was made a member of the DSO in 1901 and promoted to captain on 27 June 1903 and Mentioned in Despatches on 10 September 1901 and 29 July 1902, and awarded the Queen's Medal with six Clasps and the King's Medal with two Clasps.

He was promoted to major on 21 June 1913 and on 29 July, just before the Great War began was made temporary lieutenant colonel and given the Brevet for that rank on 1 January 1916. On 29 November he was made full lieutenant colonel

Prior to the war Campbell lived at Broom Hall, Oswestry, Shropshire and was master of the Tanat Side Harriers. He was a well-known rider to hounds and had ridden in many steeplechases.

John Campbell married Amy Dorothy Penn, daughter of John Penn MP, on 18 July 1904 at the Chapel of Wellington Barracks, Birdcage Walk, London. They were to have two children, Diana and John Ronald who joined the Coldstreams, rose to major and who was killed in May 1940.

John was made GOC 3rd Guards Brigade on 8 November 1918 and created a CMG on 1 January 1918, having been Mentioned in Despatches on three occasions on 31 December 1915, 7 November 1917 and 16 March 1919. In 1919 he was appointed ADC to the King and retired from this post in 1933 when he was given the honorary rank of brigadier general. He unveiled the war memorial at Bellenglise which was on the site of a former German gun emplacement and he was one of seven holders of the VC at the unveiling of the Guards Memorial in St James's Park

When he rode to hounds after the war he still took with him his famous hunting horn. His wife Amy died in 1927 and at her funeral her coffin was conveyed by farm wagon from Broom Hall, Oswestry to Trefonen for burial.

He remarried Margaret Emily Robina, a daughter of Dr and Mrs A. Tennyson-Smith and moved to the Stroud district of Gloucestershire in 1937. In August 1939, just before the Second World War began, Campbell served as an honorary flight lieutenant in the RAF Volunteer Reserve until February 1941. He then took over command of the 8th Gloucestershire Battalion Home Guard, a position which he held until his death in 1944. On Saturday 20 May he took the salute at Dursley in connection with 'Salute the Soldier' week and two days later, in the morning of 22 May, he died suddenly at his home at Benwell House, Woodchester, Stroud. His body was cremated at Cheltenham Crematorium and his ashes taken to Scotland where they were scattered into the River Findhorn off the Banchor Bridge, Drynachan on the Cawdor Estate. A memorial plaque was later erected on one of the walls of Cawdor Parish Church in his memory.

Campbell's second wife outlived him by forty-one years, dying on 11 November 1985. His VC and hunting horn had been bequeathed to the Coldstreams and his other decorations are on loan to them. Throughout his life after 1916 Campbell was known as 'Tallyho VC'.

J.C. KERR

Zollern Graben was a major German Second Line defensive position and stronghold on the crest of a ridge between Mouquet Farm to the south-west and Courcelette to the north-east. Attempts to capture the whole of it had been made by troops of the Canadian Army on 15 September and had only narrowly failed. In particular the much fought for Sugar Refinery had at last fallen to the attackers. They had also overrun Mouquet Farm itself, but did not totally clear it and were subsequently driven out.

The enemy from the Zollern positions had a clear view of any attackers and could also enfilade adjoining trenches with machine-gun fire. The 3rd Canadian Division was given these positions to capture on the evening of the 16th. The division was made up of the 7th, 8th and 9th Canadian brigades. The 7th were to strike at Fabeck Graben, which was part of a trench running from Courcelette to Mouquet Farm. If successful the 9th Brigade were then to carry on to attack the Zollern from the east. The first part of the plan failed because the artillery overshot but two bombing parties of the 7th Brigade were able to enter the Fabeck Trench from both ends, thus sealing off a party of the enemy, in a section of the trench which measured 250 yards. The defenders were in an impossible position as if they retreated they would be cut down by the Canadians to the left and right flanks. It was at this point that Private John Kerr of the 49th (Edmonton) Canadian Infantry Battalion was to win the VC. He moved forward as bayonet man in advance of his companions, he climbed over a 'block' and moved 30 yards along the enemy position before being challenged. Eventually he was seen and a grenade thrown at him, and in defending himself with his arm he lost part of his right fore-finger and his right side was also injured. A bomb fight ensued between the Canadians and the Germans, but Kerr grew impatient and wanted to hurry up the capture of the German position. He then ran along the top of the Fabeck Trench, fired down at its defenders killing several and the remaining sixty-two Germans surrendered. Although Kerr acted mostly on his own, the Germans probably thought that he was part of a large party of attackers. That night Mouquet Farm was attacked again and the British II Corps began to relieve the Canadian Division.

Kerr's VC citation was published on 26 October 1916 and read as follows:

> For most conspicuous bravery. During a bombing attack he was acting as a bayonet man, and, knowing that bombs were running short, he ran along the parados under heavy fire until he was in close contact with the enemy, when he opened fire on them at point-blank range, and inflicted heavy loss.
>
> The enemy, thinking they were surrounded, surrendered. Sixty-two prisoners were taken, and 250 yards of enemy trench captured.
>
> Before carrying out this very plucky act, one of Private Kerr's fingers had been blown off by a bomb.
>
> Later, with two other men, he escorted back the prisoners under fire, and then returned to report himself for duty before having his wound dressed.

He received his VC from the King on 5 February 1917.

John Chipman Kerr was born at Fox River, Cumberland County, Nova Scotia on 11 January 1887. Before the war he had moved north-west of his birth place in order to become a farmer and he purchased some virgin land at Spirit River. After war was declared however, Kerr and a small group of other 'homesteaders' walked 50 miles to the nearest railway and arrived at Edmonton where they enlisted in the 66th Battalion.

At the beginning of June 1916 when being trained in England, 400 men of the 66th were transferred to the 49th (Edmonton) Battalion who were in Belgium in the area of Sanctuary Wood near Ypres.

The Canadians later went south to the Somme battlefield, arriving at Albert on 13 September 1916 and less than forty-eight hours later they took up positions at a point near the Sunken Road in front of and to the west of the village of Courcelette.

After the war Kerr returned to Canada, and when the Second World War began he re-enlisted in the army. Hoping to serve overseas he transferred to the Royal Canadian Air Force. Instead he ended up as a service policeman and sergeant-of-the-guard in Sea Island, British Columbia. After the war he returned to Port Moody and died there on 19 February 1963 at the age of 76. He was buried in Mountain View Cemetery, Prince Edward Avenue, Vancouver. His grave reference is Veteran's Division, Albray Section, Block 5, Plot 8, Lot 12.

John Kerr's VC and medals are now held in the collection of the Canadian War Museum in Ottawa. His other commemorations include a plaque set up beside a ferry which he used to run in Dunvegan, Alberta and in 1951 he was commemorated with Mount Kerr being named after him in the VC range at Jasper National Park, Alberta. Finally, in 2006 the Chip Kerr Park in Port Moody was dedicated to his memory.

T.A. Jones

After the Allied successes of mid-September not a great deal happened in the way of ground captured, but all this changed on the 25th when the Somme battle was continued in earnest. Les Boeufs and Morval were both captured and as a result Combles to the south-east became hemmed in by the British and the French.

On the right flank the 56th (1/1st London) Division (TF) were facing the west side of Combles and Bouleaux Wood. To their left was the 5th Division, and then came the 6th Division and the Guards Division. The 5th, 6th and Guards Division were ordered to attack the line Morval–Les Boeufs, which if successful would allow Combles to be captured. For the moment we are concerned here with the progress of the 1st Battalion, The Cheshire Regiment, 15th Brigade, 5th Division. They were situated between the 95th Brigade, with their right on the Ginchy–Morval Road, and the 16th Brigade, 6th Division. The Cheshires had had only ten days to recover from some strenuous fighting near Faffemont Farm to the south west of Combles. The 1st Battalion, The Bedfordshire Regiment, 15th Brigade took the German frontline position at the bottom of the slope between Ginchy and Morval and then the 1st Battalion, The Norfolk Regiment, 15th Brigade took the German support line halfway up the slope to Morval. The Cheshires took the eastern side of Morval itself and the 16th (Service) Battalion (3rd Birmingham), The Royal Wawickshire Regiment, 15th Brigade took the final objective, a position from which observation could be had over Le Transloy and Sailly-Saillisel. The Cheshires arrived at their objective at about 2.55pm when they began immediately to consolidate their positions. It was at this point in the fighting that Private T.A. Jones was to gain his VC.

Some enemy snipers were still active and Jones was stung by the loss of a friend to the German marksmen and set off to 'settle the score'. Jones succeeded with interest and managed to capture 102 prisoners, including four officers. He had been shot twice by a sniper, once in his coat and once through his helmet, despite this he was uninjured, and managed to kill his assailant. He had been warned about the enemy misusing the white flag and took on two Germans who were using the flag but firing at him. He shot them both and continued on until he came to some enemy dugouts and partly dug trenches where he shot two officers and managed to disarm the rest of the occupants and then rounded them up. He brought them in with the help of four of his comrades. All this was within about 150 yards of the Cheshires' position and was seen by at least eleven officers who were to recommend the award of the Victoria Cross. The day had gone well for the Allies and the British had advanced over 2,000 yards and as a result Combles fell without the necessity of a direct attack. The Cheshires were relieved on the following day and returned to Oxford Copse, their casualties had been 144 and the battalion left for the Bethune district on 1 October.

Thomas Jones' citation was published on 26 October 1916 and read as follows:

> For most conspicuous bravery. He was with his company consolidating the defences in front of a village, and, noticing an enemy sniper at 200 yards distance, he went out, and, though one bullet went through his helmet, and another through his coat, he returned the sniper's fire and killed him. He then saw two more of the enemy firing at him, although displaying a white flag. Both of these he also shot. On reaching the enemy trench he found several occupied dug-outs, and, single-handed, disarmed 102 of the enemy, including three or four officers, and marched them back to our lines through a heavy barrage. He had been warned of the misuse of the white flag by the enemy, but insisted on going out after them.

Jones was presented with his VC by the King at Buckingham Palace on 18 November 1916.

Thomas Alfred Jones was the son of Edward and Elizabeth Jones and was the couple's sixth child. He was born on Christmas Day 1880 at 39 Princess Street, Runcorn, Cheshire. His father was a labourer at the Hazelhurst soap works where he worked for sixty-two years. Originally the family had moved from Wales to seek employment in the local chemical industries and in his spare time Edward was also a local preacher and a volunteer with the Oddfellows & Friendly Society. His son Thomas attended the former Runcorn National School at Church Street in a building which was later knocked down in 1976 but then rebuilt. He left school in 1894 and included billiards and football amongst his recreations. He was an excellent 'dribbler' of a football, a descriptive word which was later adapted to 'Dodger' and then 'Todger', which he was stuck with for the rest of his life. In 1900 Jones joined the local Runcorn Volunteer battalion of the Earl of Chester's Rifles and clearly had a ' good eye' as he became a crack rifle shot. The young man spent eight years with the Volunteers and four with the Terriers. In 1913 Jones became one of the first men from Runcorn to join the National Reserve. By trade he had been a fitter and begun work at Hazlehursts as a fitter and turner. After the completion of his apprenticeship he had gone to work with the Salt Union Company at their works at Weston Point, Runcorn. When war broke out in 1914 Jones was the second man to enlist with the 1st Battalion of the 22nd (Cheshire) Regiment, which he did on 5 August at Runcorn Drill Hall. The volunteers were then sent to Birkenhead for training and on to Codford in Wiltshire. After leaving for France and arriving at Le Havre on 16 August, the 1st Cheshires' service included La Bassee in October and Hill 60 in April and May 1915. After leaving the Western Front in December 1915 the battalion returned to France and Flanders for a year's duty between July 1916 and July 1917. During this time Jones was wounded twice but wasn't invalided home.

After the announcement of their son's VC on 26 October 1916 his parents at home in Princess Street were showered with messages of congratulation. A fortnight later 'Todger' returned to Runcorn on 9 November to a great welcome when he was met at the railway station. He was also given a similar rapturous welcome in Chester eleven days later where he was also given a celebratory dinner. Amongst the gifts that he received were; a gold wrist watch, a silver teapot, a case of cutlery and a pair of field glasses. He was also presented with an illuminated two foot scroll by the Runcorn UDC which is now housed in the Cheshire

Military Museum. His parents didn't miss out either as they were awarded an annual annuity by Jones' employer. Their son's deed of capturing and taking 102 German prisoners clearly struck a chord in the public imagination. Accounts of his daring action appeared in newspapers across the country including in *The Times History of the War* and a journal called *The Wide World*, which was described as a magazine for men. In April 1917 an account based on an interview with Jones was published under the title of 'Todger Jones, VC: The Man who captured a Hundred Germans single handed. His own wonderful story as told by himself'. The magazine also stated that it could be sent free to soldiers and sailors via any Post Office.

At this time he was described as a quiet, unassuming sort of man, he was smallish in stature and very lithe. After he had been awarded his VC his supply of gallantry was not exhausted for in September 1918 he was to add the DCM to his medals. These later heroics were performed during the Second Battle of Arras at Beughny, during which time Jones, through a heavy barrage, went forward carrying messages on five occasions. In addition he led some stragglers and re-organised them. The citation for this award was as follows:

> For his utter fearlessness of danger and carrying messages safely through intense barrage fire, also guiding his comrades to their proper positions.

On demobilisation Jones returned to work at the Salt Works in Runcorn where he was to be employed for thirty-six years prior to retiring in 1949. He was further honoured by having his name included on a Roll of Honour board at the Parish Church School and apart from his investiture, he met up with King George V on two other occasions. These were at a Buckingham Palace garden party for VC holders and also during the King's visit to Runcorn in 1925. Jones also attended the 1929 VC Dinner in the House of Lords, hosted by the Prince of Wales. In 1928 a film company based in Wardour Street, Soho, London came up with an idea of producing a film to be called 'For Valour'. It was to be a film about how the war VCs had been won. The company wrote to many of the surviving VC holders and there are letters on file between Jones and the film company. However there was such a public outcry against the project that the whole idea was dropped.

Jones' mother died in 1927 and his father in 1932. He remained unmarried, but my information suggests that prior to the Great War he fathered a son (now deceased) by Robena Abram, who was born in April 1915.

Jones was a member of the Home Guard in the Second World War and after the war, Jones' firm was taken over and he retired in 1949. In 1954 he was present at a ceremony to mark the return of the 1st Cheshire Battalion from a tour of duty in the Middle East, when he was one of the guests at the saluting base as the troops marched past.

Jones had always lived at 39 Princess Street and his elder sister Mrs E. Lightfoot had looked after him there after their parents had died. On 4 January 1956 he was admitted to the Victoria Memorial Hospital, Runcorn with cardiac problems and died there a few weeks later on 30 January at the age of 75. For his funeral on 3 February the whole town of Runcorn turned out to pay a final tribute to their local hero 'Todger Jones'. The pavements were lined with people from his home as far as St Michael's Church where his full military funeral took place. Flags in the town flew at half mast, the coffin was draped with a Union Jack and the hero's decorations were displayed on top of it. Jones was buried across the road from the church in the family grave plot of the town cemetery.

After his death, Mrs Lightfoot presented her brother's decorations to the Cheshire Regimental Museum at Chester Castle, where they are on permanent display. In addition to the VC and DCM, Jones had been awarded the 1914 Star, the British War Medal and the Victory Medal. As an expression of their gratitude the regiment wrote an official letter of thanks to Mrs Lightfoot and in turn presented her with a small brooch incorporating the regimental badge. They also paid for and arranged for a small memorial of white marble about ten inches high in the design of a VC which was placed on the family grave where Jones was buried. A short service was held when this memorial was dedicated on 17 June with the chaplain to the local branch of their British Legion in attendance; unfortunately Mrs Lightfoot was too ill to attend the short service but a younger sister was present. In the following years the grave fell into a bad state of repair but was later rescued and restored through the efforts of Stan Ellison, a local resident. Jones was also commemorated in a memorial in the floor of Chester Cathedral.

A reflection of the publicity given to Jones' VC has been the creation of several artists' impression of him winning his VC. A plaque to his memory was set up in the town centre in 2000 by Halton Borough Council, which is on the wall of the Halton Partnership Centre in Runcorn High Street. A bowls trophy was also named after the hero but that particular competition has now lapsed. With the naming of a crescent in Runcorn after Morval, there is also another link with Jones winning the VC, and lastly a plaque was set up at the Weston & Weston Point British Legion Club which was later transferred to the Cheshire and Manchester Regiment Barracks in Warrington. Apart from his former school building, his home in Princess Street has also been demolished and indeed many of the places associated with him have gone.

F.J. Edwards and R.E. Ryder

F.J. Edwards

On 26 September 1916 the Allies were brought more good news. On the day before, Morval and Les Boeufs had both been captured and on the 26th Combles was taken, as was most of the German fortress village of Thiepval. Thiepval had been an objective for the 1 July attack nearly thirteen weeks before it finally fell.

The Middlesex Regiment was to gain two VCs with its 12th battalion; one by Private F.J. Edwards and the second by Private R.E. Ryder. Not surprisingly the two men were to become great friends for the rest of their lives.

The 18th (Eastern) Division were positioned to the north-east of Authuille and faced the south-west face of the village of Thiepval. On their left the 49th (West Riding) Division (TF) was based on Thiepval Wood, facing the west side of Thiepval. We are concerned here with the 54th Brigade, whose battalions were made up of the 11th (Service) Battalion, The Royal Fusiliers (City of London) Regiment, the 7th (Service) Battalion, The Bedfordshire Regiment, the 6th (Service) Battalion,

R.E. Ryder

The Northamptonshire Regiment and finally the 12th (Service) Battalion, The Middlesex Regiment (Duke of Cambridge's Own). According to the *Official History*:

To the 54th Brigade fell one of the most difficult tasks of the day: the capture of the western half of Thiepval and the original German front system. The final objective was Schwaben Redoubt, which crowned the top of the ridge nearly half a mile beyond the village.

The Middlesex Battalion was to attack on what was a narrow frontage and was to go through Thiepval. A company of the 11th Royal Fusiliers was to advance up to the German front system and to also mop up behind the Middlesex Battalion. The 6th Northamptons were to help with the clearing of Schwaben Redoubt and the 7th Bedfords were to be held in reserve. Two tanks concealed in Caterpillar Copse, to the south of Thiepval Wood were also to move forward as far as Thiepval Chateau, to the south-west of the village. The assault began well, having started from a line across the Thiepval–Authuille Road with B and C companies moving up at 12.35pm, and the Middlesex got as far as the chateau, where they were checked until one of the tanks crushed the German resistance. The right side of the Middlesex Battalion then moved forward while the left side was held up. In the early afternoon the German artillery inflicted casualties on the supporting Northamptonshire Battalion.

At 2.30pm, Lieutenant Colonel F.A. Maxwell, commander of the Middlesex Battalion, established his HQ at Thiepval Chateau, and reported this situation to brigade. A defensive barrage was put down on an east–west line through the cemetery in mid-afternoon and the 6th Northamptons began to arrive in support of the beleaguered battalions. Maxwell had assumed command of men from all three battalions, and when darkness fell the German front trenches, as well as the north-west corner of the village, were still in German hands. The attack was called off for the time being and as a result the day's operations had ended in only a partial success. The 54th Brigade had achieved all it could and the enemy had 'fought to the death'. Private Edwards of B Company, 12th Middlesex Battalion had at one point in the fighting rushed forward alone and bombed out a German machine-gun position which had been holding up the advance. At a similarly critical point Private R. Ryder, also of B Company, cleared a German trench when he brought a Lewis gun into action under a hail of bullets. Both men were awarded the VC and Ryder's award included his gallant conduct in later fighting.

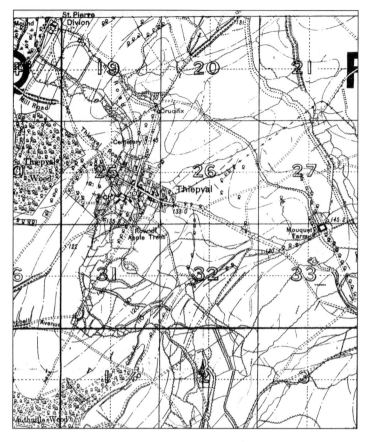

Detail from OS sheet 57D S.E. of 6 July 1916. The abbreviation of the word 'Château' in Thiepval appears beneath the number 25 identifying that square; the location is now that of the massive memorial to the missing. The Schwaben Redoubt is in the lower right of square 19, and the Leipzig Salient is in the lower side of square 31. (TM)

The three frontline battalions had a total of 840 casualties out of 2,290 men. Edwards was recommended for the VC by Lieutenant Colonel Maxwell. The citation was published on 25 November 1916 and read as follows:

For most conspicuous bravery and resource. His part of the line was held up by machine-gun fire, and all officers had become casualties. There was confusion and indication of retirement.

Private Edwards, grasping the situation, on his own initiative dashed out alone towards the gun, which he knocked out with bombs.

This very gallant act, coupled with great presence of mind and a total disregard of personal danger, made further advance possible and cleared up a dangerous situation.

Edwards was presented with his VC by the King on 5 February 1917.

Private Ryder's citation was also published on 25 November and read as follows:

For most conspicuous bravery and initiative during an attack.

His company was held up by heavy rifle fire, and all his officers had become casualties. For want of leadership the attack was flagging.

Private Ryder, realising the situation, without a moment's thought for his own safety, dashed absolutely alone at the enemy trench, and by skilful manipulation of his Lewis gun, succeeded in clearing the trench. This very gallant act not only made possible, but also greatly inspired the subsequent advance of his comrades and turned possible failure into success.

Ryder was awarded his VC at Buckingham Palace on 29 November, four days after it was announced.

Frederick Jeremiah Edwards was born in Queenstown, later Cobh, County Cork on 3 October 1894. He was the son of Quartermaster Sergeant Henry J. Edwards of the Royal Garrison Artillery and of Mrs Anne Edwards. He was educated at the Royal Hibernian Military School, Phoenix Park Dublin, which was a school for the sons of soldiers, where he was also taught drumming. When still less than 5ft tall he enlisted as a schoolboy in Dublin with the Royal Regiment of Artillery on 30 October 1908. Later while serving in Hong Kong in September 1912 he was charged with being drunk on parade and was punished with a sentence of ten days' detention. His behaviour didn't improve as five months later he was discharged from the army for misconduct. This was on

5 February 1913. However, he was soon back in the ranks and was able to rejoin the army the following year on 31 August. He served with the Middlesex Regiment in the newly formed 12th Battalion as a drummer and was to become the second drummer in the regiment to be awarded a VC.

At some point he returned to his old school in Dublin, where a presentation was made which included a solid silver flask and a cheque for the investment of War Loan certificates. In February 1918 the 12th Middlesex were disbanded and Edwards transferred to the Royal Fusiliers, and was promoted to the rank of sergeant. In April 1918 he was taken prisoner by the Germans close to Amiens on the Somme. He was demobilised on 20 March 1921, and had several jobs before becoming mace bearer to the Mayor of Holborn in London. In 1928 he was hard up and pawned his VC; when a national newspaper came to hear of this they organised its recovery, only for Edwards to sell it again when he was short of money. In 1954 he suffered a stroke which seriously affected his mobility and he could only walk with the aid of a tripod stick, and then only for short distances. His speech was also affected. In April 1955 he became a resident of the Royal Star and Garter Home at Richmond, Surrey. The home had been formerly a hotel and the deeds for it were presented to Queen Mary in 1916. It opened its doors to sixty-five wounded men who mainly occupied the former banqueting hall and ballroom. After the war it was converted into a hospital with proper facilities and now houses 200 men from the three services. Running it cost just over £11,000 in 1916. Edwards used a wheelchair when away from the home.

In May 1963 Edwards was present at Horse Guards Parade when the Middlesex Regiment held a special ceremony there. On 7 March 1964 he had a severe attack of bronchitis, and appeared to be recovering before he had an acute coronary thrombosis and died at 12.35pm on 9 March at the age of 69.

A detachment of the Middlesex Regiment provided an escort for Edwards' coffin when he was given a full military funeral at the Soldier's Plot, Richmond Cemetery where he was buried on 16 March. Amongst the mourners were several veterans including T.W.H. Veale VC and Bob Ryder VC, Edwards' life-long friend and pal, who also had difficulty with walking and hobbled along behind the coffin with the use of sticks. Ryder, also aged 69 had journeyed from Hucknall to attend the funeral and wore his medals in honour of his dead friend. The Last Post and Reveille were played by two regimental buglers. The reference for his grave is 87 of Section 22.

As we have seen, Edwards had sold his medals eventually at a time when he was hard up, for £180, so he wore a dummy set. A Canadian had owned them for twenty years and they came on the market in 1965. They were offered to the Middlesex Regiment but the regiment could not afford the asking price. However they asked to be informed where the medals went. This did not happen and Major Harold Couch of the 'Die-Hards' noticed that they were being offered for sale by auction. The regiment wrote to present and past members and asked what they thought that they could contribute to a purchase fund and also what they thought that the bidding could go up to. The response was a very generous one and Messrs Baldwins were instructed to bid for the set at Glendining's Auction Rooms on 26 October 1966. The medals were knocked down to the Middlesex Regiment for £900. In addition to the VC, which by this time in its chequered career was in a pretty battered state, the other medals were the 1914–15 Star, the British War Medal and the Victory Medal. These decorations are now in the collection of the National Army Museum.

During his life Edwards was a strong supporter of the various commemorative functions organised for the VC and GC holders but could neither read nor write. He was a 'mercurial, colourful character... and loved a fight with or without gloves.' At the time of his death his life-long friend Bob Ryder described him as 'my mad friend Patsy'.

Robert Edward Ryder was born in Brakspear Road, Harefield, Middlesex on 17 December 1895. He was educated at the Old Council School before finding work as a labourer. He enlisted with the 12th Middlesex (Duke of Cambridge's Own) in 1914. Six weeks before he left for France his wife died tragically early of consumption, which she had contracted through asbestos dust when working at a gasmask factory. After his award for the VC was published he received a letter from Brigadier-General Maxwell and also from his platoon officer W.E. Inskip-Read who wrote:

My Dear Ryder,

My most heartiest congratulations. I am not surprised to hear you have won the VC as I have always had a very high

opinion of you and knew, if ever you had the opportunity,
you would rise to the occasion. Your wife and family have
good reason to be proud of you.

On 1 December 1916, after the Battle of the Somme ended and two
days after he was awarded the VC by the King, Ryder was severely
wounded in the hip and was also peppered with shrapnel splinters.
The next thing that he was aware of, having lost consciousness, was
that he was in hospital in Norwich. He was out of action for some
time but asked to be returned to the fray and in 1917 fought on the
Italian Front and went on to win the Italian Bronze Medal for swim-
ming across the River Piave under the eyes of the enemy in order to
rescue some troops who were under heavy fire.

After the war Ryder found employment difficult and in 1939 he
quickly rejoined the army, this time becoming a sergeant instructor
with the Royal Sussex Regiment. At the end of the war in 1945
Ryder was demobilised in Uxbridge and on coming out of the
centre stopped two galloping horses who were careering down the
main street at a time when children were coming out of school.

He farmed in New Brunswick, Canada until 1965 and then
returned to England where he lived in Enfield, Middlesex. It was
at this time that it was discovered that a piece of shrapnel was still
lodged in his left leg.

In 1966 he was one of twelve VC holders who were invited by
the government to attend the 50th anniversary of the Battle of
the Somme at Thiepval, France. Their expenses were to be paid;
however, Ryder, who had married again, stated that he needed
his wife to accompany him as his wounds gave him trouble and
he needed assistance. He said that he would not go unless the
government paid, although the British Legion and the Middlesex
Regiment both said that they would pay for his wife's expenses.
The problem must have been resolved and the couple travelled to
France with the group of VC holders.

In 1970 the couple moved from Albuhera Close, Enfield to
Hucknall, Nottinghamshire. Edna, his wife, came from the town
and over the years they had six children, three boys and three girls.
Two of the boys had served with the Middlesex Regiment at some
time, and one with the Buckinghamshire Constabulary.

For a time Ryder worked at a local ordnance factory at Chilwell
and it was during this period that his health began to fail, a contribu-
tory factor to his ill health were his war wounds. He fought for

greater pensions for VC holders and having lost this battle he was 'too proud' to claim social security. In 1976 Ryder had been invited to Buckingham Palace with other holders of the Victoria Cross and was greeted as 'Bob' by Prince Philip, and in 1977 he was presented with the Queen's Jubilee Medal. In May of the following year Mr Alf Morris, Minister for the Disabled, visited Ryder at his home in Annesley Road.

After having been a patient at Nottingham General Hospital, Ryder died at his home on 1 December 1978, he was 82 years of age. Although the Ryders had been hard up, they had refused to either sell his decorations or to claim social security. Bob had expressed a wish to be buried in Harefield, his birthplace.

Ryder had put aside enough money for this eventuality and was given a military funeral at St Mary's, Harefield. A childhood hero of Ryder's and another VC holder, Major Gerald Goodlake had also been buried in the same cemetery in 1890. Ryder's funeral took place on 11 December and buglers were supplied from the Queen's Divisional Depot, as well as seven men who acted as pall bearers. A Nottingham firm offered to gild a wooden cross for Ryder's site but a standard Commonwealth War Grave Stone now marks the grave. On his grave, reference 1948, is a single inscription under his name and it is 'A Diehard', taken from the Middlesex Regimental Nickname. Ryder is also commemorated in the Middlesex Guildhall, Westminster.

Although it was possible that Ryder, in saving his companions at Thiepval on 26 September 1916, had killed over 100 Germans, he later reflected, 'I don't know why I did it... Normally I wouldn't hurt a fly.' On his death the *Sunday Express* described him 'as a shy but proud VC'. In 1979 news got out that Mrs Ryder was hard up, as she only had a pension and a small allowance to live on, and still steadfastly refused to sell her husband's decorations which could have fetched £12,000. Edna had to appeal to people to stop sending her money, she had been sent over £600 from well wishers all over the country and had no way of returning it as most of the donations were sent anonymously.

In 1980 when she was 84, Edna presented her late husband's medals to the Imperial War Museum and at the opening of a special VC Exhibition was introduced to Prince Charles and Bob Ryder's medals formed part of the display.

T.E. ADLAM

F.J. Edwards and R.E. Ryder of the 12th Middlesex, 54th Brigade, 18th (Eastern) Division were not to be the only members of the 54th Brigade to win the VC during the struggle to capture Thiepval. They were joined by Second Lieutenant T.E. Adlam, a company commander of the 7th (Service) Battalion, The Bedfordshire Regiment.

It will be remembered that the 54th Brigade had made considerable progress in the attempt to capture the German stronghold on the 26th. On the 27th the brigade arranged for the 7th Beds, who were in reserve in Thiepval Wood, to take over the front from the other three battalions: the 12th (Service) Battalion, The Middlesex Regiment (Duke of Cambridge's Own), 11th (Service) Battalion, The Royal Fusiliers (City of London) Regiment, and 6th (Service) Battalion, The Northamptonshire Regiment. This was to be carried out by 7am and the Bedfords, together with the 1/5th Battalion (TF), The Prince of Wales's Own (West Yorkshire) Regiment of the 49th (West Riding) Division, were to attack the final objective at a later hour. However when it was seen just how exposed the frontline troops were, the relieving battalions were given the less arduous task of capturing the north-western part of Thiepval. The relief went well despite the darkness and the unfamiliarity of the featureless landscape, and the attacking troops were in position at 5.45am. They moved forward using bomb and bayonet and considered that not using artillery support was the best plan. After slight progress on the right, enemy machine-guns started up and members of Adlam's company were forced to seek shelter in a trench. Realising the importance of the situation, Second Lieutenant Adlam began to go from shell hole to shell hole to collect them up. When giving orders to his men about bombs, he said: 'You all got a bomb?' and 'Well, get one in your hand, pull out the pin. Now hold it tight. As soon as I yell 'Charge!' stand up, run 2 or 3 yards and throw your bomb. And I think we'll get into that trench! There's practically no wire in front of it...'.

Then leading his men across the open ground the plan worked and the group managed to scramble into a small section of still usable trench. Having run out of their own bombs they discovered a plentiful supply of enemy ones. Adlam knew how they worked and he and his men began to lob them back at the enemy, the time fuse being about five seconds. Adlam thought that seeing their own bombs being used against them would dishearten the foe and he admitted that 'it rather put the wind up them'.

Approaching a machine-gun post and continuing to hurl bombs, the group managed to drive the crew out. They then dealt with a second machine-gun and made progress with other troops, the 1/5th (West Yorks) Regiment coming up behind to the south of the village in support before dark.

All told, at least seventy Germans had been taken prisoner including the dozen brought back by Adlam. The battalion objective had been secured by 11am and positions to the north of Thiepval consolidated, they were also in touch with the 53rd Brigade on the right. The Bedfords had suffered ninety-eight casualties killed or wounded.

Adlam's commanding officer wanted an advance post established leading up towards Schwaben Redoubt and Adlam, though having been badly wounded in the leg, volunteered to make a bombing advance on his own, although it was the turn for the 53rd Brigade, supported by the 55th as reinforcements, to capture the redoubt. More prisoners were taken and two advance posts were established.

On the 28th Stuff Redoubt was to be captured prior to the attack by the 7th Bedfords, with all their companies committed, on Schwaben Redoubt itself. This time they were the last company in the line of attack and were in their positions by noon, although they then had to wait for an hour while the men kept their spirits up. Shells were coming over when they went forward and once again Adlam's bombing skills came into play. Making progress as they advanced, they came to a large mine crater about 50 feet across, close to the redoubt itself which was lined with Germans firing at them, but Adlam's men promptly began to bomb them out. Once more the gallant lieutenant was wounded and prior to the 54th Brigade's relief, the battalion casualties were 122 killed or wounded. The 54th Brigade withdrew to Thiepval on the 29th and to Mailly-Maillet Wood the following day.

Adlam had been in the trenches for only two months and was 22 years of age. Adlam's ability to out-throw the German bombers was acquired at school, where he had been known to throw a cricket ball as far as 100 yards. His party had gathered up as many German bombs as they could find on the battlefield and began a whirlwind attack on the enemy with these. In order to improve his throwing aim Adlam pulled off his equipment to allow him more manoeuvrability. It is likely that the speed of this attack totally stunned the German troops and when he led his men forward they had little trouble in killing or capturing their assailants. They had reached their first objective by 8.30am before moving on another 300 yards. By 11am the north-west corner of Thiepval Village was in Allied hands and Major General F.I. Maxse of the 18th Division singled out Adlam for special praise and thanks. The next day Adlam continued to lead his men into action with no sense of danger to himself at the successful fight for the Schwaben Redoubt, but as his right arm was wounded this time he was unable to throw any bombs.

At around the same time, at the end of September, his mother had died and his family wanted him home on compassionate leave. He was advised however to stay put 'as you can't do any good going home'. If he had returned home, he would not have won his VC at Thiepval.

Lieutenant Colonel Frank Maxwell (Middlesex) in his letters wrote:

This morning (27th) I had orders to clear out on relief by another regiment, but, much to the CO's delight, I disobeyed the order and stayed on to see him through his attack on the stronghold that had beat us till then. I was in no mind to lose what we had so hardly won by going before he had done his job. And we only did it after three hours' attempt. But I have paid the penalty of a dressing-down by the general, who is furious...

It is very clear from Maxwell's letters that he was genuinely surprised that the brigade had done so well in such an exposed situation against troops who had known the ground for over a year.

Later in the year, when back from an evening out in camp at Colchester, Adlam found a stack of congratulatory telegrams pinned to the mess notice board from people who clearly knew about the announcement of his VC before he did. Adlam's citation was published on 25 November 1916 and read as follows:

> For most conspicuous bravery during operations.
>
> A portion of a village which had defied capture had to be captured at all costs, to permit subsequent operations to develop.
>
> This minor operation came under very heavy machine-gun and rifle fire.
>
> Second Lieutenant Adlam realising that time was all-important, rushed from shell hole to shell hole under heavy fire collecting men for a sudden rush, and for this purpose also collected many enemy grenades. At this stage he was wounded in the leg, but nevertheless he was able to out-throw the enemy, and then, seizing his opportunity, and in spite of his wound, he led a rush, captured the position, and killed the occupants. Throughout the day he continued to lead his men in bombing attacks.
>
> On the following day he again displayed courage of the highest order, and though again wounded and unable to throw bombs, he continued to lead his men.
>
> His magnificent example and valour, coupled with skilful handling of the situation, produced far-reaching results.

Adlam was presented with his VC by the King at Buckingham Palace on 2 December 1916. Because of his wounds sustained at Thiepval on 27/28 September, Adlam was taken off infantry duties and transferred to the Army Educational Corps. Towards the end of the war, when he was with the RAF, he was due for posting to Singapore but the order was cancelled at the last minute.

Thomas Edwin Adlam was the son of John Adlam and Evangeline Adlam and was born in Waterloo Gardens, Salisbury on 21 October 1893. He was one of six children and his first school was St Martin's Primary School. He was educated at Bishop

Wordworth's School in Salisbury and trained to be a teacher in Basingstoke. He became keen on football and played for Salisbury City. He joined the Hampshire Territorials on a two year course in 1912 and during training at Sittinbourne in Kent, he honed his famous bomb throwing skills when he was bombing officer. He was able to throw a Mills bomb as far as 40 yards using either arm. In August 1914 while at the annual summer camp in he was called up and left the camp to catch a train to Salisbury in order to reach the collecting centre at Hillsea. He had already started a career by training at Brook Street Council School in Basingstoke which was when he was to meet Ivy Mace, who he was later to marry. He joined the Territorial Force in 1912 and on 16 November 1915 was commissioned as a second lieutenant. Between April 1916 and January 1919 he served as an instructor at No. 2 Officer Cadet Battalion, Cambridge. There must have been at least a two or three month break in these duties when he served with the infantry on the Western Front. On 21 June 1916 he married Ivy Annete, daughter of Mr and Mrs W.H. Mace of Farnborough, Hants, and the ceremony took place at St Mark's Church, South Farnborough. At the time his address was Lynchford House, Farnborough.

Adlam was demobilised on 15 November 1919 but for a time remained with the army and served in Ireland during the 'The Troubles.' He then officially retired in March 1923, and his address at this time was Guildford House, South Farnborough. He was made the headmaster of Blackmoor C.E. School at Blackmoor, Liss, and his wife was also a teacher at the school. He had become known as the 'Salisbury VC' and in the 1920s was presented with a gold watch by the Mayor as well as being invited to unveil the city's war memorial. His name remained on the Officers Reserve List and two weeks before the Second World War broke out in 1939, he was recalled to the Colours. He enlisted with the Royal Engineers which took him to Avonmouth Docks, and then later he became deputy assistant quartermaster general at Glasgow, Dover and Tilbury where he was serving at the time of the D-Day landings in June 1944.

Adlam ended the war with the rank of lieutenant colonel and returned to his school at Blackmoor. His family had grown to four children and when his school was closed he purchased it for his family, converting it into a house. Adlam had retired early and performed a number of different jobs, especially enjoying his work on the Woolmer Estate of Lord Selborne. In 1966 he was one of a group of VC holders who were invited by the Ministry of Defence to take part in the 50th anniversary commemoration of the Battle of the Somme at Thiepval.

Tom Adlam always regarded himself as a schoolmaster first and as a soldier second. He was also a keen gardener and cricketer, keeping wicket for a local team until the age of 71. He died while on holiday with one of his daughters on Hayling Island on 28 May 1975. He was 81 years of age and was buried at St Matthew's, Blackmoor, across the road from where he formerly lived, in a grave that he shares with his wife.

During his life, when questioned about his gallantry on the Somme, Adlam was like many VC holders, reticent on the matter. He often made the point that 'others had suffered and had nothing to show for their efforts and that thousands had done what he had done and he was always conscious of the terrible price that his comrades had paid in those battles of 1916.' Tom Adlam does come over from transcript of his interviews as a very nice man indeed and in addition never critical at the way the war was conducted.

On 27 September 2003, Adlam's VC together with seven other campaign medals were handed over by the current regiment and members of the Adlam family at a civic ceremony on permanent loan to Salisbury for display in the city's Silver Cabinet of the Grand Jury Room in the Guild Hall. The City Gold Watch presented to Adlam in the 1920s is also with the collection.

A.C.T. WHITE

The battle for possession of the Thiepval Ridge continued to 1 October when Stuff Redoubt was consolidated and the last section of Schwaben Redoubt taken.

Stuff Redoubt was one of several German redoubts to the north of Mouquet Farm and to the north-east of Thiepval. It was north-west of Zollern Redoubt and due east of Schwaben Redoubt. Pozières was to the east and Grandcourt to the west.

On 28 September the 32nd Brigade of the 11th (Northern) Division was supposed to capture Stuff Redoubt and then link up with the Canadian Army's left flank by capturing Hessian Trench which ran eastwards from Stuff. Two companies of the 8th (Service) Battalion, The Duke of Wellington's (West Riding) Regiment were positioned in Zollern Trench, ready for the assault. A mixture of men from the 9th (Service) Battalion, The Prince of Wales's Own (West Yorkshire) Regiment and 6th (Service) Battalion, The Princess of Wales's Own (Yorkshire) Regiment, or Green Howards, who were holding on to their positions in Stuff Redoubt, were meant to complete its capture.

When zero hour at 6pm arrived, the 8th DWR found that they could not advance owing to the German barrage and congestion in the trenches. However, the other two Yorkshire battalions under the leadership of Captain A.C.T. White (Green Howards) did have some success later on in the evening when they managed to bomb their way forward and were able to capture most of Stuff Redoubt's northern face. However they were not able to hang on to what they had taken, as they lacked both the men and ammunition. Despite this they somehow clung onto the positions that they had gained.

On 30 September, having been resupplied with ammunition, the survivors from the bombing party led by the inspired Captain White was once again in the thick of the fighting in the attack from the southern face of Stuff Redoubt. Convergent bombing attacks were made and a party of the 6th (Service) Battalion, The York and Lancaster Regiment, 32nd Brigade moved along eastwards from Hessian Trench and the 7th (Service) Battalion, The South Staffordshire Regiment moved up the Zollern Trench. The joint attack worked and before darkness fell the 11th Division were in control of all of its objectives except for the northern half of the redoubt. The 11th Division was relieved by the 25th Division and the Green Howards moved to hutments at Varennes, south of Acheux. Casualties had been 396 killed or wounded.

Captain White was awarded the VC for his leadership in the period of fighting for Stuff Redoubt between 27 September and 1 October. The citation was published on 26 October 1916 and read as follows:

> For most conspicuous bravery. He was in command of the troops that held the southern and western faces of a redoubt. For four days and nights, by his indomitable spirit, great personal courage, and skilful dispositions, he held his position under heavy fire of all kinds and against several counter-attacks. Though short of supplies and ammunition, his determination never wavered. When the enemy attacked in greatly superior numbers and had almost ejected our troops from the redoubt, he personally led a counter-attack, which finally cleared the enemy out of the southern and western faces. He risked his life continually and was the life and soul of the defence.

Captain White was presented with his VC by the King at Hyde Park, London on 2 June 1917. He was the fourth VC in the Somme battle, a record for the battalions taking part.

Archie Cecil Thomas White was born at Boroughbridge, Yorkshire on 5 October 1891. He was the elder of two sons of Thomas, a tailor, and his wife Jean who lived at Norwood House,

Langthorpe, Boroughbridge. The ancient Yorkshire market town had at one time sent two Members of Parliament to Westminster.

White was educated at Harrogate Grammar School, where he was a contemporary of Donald Bell, and King's College, London where he graduated in 1912. He then became a teacher at Westminster School. He enlisted with the Yorkshire Regiment and was commissioned into the 6th Yorkshire Regiment (Green Howards) as a second lieutenant on 14 October 1914 and was promoted to temporary lieutenant on 10 December 1914. He served as a temporary lieutenant in Gallipoli in 1915 and a severe case of dysentery probably saved his life as he could not take part in an attack at Lala Baba, Suvla Bay on 6/7 August in which almost all the officers were killed. His younger brother, Second Lieutenant John Finlayson, also in the Green Howards, died in the same operation. Archie White himself was wounded in the Dardanelles and was later transferred to France, gaining the MC before his VC at Stuff Redoubt. He was to write of his experience fifty years later in 1966 and said that:

> When after 48 hours a message got through from Corps HQ (Lt Gen Sir Claud Jacob) asking how long we could hold on, being a very bumptious person I replied 'Till the cows come home'.

After the Somme battle White became a staff officer in France, firstly as a GSO3 on 30 June 1917 and later as a brigade major on 28 March 1918 when he joined the staff of another Somme VC holder, Brigadier General J.V. Campbell of the Coldstream Guards. White found him a difficult man to serve and he had already got through three or four brigade majors before White's appearance. Despite early misgivings the two men did hit it off and in time also became good friends. In 1919 White later served as a brigade major with the Archangel Relief Force in North Russia between 29 May and 5 October.

During the war he had been wounded twice and Mentioned in Despatches on three occasions. After the war he resigned his commission with the Green Howards on 13 November 1920 and then joined the new Army Education Corps on the 25th. At the time he was the youngest major in the British Army. He was appointed as an instructor at Sandhurst from 1921 to 1925 and four years later he was back there as a senior AEC Instructor from

1929 to 1933. He then filled various positions, mainly during tours of duty in India and Burma. On the outbreak of war he was made a lieutenant colonel and joined the Cypher Office. He became Command Education Officer in the Northern and Southern AA Commands and between 1943 and 1945 was Chief Education Officer of the newly formed 21st Army Group. He served with the British Army of Liberation throughout north-west Europe. In connection with his education work he was Mentioned in Despatches on 9 August 1945.He became the principal of the City Literary Institute in London between 1948 and 1956. The institute had 10,000 adult part-time students and a wide-ranging syllabus. Although he had retired from the position of head, he returned to give classes on retirement. He then became a member of the Senate and fellow of Kings College, London.

He later married Jean Wells, a widow and they had three daughters. When Sir Hugh Stockwell became colonel commandant of the Royal Army Educational Corps and was also appointed to Surpreme Headquarters, Allied Powers in Europe, White became deputy colonel commandant.

In 1963 he published a book on the history of Army Education. In 1966 he was one of twelve VC Holders invited by the Ministry of Defence to take part in the 50th anniversary commemoration ceremonies of the Battle of the Somme at Thiepval. He was then 65 years of age and still looked a very upright and distinguished English gentleman. He was a man of Christian beliefs and a great supporter of his former regiment, the Green Howards. He was also a prominent member of the Victoria and George Cross Association. Archie White died at his home, 'Brucklay', Upper Park Road, Camberley on 20 May 1971 at the age of 80. His wife predeceased him by twenty-one years. White was cremated at Brookwood Crematorium,Woking and his ashes scattered in Tennyson Lake Garden. The reference was 76649 and his name is listed on North Cloister Bay, 19–173. A blue plaque was put up at the former family tailor's shop in Boroughbridge. His VC and medals are in the possession of the Green Howards Museum, Richmond, North Yorkshire.

R.B. BRADFORD

As a continuation for the battle for possession of the Transloy Ridges, the Allied plan for 1 October 1916 was for the Fourth Army to capture Eaucourt l'Abbaye and the Flers line as far as Le Sars. The l'Abbaye consisted of two large farms built on the site of an Augustine abbey that were in the same enclosure. The Flers line at the end of September ran in a south-easterly direction from the south of this position to the south-west of the village of Flers.

The 2nd New Zealand Brigade was on the right in a line that stretched from Flers Trench to Gird Trench; on their left was the 47th (1/2nd London) Division (TF) and on their left was the 151st Brigade of the 50th (Northumbrian) Division (TF). We are concerned here with last named infantry brigade which contained four battalions: the 1/5th (Cumberland) Battalion (TF), The Border Regiment, and three battalions of the Durham Light Infantry, 1/6th, 8th and 9th (TF). The 1/6th was, on 1 October, a composite battalion made up from men of the 1/5th Borders, the 1/8th Durhams, and the 1/5th Battalion TF, The Northumberland Fusiliers, from the 149th Brigade.

In the subsequent fighting, the right flank of the 1/6th Durhams became exposed by the failure of the left flank of the 47th Division, which had been caught very badly by enemy machine-gunners.

However, the Durhams were able to cling on to a weak position in Flers Trench. Major G.E. Wilkinson, commander of the 1/6th Durhams, was severely wounded in the arm and retired from the action and sought out Lieutenant Colonel Roland Bradford, commanding officer of the 1/9th Durhams who were in support of the attacking battalions. Bradford was in his headquarters position called Seven Elms, about half a mile in front of High Wood. Wilkinson told Bradford of the situation and suggested to him that he should assume command of the 1/6th in addition to the 1/9th and to go up the line and take charge of what was a precarious situation. Wilkinson had no suitable senior officer on his own staff, only junior officers.

As a consequence of Bradford taking control of the two battalions, Flers Trench was captured by 9.30pm and Bradford was later to be awarded the VC for his inspired leadership and organising ability. He was first recommended for the DSO by Brigadier General Cameron of the 151st Brigade, but as more details of his action filtered through, this was changed to the VC. Bradford and his troops withdrew to Bécourt Wood on the 3rd and then to Hénencourt Wood the following day, and after a week they were occupying the south-west corner of Mametz Wood.

The citation for Bradford's VC was published in the *London Gazette* on 25 November 1916 as follows:

> For most conspicuous bravery and good leadership in attack, whereby he saved the situation on the right flank of his brigade and of the division.
>
> Lieutenant Colonel Bradford's battalion was in support. A leading battalion having suffered very severe casualties, and the commander wounded, its flank became dangerously exposed at close quarters to the enemy. Raked by machine-gun fire, the situation of the battalion was critical. At the request of the wounded Commander, Lt Col Bradford asked permission to command the exposed battalion in addition to his own.
>
> Permission granted, he at once proceeded to the foremost lines.
>
> By his fearless energy under fire of all description and his skilful leadership of the two battalions, regardless of all danger, he succeeded in rallying the attack, captured and defended the objective, and so secured the flank.

It is unlikely that Bradford waited for permission from Brigadier Cameron before taking charge as Wilkinson did not inform the brigadier until reaching Brigade HQ, which was 2 miles behind the lines. There would have been no time to lose as the situation was so critical on the right flank of the attack.

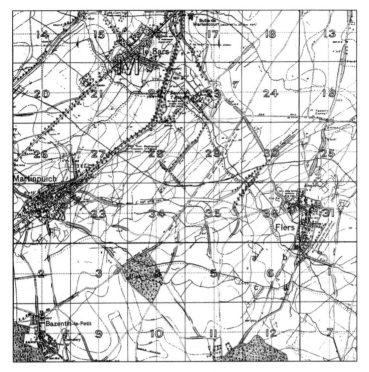

Detail from OS sheet 57C S.W. corrected to 3 September 1916. The line running through square M 20, 27, 28, 29, 30 and N25 was marked in pencil the night after the attack and gives an idea of the ground gained and the bulge around Flers demonstrates the advantage gained by the surprise use of tanks.' Switch Trench runs from square 2, across the edge of High Wood and on through square 6. (TM 2458)

On 5 November the 151st Brigade of the 50th Division were again in the thick of the action, this time in an attack against the Butte de Warlencourt, a small hillock to the north-west of Eaucourt l'Abbaye. Australian troops were to the right and the 46th (North Midland) Division (TF), to the left. The objectives were the Butte itself and a quarry to the south-west, close to the Bapaume Road. By the road to l'Abbaye, the Gird position was also to be consolidated.

The attack, which was an impossible one for the Durham battalions to succeed with, failed, although small parties did actually reach the Butte itself before German counter-attacks removed them. The attacking troops had been enfiladed by machine-gun fire from both flanks and as the ground was so muddy and the position so exposed, there was no chance of any progress. Indeed Bradford was doubtful of the value of the capture of the small hill; however, he did note that it 'had become an obsession. Everybody wanted it'.

Lieutenant Colonel Roland Bradford was presented with his VC by the King at Hyde Park on 2 June 1917. He was the 14th person out of 350 to receive an award from the King and the number 13 had been left out of the programme.

Roland Boys Bradford was born on 23 February 1892 at Carwood House, Witton Park, Bishop Auckland. He was the fourth of five children, four boys and one girl, of George and Amy Marion (née Andrews) from Willesborough in Kent. George was a mining engineer for Stobart Collieries and a colliery manager. He later became a chairman of a group of mines in South Wales and a steel company in Darlington. Roland was baptised at St Paul's Church, Witton Park by the Reverend Charles Aubrey on 23 March 1892. He was educated at Darlington Grammar and then at Epsom College (1907–1909) where he became a member of the school Cadet Force and later a section commander. On leaving college he joined the Church Lads' Brigade and was made a second lieutenant in the local Territorial Force before being commissioned into the 2nd Battalion, Durham Light Infantry (DLI),18th Infantry Brigade, 6th Division in May 1912. He was a keen horseman and was fond of competitive sports.

At the beginning of the war in 1914 Roland Bradford embarked with the 2nd DLI and landed at St Nazaire on 10 September 1914, taking part in heavy fighting at Troyon in the first Battle of the Aisne. He was made a lieutenant on 25 September and was eventually to become a brigadier general. He was awarded the MC on 18 February 1915 for leading an attack the previous year at Armentières, and in May was made adjutant of the 7th DLI, holding this position until early 1916. In April he was transferred to the 9th DLI as second-in-command before taking over as its commanding officer. On 4 August he was promoted to lieutenant colonel and was to remain with the 9th DLI until

November 1917. At the age of 25 he became the youngest briga-dier general in the British Army when he took command of the 186th Brigade, 62nd (West Riding) Division. When involved in an attack against the enemy Hindenburg Line near Graincourt, he was killed by a stray shell that hit his brigade headquarters near Lock 7 on the Canal du Nord, Hermies on 30 November 1917. He was buried at Hermies British Cemetery, Row F, Grave 10. Roland Bradford is commemorated at St Paul's, Witton Park with a Rose Window, situated high up on the west wall of the church. He is also commemorated in St Cuthbert's Church, Darlington; Queen Elizabeth Sixth Form College; Holy Trinity Church, Darlington; and at the Territorial Drill Hall. Furthermore, dona-tions to a Bradford Memorial were used to pay for Darlington Memorial Hospital to have new entrance gates. The writer Henry Williamson also painted a pen portrait of him in his book *Love and the Loveless*. His brother George Nicholson Bradford, a lieutenant commander in the Royal Navy won a posthumous VC during the attack on the Mole, Zeebrugge, Belgium on St George's Day, 23 April 1918. A third brother, James Barker Bradford of the 18th DLI, also died of wounds in May 1917. Captain Thomas A. Bradford, later Sir Thomas, was awarded the DSO and survived the war, he lived in Darlington. The boys' mother, Amy, used to place an 'In Memoriam' notice in *The Times* every anniversary of the deaths of her three sons, and wear her sons' decorations every Armistice Day at services at the town's war memorial. She herself died in January 1951 in Folkestone.

Roland, who was obviously a born soldier, was also awarded the MC in addition to the VC and his medals are in the possession of the Museum of the Durham Light Infantry.

Perhaps the final word on Bradford as a soldier should be left to Charles Gee, who served with him when an adjutant with the 9th DLI in 1917 and was interviewed by the Imperial War Museum (13717). Bradford was considered to be an outstanding soldier and was always concerned about the welfare of the men under his command, and even tried unsuccessfully to obtain a better alloca-tion of leave for them. In return his men had a huge respect for him and implicitly trusted him.

Bradford was quite happy to tear up or ignore orders, often telling Gee to 'lose it' if he felt it was not worth consideration, and High Command often turned a blind eye to this rebellious behaviour. Gee also implies that he could be a bit of a martinet and certainly a total perfectionist who missed no undone button. However, he admitted that he also 'sort of worshipped him'.

The Bradford family were one of the most highly decorated of the war, with the distinction of two brothers winning a VC. On 8 September 2001, during a Victoria Cross celebration, a commemorative Stone was unveiled at the Durham Light Infantry Museum.

H. KELLY

On 2 October 1916 the enemy counter-attacked the Eaucourt l'Abbaye position and the British failed to hold onto the village of Le Sars to the north-west. The British did, though, manage to recover Eaucourt l'Abbaye the next day and on the 4th, Second Lieutenant H. Kelly of 10th (Service) Battalion, The Duke of Wellington's (West Riding) Regiment, 69th Brigade, 23rd Division gained a VC for extreme bravery during a further attack towards Le Sars.

Flers Support Trench naturally ran alongside Flers Trench and they both ran in a south-easterly direction of the village of Le Sars, in front of Eaucourt l'Abbaye and towards Flers itself. The two divisions involved in the fight for the village were the 47th (1/2nd London) Division (TF) to the right and the 23rd Division to the left. On 4 October 47th Division took the rest of Flers without much opposition and then pushed on towards a position to the north-west of Eaucourt l'Abbaye. The 23rd Division endeavoured to carry the sections of Flers Support Trench to the north of the Bapaume Road. The 10th DWR, 69th Brigade relieved the 8th (Service) Battalion, The King's Own Yorkshire Light Infantry, 24th Brigade, 23rd Division on the afternoon of 2 October. The relief was very much delayed owing to congestion in the trenches and was not completed until dawn on the 3rd. *The Iron Duke*, which is the journal of the Duke of Wellington's Regiment (Vol. VIII, No. 23 October 1932), suggests that the action for which Kelly was decorated actually took place on the 3rd and not on the 4th of October. The journal says the action took place as part of a 'small operation, preliminary to the Battle of Le Sars....' The history of the 23rd Division by Lt Col H.R. Sandilands described the situation as follows:

But as a preliminary to this big attack the GOC 69th Brigade determined to endeavour to improve his position by two small operations, designed to capture the portion of Flers 2 still held by the enemy, and a short length of Flers 1 to the south of the Bapaume Road, in which the enemy had again obtained a footing.

On the evening of 3 October, following artillery preparations, two small companies of the 10th Duke of Wellington's attacked Flers 2, north of the Bapaume Road, while a party of the 8th Yorkshire Regiment carried out a simultaneous bombing attack against the enemy in Flers 1.

To gain their objective, the Duke of Wellington's had but 100 yards to cross. But their advance lay across mud and mire of the most appalling description, and was met by a withering fire of rifles and machine-guns. Following their leaders, among whom Second Lieutenants Stafford, Harris and Kelly were conspicuous in the example they set, the men pushed forward with the greatest gallantry, and gained the enemy's wire. Here they were held up. To cross a greater distance in these conditions would have been scarcely possible, but the distance of the assembly trenches from the objective had been insufficient to enable the artillery to deal effectively with the wire. Stafford and Harris were killed, and the attack broke down.

Henry Harris and Henry Stafford are both listed in *Officers Died in the Great War* as having been killed on 4 October.

The citation for Kelly's VC was published on 25 November and read as follows:

For most conspicuous bravery in attack. He twice rallied his company under the heaviest fire, and finally led the only three available men into the enemy trench, and there remained bombing until two of them had become casualties and enemy reinforcements had arrived.

He then carried his company sergeant major, who had been wounded, back to our trenches, a distance of 70 yards, and subsequently three other soldiers.

He set a fine example of gallantry and endurance.

Kelly was presented with his VC by the King at Buckingham Palace on 14 February 1917.

Henry Kelly was born at Rochdale Road, Moston, Manchester on 10 July 1887, the eldest son of a family of ten children to be born to Charles Kelly of Sandyford, Dublin and Jane (formerly McGarry) of Manchester. Henry attended St Patrick's School Manchester, and the Xaverian Brothers College, Victoria Park, Manchester. His father died in 1904 and Henry was left as head of the family, taking up a post as a sorting clerk at Newton Street Post Office in Manchester. He trained with the Manchester Royal Engineers Territorials and later left his home in King Street, Moston, Manchester to enlist in the Cameron Highlanders as a private on 5 September 1914 at the age of 27. He transferred to the Manchester Regiment where he gained his first stripe before becoming a sergeant major two weeks later. He was commissioned on 12 May 1915 into the 10th Duke of Wellington's and went overseas to France in the same month. On 11 September 1916 he was made a temporary lieutenant. After he had won the VC in October 1916 his corps commander decorated him with the ribbon of the VC.

In 1917 Kelly was present at the Battle for Messines Ridge (6 June 1917) and at the Menin Road in September as part of the Third Battle of Ypres, and was made a temporary captain on 21 September. In 1918 he was involved in the fighting in Italy on the Asiago Plateau and gained the MC for his role in a raid on the enemy trenches during the night of 21 June. A large number of the enemy were killed. A few months later he gained a Bar to his MC in an attack on the Austrian positions across the Piave on 27 October, where again his leadership resulted in the capturing of many prisoners and the capture of enemy machine-guns.

By the end of hostilities Kelly was to become one of the most highly decorated officers of the war and in addition to gaining the VC and two MCs he was also awarded the Belgian Croix de Guerre and the French Military Medal. He left the army in January 1920 after having been promoted to the rank of temporary major and put in charge of a Rest Camp in France.

After the war he returned to Ireland and in 1922 was appointed chief of staff for overseas operations of the Irish Free State Army. At around this time he married Eileen Guerin from County Kerry. He resumed working for the Post Office but in 1936 went to Spain in order to take part in the Civil War, becoming commandant-general of the International Brigade until 1938. He was awarded yet another medal, the Grand Laurelled Cross of San Fernando. When the Second World War began Kelly served as a lieutenant in the Cheshire Regiment and from October 1943 to February 1944 he was in charge of the District Claims office of the London District at Curzon Street. Unfortunately, and probably owing to the pressure of work at the time, he allegedly made fraudulent claims for travel expenses to the value of two pounds ten shillings. He was court-martialled and severely reprimanded. He resigned his commission and rejoined the Post Office in 1944. He lived at 178 Hall Lane, Baguley, Wythenshawe with his wife Eileen and two children.

Kelly died after a long illness at Prestwich Hospital, Manchester on 18 January 1960. He was given a private funeral which was attended by representatives of his former regiment as well as members of his family. He was buried in a grave without a memorial stone in the Roman Catholic Section, Plot 1, Grave 372. His wife joined him there twenty-five years later in 1985 and the couple now share a headstone set up by the family and his regiment in October 1986.

Kelly's decorations are in the keeping of the Regimental Museum of the Duke of Wellington's Regiment in Halifax. It is to be hoped he will be remembered as an outstanding soldier and also one of the most decorated officers in the Great War.

J.C. RICHARDSON

In the four days that elapsed between Lt H. Kelly winning his VC at Le Sars and 8 October when Piper Richardson was to win his, there had been slight Allied progress in the battle. The British had advanced to the north-west of Eaucourt and the French Army had made progress to the north-east of Morval. On the 8th the 1st Canadian Division were to advance to The Quadrilateral on the Le Sars Line, which was to the north-west of the village itself, and also reach Regina Trench which ran across their lines in a south-westerly direction. Regina ran from the north of Courcelette to Stuff Trench, which in turn joined the Schwaben Redoubt.

The attack began at 4.50am on the 8th when it was still dark and also raining. The two Canadian brigades under the leadership of Major General Currie were the 1st on the right and the 3rd on the left. The 3rd and 4th Canadian Infantry battalions of the 1st Brigade attacked the right-hand objectives, the Le Sars Line and The Quadrilateral. They reached the former but, owing to uncut wire, were held up at the second and also had to swerve to the left when looking for gaps in the wire. The two battalions therefore mingled together on the left. In the afternoon a threatened German counter-attack was delayed by the intervention of the artillery, but the Canadians were forced back, being greatly outnumbered and also out of bombs. They ended the day at their jumping-off trenches.

On the left of 1st Canadian Brigade was the 16th Canadian Infantry Battalion (Canadian Scottish) and the 13th Canadian

Infantry Battalion (Royal Highlanders), with the former battalion managing to enter Regina Trench after forcing its way through the wire. However as the 3rd Battalion on its right fell back, the 16th found that it could not hang on. The Royal Highlanders on the left were also held up by uncut wire, and after suffering heavy casualties fell back before dark. It seems that the uncut wire was a huge problem all along the line, and one can only assume that the artillery should either have been more destructive or that over-optimistic reports allowed the attack to take place. In addition the Canadian lines were crescent-shaped and the Germans had a concave front on this sector, which gave them a distinct advantage over their attackers.

However we are concerned here with the role of the 16th Battalion and in particular that of Piper James Cleland Richardson. To quote the diary of the battalion:

'When our barrage started,' said Company Sergeant Major Mackie, who was advancing on the left flank of the leading wave Number 4 Company, 'Major Lynch, Captain Bell, Piper Richardson and myself went out of the trench. After waiting for five minutes we bade goodbye to Captain Bell who was to take over the second line of the company, and Major Lynch gave the order to advance. The three of us walked in front of the leading line; Piper Richardson on the Major's left and I on his right. The going was easy as the ground was not cut up. About half way over I commenced to wonder why the piper wasn't playing and crossed over by the side of him to ask the reason. He said he had been told not to play until ordered to do so by the major.'

The party reached the wire, which they found to be uncut, and when they were searching for an opening the Germans began to open fire and throw bombs, and Major Lynch fell mortally wounded. Richardson asked Mackie if he could play his pipes and was told to go ahead. The wire still slowed down the Canadian advance and many men from the first two waves became casualties because of the intense fire. Richardson, according to eyewitnesses, walked up and down in front of the wire for fully ten minutes, thereby inspiring about 100 men of the Canadian/Scottish battalions to greater effort in their attack against Regina Trench. Richardson must have been leading a charmed life and he also helped with the bombing attack against the enemy. He later helped a wounded colleague back to safety and on realising that he had mislaid his pipes, he went back to recover them. He was never seen alive again, although his body was recovered from the battlefield.

Richardson's gallantry on 8/9 October 1916 inspired a great deal of the image of the lone piper walking up and down in no man's land under intense fire but seemingly untouched by it all. Much of this publicity was written up for reasons of propaganda and was of a *Boy's Own Paper* type. As late as September 1965 a comic strip version of Richardson's bravery was published in a magazine called *The Victor*.

Richardson's posthumous award was not announced until 22 October 1918, owing to some administrative delay, and read as follows:

> For most conspicuous bravery and devotion to duty when, prior to attack, he obtained permission from his commanding officer to play his company 'over the top'.
>
> As the company approached the objective, it was held up by very strong wire, and came under intense fire, which caused heavy casualties and demoralised the formation for the moment. Realising the situation, Piper Richardson strode up and down outside the wire, playing his pipes with the greatest coolness. The effect was instantaneous. Inspired by his splendid example, the company rushed the wire with such fury and determination that the obstacle was overcome and the position captured.
>
> Later, after participating in bombing operations, he was detailed to take back a wounded comrade and prisoners.
>
> After proceeding about 200 yards Piper Richardson remembered that he had left his pipes behind. Although strongly urged not to do so, he insisted on returning to recover his pipes. He has never been seen since, and death has been presumed accordingly, owing to lapse of time.

James Cleland Richardson was born at Bellshill, Lanarkshire, Scotland on 25 November 1895. He was the son of Davis Richardson and Mary Prosser who lived in Princess Avenue, Glasgow. The family moved there in around 1913 and James attended school at Bellshill Academy, Auchwraith Public School,

Blantyre and John Street Public School, Bridgeton, Glasgow. His family moved to British Columbia, Canada a few years before the war and his father became a chief of police in British Columbia.

Prior to the war Richardson had been a well-known piper and had worked as a driller for about six months before joining the Canadian Forces on the outbreak of war in August 1914 at the age of 18. His battalion was the 72nd Seaforth Highlanders. When he left for France he was attached to the 16th Canadian Scottish and was with them in the famous Canadian stand at St Julien in April 1915.

In 1916 it was Major C.W. Peck who recommended that Richardson should be awarded a posthumous VC. Peck later became commander of the 16th Battalion (Canadian) Scottish and won a VC himself at Cagnicourt in early September 1918.

Richardson was buried at Adanac Military Cemetery, Plot III, Row F, Grave 36. He was not yet 21 when he was killed. His decorations were left to his sister, Mrs Charles A. Murray of Blackburn, White Rock, British Columbia but are now in the Canadian Scottish Museum in Victoria.

Richardson's name is commemorated along with those of thirteen other VC holders on a Memorial Arch in Hamilton, Lanarkshire and he is also remembered with the Richardson Chapter of OIDE in Chilliwack, British Columbia. A bronze statue of him designed by John Weaver was unveiled on 11 October 2003 at the front of the grounds at Chilliwack Museum, and finally his famous bagpipes were rediscovered in 2002 and are now on display in Canada at the British Columbia Legislature.

R. DOWNIE

Little Allied progress was made for the fortnight after Piper Richardson gained a Victoria Cross on 8 October, and on 23 October the 4th Division was ordered to capture enemy positions in front of the village of Le Transloy to the north-west of Les Boeufs where a line was established beyond the crest of a spur. From this point it would be possible for an advance to be made on Le Transloy itself.

Owing to the morning being misty, the time of the advance was delayed from 11.30am to 2.30pm. The Allied artillery had begun to shell the village and the cemetery, and this shelling was later reduced to a creeping barrage 50 yards in front of the attacking infantry. On the right was the 11th Brigade, made up from the 1st Battalion, The Hampshire Regiment and the 2nd Battalion, The Royal Dublin Fusiliers attached from the 10th Brigade. The former battalion together with the French 152nd Division were stopped almost immediately by attacking fire from Boritzka Trench, which was the attackers' objective.

The advance was also troubled by machine-guns concealed in shell holes. When the 1st Battalion, The Rifle Brigade (Prince Consort's Own) arrived to give assistance, the advance progressed and positions were established north-west of the objective. After darkness fell it was found that the Dubliners had captured a position called the Gun-Pits to the east of Les Boeufs, and also a strongpoint beyond them. It was at this time that Sergeant R. Downie of the 2nd Battalion, Royal Dublin Fusiliers gained the VC.

It was said that after the Dubliners had lost their officers Sgt Downie had taken immediate control and with the rallying cry of 'Come on, the Dubs!' rushed the German machine-gun crew and scattered them. There was a determined series of counter-attacks but Downie's men beat them off and established their defences. It was said that Downie was 'everywhere, directing, counselling, and cheering the men who he had led so bravely forward!' The battalion then retired to Trônes Wood and Mansell Camp before leaving the area a week later. Their casualties had been 182.

His VC citation was published on 25 November 1916 and read as follows:

> For most conspicuous bravery and devotion to duty in attack. When most of the officers had become casualties, this non-commissioned officer, utterly regardless of personal danger, moved about under heavy fire and reorganised the attack, which had been temporarily checked. At the critical moment he rushed forward alone, shouting, 'Come on, the Dubs!' This stirring appeal met with immediate response, and the line rushed forward at his call. Sergeant Downie accounted for several of the enemy, and in addition captured a machine-gun, killing the team. Though wounded early in the fight, he remained with his company, and gave assistance whilst the position was being consolidated. It was owing to Sergeant Downie's courage and initiative that this important position, which had resisted four or five previous attacks, was won.

Downie was presented with his VC by the King at York Cottage, Sandringham, Norfolk on 8 January 1917.

Robert Downie was born at Springburn Road, Glasgow on 12 January 1894, a son of Mr Francis Downie and Mrs Elizabeth Jane Downie. Robert was one of sixteen children, five of whom were to serve in the Great War, with two of them being killed. He was educated at St Aloysius's School, Springburn, and went to work at Hydepark Locomotive Works, Glasgow, where his father had worked for most of his life.

On 12 January 1912 Robert joined the army and on 4 April 1914 married Ivy Louise Sparks at Gravesend. He left for France in August 1914 and by the end of the war he had been wounded five times, including being gassed. By the end of the war the Downies had given birth to three children, one son, one daughter and one who died in infancy.

Eight days before the King was to present Downie with his VC, the sergeant returned home to Glasgow where he was given a public welcome at the Springburn Town Hall. In the evening he attended a special reception given by the United Irish League and was presented with a gold watch by his former school and a purse containing treasury notes.

Downie left the army in March 1919 and in addition to the VC gained the Military Medal and the Mons Star, as well as the Russian Order of St George. In addition he was Mentioned in Despatches on two occasions.

After the war he became an avid supporter of the various functions organised for holders of the VC and GC and attended these functions at least a dozen times. At the end of July 1941 he attended the funeral of Lieutenant Henry May VC in Glasgow, who was the first Glasgow man to win the VC in the Great War. Walter Ritchie, another Somme VC winner, also attended. He was a member of the Home Guard until they were stood down in December 1944. He was also a supporter of Celtic Football Club where he worked at the turnstiles.

Robert Downie died on 18 April 1968 at the age of 74, and was buried at St Kentigern's Cemetery, Glasgow, Section 21, Lair 506. He was joined in 1970 by his daughter, Annie and his wife Louise. At the present time his decorations are still in private hands.

E.P. BENNETT

There was a gap of thirteen days between Sgt Downie winning his VC at Les Boeufs and Lt E.P. Bennett winning his in the fighting for Le Transloy. Not a great deal of progress had been made by the Allies during this time on the Somme front due to rain, and the author calculates that about 41mm of rain fell in this period, making conditions for fighting well nigh impossible. Despite this the French Army did make some progress to the north-west of Sailly-Saillisel and the British progressed slowly towards Le Transloy. On other fronts, the French had re-entered Vaux.

General Rawlinson, commander of the Fourth Army, had proposed to limit this attack planned for 5 November to the capture of ground to the east and north-east of Les Boeufs. The French at the same time were planning to capture St Pierre Vaast Wood, which when accomplished would create a dangerous salient which Lord Cavan (XIV Corps) undertook to cover.

The 33rd Division were situated at Les Boeufs and consisted of the 19th, 98th and 100th brigades. The 100th Brigade contained the 2nd Battalion, The Worcestershire Regiment who we are concerned with here. On 4 November, the 2nd Battalion, The Royal Welsh Fusiliers, 19th Brigade were ordered to dig trenches on the crest of the ridge in front of Le Transloy, but little was achieved because of the openness of the position. The actual objective at Le Transloy was the cemetery and the enemy machine-gunners were on the alert. The 2nd Worcesters made a flank attack from the French positions, to the right of the 33rd Division, and captured Boritzka and Mirage Trenches before joining up with the 16th (Service) Battalion (Church Lads' Brigade), The King's Royal

Rifle Corps. The Worcesters' first wave had been unsuccessful and the leader of the second wave, Lt E.P. Bennett of C Company took over both units and urged the infantry on. He had recently been blown up by a shell and his wounds had been bandaged by a Frenchman, and he carried on leading the advance with a spade in his hand. The *Regimental History* describes the incident in the following manner:

> Lieutenant Bennett found a spade and cut himself a step in the embankment. Then he ran forward through the bursting shells. As he ran, he passed the little second lieutenant (possibly Jack Oswald Couldridge) struck dead. Still grasping the spade, he reached the troops, dashed through them and signalled them to advance. The whole battalion rose behind him and flooded forward in one wave over the crest-line and down onto the flank of the German trenches.

This was when the German positions at Mirage and Boritzka trenches gave way. The Worcesters advanced down the slope towards Le Transloy for a distance of 500 yards and then dug in and consolidated their positions. They then linked up with the 16th KRRC. The Worcesters were later relieved by the 1/5th (TF), The Cameronians (Scottish Rifles), 19th Brigade, and the battalion withdrew to Guillemont, and then to camp at Fricourt. Casualties had numbered 200. Bennett returned with a party of only sixty men to receive congratulations from Battalion HQ at Les Boeufs. The trench that they had occupied was later named Bennett's trench.

Bennett's citation was published on 30 December 1916 and read as follows:

> For most conspicuous bravery in action when in command of the second wave of the attack. Finding that the first wave had suffered heavy casualties, its commander killed and the line wavering, Lt Bennett advanced at the head of the second wave, and by his personal example of valour and resolution reached his objective with but sixty men.
>
> Isolated with his small party, he at once took steps to consolidate his position under heavy rifle and machine-gun fire from both flanks, and although wounded, he remained in command directing and controlling.

He set an example of cheerfulness and resolution beyond all praise, and there is little doubt that but for his personal example of courage, the attack would have been checked at the outset.

Bennett was decorated by the King on 5 February 1917 at Buckingham Palace and was the second man from the Worcester Regiment to gain the VC during the Battle of the Somme.

Eugene Paul Bennett was the fourth of five sons of Mr Charles Bennett, a former headmaster and accountant, and Florence Emma Sophia Bennett, there was also a daughter, Dora. Paul was born at Cainscross, Stroud, Gloucestershire on 4 June 1892. Bennett was educated at Marling School in Stroud between 1905 and 1908. He was a good cricketer and footballer. He later joined the staff of the Bank of England. In October 1913 he joined the 1st Artists Rifles as a private and went with the 1st Artists to France in October 1914. He was commissioned into the 2nd Worcesters on 1 January 1915, and remained with them until the day he gained his VC. He was present at the Battle of Neuve Chapelle and on 26 September he was awarded the MC during the Battle of Loos and was Mentioned in Despatches. He received the MC at Buckingham Palace from the King on 10 May 1916. His parents whose address was 'Fromehurst', Frome Park Road, Stroud were with their son at the ceremony. At the time that Bennett was gaining his VC in November 1916, he had been wounded and spent several months recovering. On his discharge he was made a captain and was fit enough to return to Stroud whose inhabitants were eager to give him a special welcome which they arranged for 21 February 1917. His train was met by members of the Stroud Council as well as by members of his family, and a guard of honour was drawn up for his inspection. Banners of welcome draped the town's streets and many shops and officers were closed to allow their employees to greet their 'local hero'. Bennett and his family were installed in a Rolls Royce which was drawn through the town to a platform where the welcoming ceremony was to take place. Bennett was greeted on behalf of the town by the vice chairman of Stroud Urban District Council and presented with an Illuminated Address. Later that evening a dinner was given in his honour at the Holloway Institute and in reply he gave a modest speech. His brother Theodore was allowed to attend the celebrations. The Bank of England also presented him with a Sword of Honour. On 18 October 1918 Bennett sustained very severe shell splinter wounds and was still confined to bed nearly a year later, which was the reason why he could not attend his father's funeral in September 1919.

Bennett had had three brothers, one of whom, Lt Harold RGA was killed in a motorcycle accident; another was Lt Theodore Bennett of the Machine Gun Corps who was also killed on 7 September 1918 when attached to the Indian Infantry.

In July 1922 Paul Bennett married Miss Violet Forster who at one time had been a song writer, and they had a daughter and a son. Bennett was called to the Bar at the Middle Temple in 1923 and was Prosecuting Counsel on the SE Circuit between 1931 and 1935 when he became a metropolitan magistrate, a position that he was to hold until 1961. He sat at the West London Magistrate Court for eleven years and then at the Marlborough Street Court from 1946 until 1961. In addition he was a governor of the Regency Polytechnic. In the Second World War the Bennetts were bombed out of their home in Marylebone twice, and after the war their son died of pneumonia in 1946. In 1949 Bennett's wife 'went missing' for a few days before being found in a distressed condition on Hampstead Heath. The Bennetts retired to Vincenza, North Italy where Paul died on 6 April 1970 at the age of 77. He was cremated at Vincenza Crematorium and his ashes are in Niche 116, and his name is on a table in the vault. Bennett's wife survived him and after her husband's death she wrote to the headmaster of Marling School telling him that she would like the school to have a picture of her late husband that used to hang in the Marlborough Street Court. It was of Bennett in the uniform of a squadron leader in the RAF when he had been an officer in the Air Training Corps in the Second World War. The portrait was later hung in the school hall. The Bennett prize for 'outstanding service to the School' was also established. He is also remembered in the window of the cloisters of Worcester Cathedral. Bennett's addresses in England after the Great War were 18 Manor Gardens, London, SW19 in the 1920s and later Homefield, Aldwich, Sussex. His decorations are in the Worcester City Museum.

On his death *The Times* described Bennett as 'Soldier and Magistrate', he excelled at both careers.

J. CUNNINGHAM

In the time between Lieutenant E.P. Bennett gaining the VC at Le Transloy on 5 November and Private John Cunningham winning his on 13 November, the Allies had been making their final preparations for the commencement of the Battle of the Ancre.

We are not directly concerned here with the main part of the battle as Cunningham's battalion, the 12th (Service) Battalion (3rd Hull), The East Yorkshire Regiment (The Duke of York's Own), 92nd Brigade, 31st Division was to the north of the battlefield protecting the left flank of the Allied attack. The 93rd Brigade was on the left of the frontline to the south-east of Hébuterne and the 92nd was on its right. This brigade consisted of four Hull battalions from the East Yorkshire Regiment, the 10th, 11th, 12th and 13th. The brigade had been in reserve at Serre on 1 July when the rest of the division suffered high casualties, but this time they were not going to 'escape' again.

In an attack against the village of Serre, Pte Cunningham's battalion the 12th East Yorkshires, together with the 13th Battalion, pushed forward from their assembly positions soon after midnight on 13 November with snipers and Lewis guns. Through this early start they were to provide support on the left flank when zero hour arrived a few hours later. The barrage was excellent and the Yorkshire battalion reached the German front trench without any major difficulty, and during the whole action 300 Germans were captured. Despite the ease of the battalion's progress, the enemy was in no mood to give up its support trench and fought back strongly with rifle fire and bombs, and on the right of the line the 13th Battalion suffered heavy casualties in the fighting. Responding mainly with Lewis guns the 12th Battalion had continued to use communication trenches that stretched as far back as Star Wood for conducting counter-bombing attacks. The British managed to hang on to what ground they had captured but had run very short of bombs. It was during this part of the action that Pte Cunningham carried out the deeds which led to his award of a VC. The citation for the decoration which was published on 13 January 1917 tells the story in the following way:

> For most conspicuous bravery and resource during operations. After the enemy's frontline had been captured, Private Cunningham proceeded with a bombing section up a communication trench. Much opposition was encountered, and the rest of the section became casualties. Collecting all the bombs from the casualties, this gallant soldier went on alone. Having expended all his bombs, he returned for a fresh supply and again proceeded to the communication trench, where he met a party of ten of the enemy. These he killed, and cleared the trench up to the enemy line. His conduct throughout the day was magnificent....

Unfortunately, later on in the day the 3rd Division on the 31st's right was unsuccessful in its fight against German positions at Serre, and the battalion had to withdraw because the enemy had a very clear view over their attackers. This situation led to an exposed flank which could only be corrected by the retreat of the 92nd Brigade to its own lines.

As a postscript, the great sacrifice of the East Yorkshire battalions on the 13th have tended to be obscured by the relative progress in the day further south, and especially at Beaumont-Hamel, Beaucourt and St Pierre Divion.

Cunningham was presented with his VC by the King in an open-air ceremony in Hyde Park on 2 June 1917.

John Cunningham, who was usually known as Jack, was the son of Charles Cunningham, a licensed hawker, and his wife Mary Ann. John was born on 28 June 1897 at Swaby's Yard, Scunthorpe, an address which no longer exists. The family later moved to Hull and John attended schools at St James's Day School, Wheeler Street (later Newington High) and Chiltern Street School. The original Chiltern School had been pulled down and a modern primary school built in its stead. His education was often interrupted as his parents were so often on the move.In Hull the family lived at Edgar Street, Hessle Road behind St James's which was later redeveloped.

After he left school John became a hawker like his father before him, and in 1915 enlisted in the 3rd Hull Battalion at the age of 17. He carried out his initial army training at South Dalton near Beverley and later served with the battalion in Egypt from December 1915 until March 1916, when its role was to protect the Suez Canal. The battalion then moved to France and the Western Front. In the following year, on 2 June 1917, Cunningham was one of the 350 men and women to be decorated at a special public ceremony of investiture that took place at Hyde Park. It was a beautiful summer's day and aircraft of the Royal Flying Corps patrolled the skies overhead in case of a surprise attack by German Gotha Bombers. A Guards Brigade provided suitable music for the occasion and the ceremony was also filmed. Cunningham was one of the first men to be decorated by the King and the other early recipients included several other Somme VC winners, Hughes, White, Allen, and Bradford. The crowd was able to follow the ceremony by reference to a programme. Each man or woman had a number and this number was displayed on boards in various parts of the crowd. This way everyone present knew who was who. It was interesting that owing to superstition the number 13 was dropped from the proceedings. Roland Bradford was number 14 in the list instead of 13, although the altering of his number did not prevent him from being killed by a stray shell nearly six months later. When Cunningham's turn came to be paraded in front of the King there was a roar from the crowd who had read of his deed in their programmes and the King talked to the 'Hull Hero' for some little time. The last people who were decorated were members of the nursing profession and they were followed by the families of those who had gained their awards posthumously.

Later that evening Cunningham left London with his parents, who had also been present at the reception, returning home on leave to Hull where he was given a huge welcome. Although his train arrived at Paragon Station at 2 o'clock on a Sunday morning, the crowds were there waiting to greet their 'local hero'. On emerging from the station at the former Anlaby Road entrance, a great roar went up from the crowds and Cunningham was immediately hoisted shoulder high and carried home. During the same leave he visited St James's Day School and although later there were plans to erect a plaque to Cunningham at Wheeler Street School, they were not carried through. The local cinema, the Hull Palace, showed the film of the investiture that had taken place at Hyde Park at 'both houses' while Cunningham was on leave.

John Cunningham, his parents and a younger brother were also invited to be guests at a crowded meeting of Hull City Council at the Guildhall, where he was given an official welcome on behalf of the city and also presented with an Illuminated Address. In reply Cunningham gave a short message of thanks and was applauded continuously. The Lord Mayor, Alderman F. Askew said this to Cunningham in his public address:

> ... It was open to him, as well as to any of the rank and file, not only in the Army, but in civil life, by his zeal, industry and determination, to achieve higher honours in the future. There was no doubt that his deed would be talked of for many years to come....'

Cunningham was quite badly wounded in the latter part of the war and was demobilised in 1919. In the same year he married Ena Harrison, who later gave birth to a daughter. Shortly after his return from the army, it appears that Cunningham was having difficulty settling down and fitting in with civilian life. As early as July 1919 we find him being summoned for physically abusing and beating up his wife. In defence he maintained that 'she left him three times a week'. The local magistrate granted Mrs Cunningham a separation order with a weekly allowance of 25 shillings. At his appearance in court Cunningham wore his VC. Summoned again nearly sixteen months later (November 1920), Cunningham was ordered once more to pay his wife a maintenance grant. Cunningham, who was again sporting his VC, said in his defence that he only had an income of an army pension of £2 a week. He received this pension for being wounded in both legs and in the lungs. However, these wounds did not prevent him from being involved in a brawl with an ex-soldier a couple of weeks

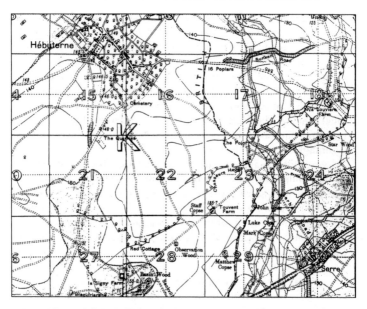

A British map of the Hébuterne–Serre area dated 16 May 1916. Only 'enemy' trenches are shown in detail. (TM453)

later, when he was put on remand for hitting the man on the head with a bottle.

In March 1922 Cunningham became the first of the Somme VC holders to be sent to prison, for failing again to keep up payments to his wife. The arrears amounted to £10. Seven years later, in November 1929 Cunningham once again made the local headlines in Hull. This time he was the victim of two fellow hawkers who had made off with his share of the value of a quantity of lino that the three had agreed to sell and split the proceeds. Cunningham was not in court on this occasion as he had a more pressing engagement with the Prince of Wales at a dinner for Victoria Cross winners!

John Cunningham died of tuberculosis in a sanatorium in Kingston-upon-Hull on 21 February 1941 at the age of 43. He is buried in the family grave which includes his parents, Charles and Mary Ann, and his brother Matthew who joined them in 1951.

The compartment number is 180, the number of the grave 17509 and all four names are included on the headstone, and in view of this it is deemed that John Cunningham does not require a separate headstone. His decorations are in the possession of The Prince of Wales's Regimental Museum in York. Like most VC winners his obituary was published in *The Times*.

Cunningham was the first man connected with Hull to win the VC in the Great War, and he was one of four members of the East Yorkshire Regiment to receive the nation's highest military honour. In view of it now being seventy years since Cunningham's death, and the end of what appeared to be a fairly tragic post-war life, it would seem high time for the people of Hull to commemorate their former hero. After all, enough fuss was made of him when he returned home in 1917, having brought glory on himself, his regiment and his home town. It would be nice to think that Cunningham's misdemeanours could be forgiven and that at the very least a fund opened that would provide enough money for the erection of a memorial stone on his grave. However, he is commemorated in the Hull Memorial Gardens together with three other VC winners with local connections, including Second Lieutenant John Harrison VC, MC. Their names are listed on a granite slab on a bevelled concrete plinth. He was also commemorated with a memorial in Chiltern School.

B.C. FREYBERG

While John Cunningham was winning a VC opposite Hébuterne on 13 November, the 63rd (Royal Naval) Division were making great progress to the south-east in their attempt to capture the enemy-held village of Beaucourt. It was for his outstanding leadership on this day as commanding officer of the Hood Battalion, 189th Brigade that Lieutenant Colonel Bernard Freyberg was to win a Victoria Cross. He had already been created a Companion of the Distinguished Service Order at Gallipoli.

The start of the Battle of the Ancre had been delayed several times because of adverse weather conditions, but finally it was confirmed that it should take place on 13 November. The plan of attack was the line Serre–Beaumont Hamel–Beaucourt–St Pierre Divion. These strong points were to be attacked by the 3rd, 51st and 63rd Royal Naval Divisions of XIII Corps, in the order left to right. The 63rd Division was allotted a front that measured 1,200 yards, and their right flank was on the north side of the River Ancre which ran in an easterly direction from the village of Beaucourt.

The 63rd Division was to reach Beaucourt, their objective was to take the intervening positions. Their jumping off trenches ran in a north–south line. The enemy, which was nearly 250 yards away, had three lines of trenches and the first line to be captured was called the 'Dotted Green Line'. Behind it was a valley which ran through the Beaucourt Station Road. Behind this was a ridge that ran from Beaumont Hamel to the Station at Beaucourt, called the 'Green Line', and this ran down as far as the River Ancre.

The third objective was called the 'Yellow Line' and was in front of Beaucourt village. The village itself was to be the final objective and was known as the 'Red Line'.

The Hood, Hawke, Howe and 1st Royal Marines from the 189th and 190th brigades moved off first at 5.45am; it was not only pitch dark but there was a Scotch mist as well. From the beginning the situation was confused and the attacking units quickly became intermixed. In the mist, the Drake Battalion got too far ahead of the advance and the battalion hadn't even noticed the enemy lines, although they had bombed several German dugouts. They also found themselves too close to their own barrage and lost some men as a result. At the line above Station Road, as it was at last getting light, Freyberg assumed command of the operation. He had been commander of the Hood Battalion and was dressed in his 'number one rig'; he was an imposing sight on the battlefield being over 6ft tall and weighing 16st. Chief Petty Officer Tobin later recalled the following greeting from Freyberg: 'Hullo, Tobin, I think we will get a VC today'.

This was after Freyberg's adjutant and signals officer had both been killed on either side of him. At the 'Yellow Line', the third line in front of Beaucourt, Freyberg gave instructions to dig two lines of trenches while the attack on the village was organised. At this time the British artillery were again causing casualties by 'dropping short'. In addition German snipers in front of Beaucourt were very active and causing casualties with accurate rifle fire, although the trenches did give the attackers some protection. Here they dug in for the night, which was a very cold one, while the British bombardment continued until the situation on the left flank was clearer. At 6am on the 14th the 90th Brigade (RND) was to attack and become level with the Naval Division's advance, and then at 7.45am the brigade was to attack and capture Beaucourt. The German machine-gunners and snipers were very active and the Allied barrage ineffectual. At zero hour Freyberg, disregarding any risk to his own life, climbed out of his trench and led the attack in person. The first wave stopped three times, and at this time Freyberg was knocked over by a bullet which hit his helmet. He scrambled up again and went on into Beaucourt with the Royal Naval Division behind him. The Germans decided not to make a fight of it and surrendered in their hundreds. They came out of their holes, tore off their equipment and gave themselves up. After the village was captured it was decided to make a trench on the far side of the village. At this stage the German snipers were still firing very accurately and, although wounded, Freyberg was able to carry on with the task of organising the battle. This was just before 9am and the German heavy guns suddenly started firing into the village. Conditions for the Marines became very hazardous and unfortunately their commanding officer Lt Col Freyberg was hit for the third time, but this time much more seriously. His wound, which was in his neck, was bleeding profusely and was dressed by The Hon. Lionel S. Montagu, a brother officer who also gave Freyberg some morphia. After about ten minutes the shelling eased and Montagu suggested that he should get three men to take him down the line for medical treatment. Freyberg, who was still giving instructions despite his wounds would not hear of such a suggestion and then asked Montagu if he would walk him down to the aid post. The distance was 300 yards and Freyberg lent on his colleague for support as they negotiated the German shelling and the various shell holes in their path. The regimental aid post was in the shelter of a bank where members of the Drake and Hood battalions were sheltering, as were a number of staff officers, according to Montagu. Freyberg was immediately administered to by the regimental doctor and gave instructions for the commander of the 13th (Service) Battalion, 111th Brigade, 37th Division, The King's Royal Rifle Corps, to take over from him.

It is hardly surprising that after being wounded three times in the same action and almost leading the attack on Beaucourt single-handed that Freyberg should be granted the VC. The citation was published very soon afterwards on 15 December 1916 and read as follows:

For most conspicuous bravery and brilliant leading as a battalion commander.

By his splendid personal bravery he carried the initial attack straight through the enemy's front system of trenches. Owing to mist and heavy fire of all descriptions, Lieutenant Colonel Freyberg's command was much disorganised after the capture of the first objective. He personally rallied and reformed his men, including men from other units who had become intermixed.

He inspired all with his own contempt of danger. At the appointed time he led his men to the successful assault of the second objective, many prisoners being captured.

During this advance he was twice wounded. He again rallied and reformed all who were with him, and although unsupported in a very advanced position, he held his ground throughout the day and the following night, under heavy artillery and machine-gun fire. When reinforced on the following morning he organised the attack on a strongly fortified village and showed a fine example of dash in personally leading the assault, capturing the strongly fortified village and 500 prisoners. In this operation he was again wounded.

Later in the afternoon he was again wounded severely, but refused to leave the line till he had issued final instructions.

The personality, valour and utter contempt of danger on the part of this single officer enabled the furthermost objective of the corps to be permanently held, and on this point d'appui the line was eventually formed.

Freyberg was the last man to be awarded the VC during the Battle of the Somme, but not the last man to have his citation published. The citation for George Evans was not published until 1920.

The Battle of the Somme officially finished on 18 November. As we have seen, Beaucourt fell on the 14th and the British were able to advance to the north and south of the Ancre and reach the outskirts of Grandcourt. Freyberg did not receive his VC from the King at Buckingham Palace until 2 January 1918.

Freyberg's wounds sustained during the Battle of the Somme took several months to heal and he was not properly fit until March 1917. He was promoted to the rank of brigadier general and placed in command of the 173rd Brigade, 58th (London) Division. He fought with them at Bullecourt and in September in the Third Battle of Ypres, Passchendaele, where he was again seriously wounded. After three months he was back in the Salient again in command of the 88th Brigade, 29th Division. He was then involved in most of the 1918 battles and was awarded two Bars to his DSO. The first was for leading an attack to capture Gheluvelt on 28 September and the second for leading a cavalry charge at Lessines on 11 November. After the Armistice he went with the British Army of the Rhine. In total he was wounded nine times and Mentioned in Despatches on seven occasions. The French awarded him with the Croix de Guerre with Palms.

Bernard Cyril Freyberg was born in 8 Dynevor Road, Richmond, Surrey on 21 March 1889. He was the seventh son of James Freyberg and the fifth by his second wife Julia Hamilton. The family left for New Zealand in 1891 where they settled in Wellington. James Freyberg worked in the Forestry Department. Bernard was educated at Wellington College (1897–1904) and became a champion swimmer, nursing ambitions to swim the English Channel. He also boxed, sailed and played rugby. In 1905 he joined D Battery of the New Zealand Field Artillery Volunteers in Wellington and in 1911 was commissioned into the 6th Hauraki Regiment. In the same year he qualified to be a dentist in Octago and in 1913 took on the job of a ship's stoker and sailed to Sydney, Australia. On returning to Wellington he obtained a stoker's certificate and sailed for America where he took on various jobs before leaving for England at the end of August 1914. Once in London he sought out an army commission and managed to obtain an interview with Winston Churchill, First Lord of the Admiralty who was busy with setting up a Naval Division which became the 63rd. The aim was to find suitable employment for the 20 to 30,000 men from the Royal Navy Reserves who would not be required to crew ships. Churchill seems to have taken a shine to Freyberg who subsequently ended up with the Hood Battalion of the RNVR as a temporary lieutenant. The Hood was part of the 2nd Royal Naval Brigade which left for Belgium in early October and arrived at Antwerp on 6 October. At this stage they joined the 1st Royal Naval Brigade and the Royal Marine Brigade in an abortive attempt to prevent the town from falling into enemy hands. The operation was a complete failure and many men were taken prisoner, and two days later the survivors had reached Ostend to sail to Dover where they arrived on the 11th.

For a time the various naval units were scattered over the country, but reassembled at the end of November in Blandford Forum, Dorset. By December, Freyberg was in command of the Hood's A Company and Sub Lieutenant Patrick Shaw-Stewart described him as being ' a tremendously strong and impressive figure'. Shaw- Stewart was joined by Sub Lieutenant Arthur Asquith known as 'Oc', a son of the prime minister, and brother of Raymond. Other luminaries included Rupert Brooke, Alan Herbert and Denis Browne. Frederick 'Cleg' Kelly joined then in February 1915.

On 6 February the Royal Marine Brigade sailed for Gallipoli and arrived at Lemnos on the 24th, and in March joined the rest of the division arriving off Gallipoli on the 19th. The Naval bombardment of the Peninsula had failed and the Naval Division was ordered to Egypt. A few weeks later they left for Mudros on 5 April and took part in the Helles and Anzac battles.

After Rupert Brooke died of blood poisoning on board a French Hospital ship, having never taken any part in the fighting, Freyberg helped to find a suitable grave site on the island of Skyros. There was some urgency to conduct the burial quickly as the division was to embark the following day. A suitable spot was found in an olive grove and eight Petty Officers took part in carrying the coffin up a rocky path on a two-hour journey. Shaw-Stewart, with drawn sword, was in command of a four man firing party and another sub lieutenant carried a wooden cross. A cortége of officers then followed, led by Major General Archibald Paris, divisional commander. After the burial service Freyberg helped to lay pieces of white marble over the grave which helped to form a cairn. The Hood Battalion left Skyros with its transports the next day.

On the 25/26 April a deception was planned concerning a proposed landing on the mainland and, being a strong swimmer, Freyberg suggested that he should swim ashore at a point between Bulair in the Gulf of Saros and set up some marker flairs to deceive the Turks. After Freyberg carried out this bold operation he was later taken from the water in a very cold state. He was subsequently awarded a DSO.

Also in April, responsibility for the 63rd (RND) was handed over from the Admiralty to the War Office. In June the Hood Battalion took part in the ill-fated attempt to capture Achi Baba, and although Freyberg was suffering from wounds he was appointed active battalion commander of the battalion. This promotion only lasted a month, owing to his wounds. However, he always had remarkable powers of recovery, and after a spell in a hospital in Egypt he returned to the Peninsula in August and was promoted as a RNVR commander. He left the Peninsula in January 1916 during the evacuation.

After the RND had been reformed, he was made a lieutenant colonel and the division then sailed for France and the Western Front in May via Marseilles. As we have seen, the division took part in the latter stages of the Battle of the Somme in which Freyberg was wounded and won the VC in the capture of Beaucourt. His wounds in the November Somme battle took several months to heal and he had returned to England to recover, which by March he did, and he was promoted to the rank of brigadier general in command of 173rd Brigade, 58th Division. He fought with them at Bullecourt and in September in the Third Battle of Ypres, where he was seriously wounded again. After three months he returned to Passchendaele as commander of the 88th Brigade, 29th Division. He won two Bars to his DSO during the remaining months of the war and ended it having been wounded six times. The French also presented him with a medal, the Croix de Guerre with Palms. In addition his name had also been Mentioned in Despatches several times.

I have dealt at length with Freyberg's record during the Great War because, apart perhaps from Carton de Wiart, Freyberg was surely the greatest soldier who was to be a winner of the Victoria Cross during the Battle of the Somme.

Passing quickly over the rest of Freyberg's career, suffice to say that he brought to bear all his unique qualities to any job or position that he was offered. Freyberg married Barbara, a widow of The Hon. Francis McLaran, daughter of Sir Herbert and Lady Jekyll on 16 June 1922. As well as being a great friend of Winston Churchill, Freyberg also became a chum of the dramatist J.M. Barrie who, like Churchill, had a soft spot for 'action heroes'. After the war he flirted briefly with politics, took a staff course at Sandhurst, served briefly with the Grenadier Guards and the Manchester Regiment and made three attempts to swim the English Channel. In the 1930s he became a senior officer in Southern Command and was made up to a major general. In 1937 he was declared medically unfit and left the army and gained a position with BSA, he also dabbled again with politics and was adopted as a prospective Conservative candidate.

In 1939 he was recalled to the army and took command of the New Zealand Army and was with them in North Africa. Before then he had an unusual setback when in command of the island of Crete and he and his troops were lucky to escape from the German airborne landing. The enemy was infinitely better equipped for the task of holding the island.

As a result of his very close ties with New Zealand, Freyberg became its governor general after the war, and held the post until 1952. He then returned to England and became lieutenant governor of Windsor Castle.

Freyberg was to receive many military and civil honours and was awarded a third Bar to his DSO in Italy for the advance on Trieste in 1945. He was appointed KBE in 1942 and GCMG in 1946. In 1951 he was created 1st Baron of Wellington, New Zealand, and of Munstead in the county of Surrey. Mrs Freyberg, by now Lady Freyberg, who had one son, Paul Richard, born in 1923 was involved in troop welfare and was made a member of the Order of the British Empire, and was as popular as her husband in New Zealand.

Bernard Freyberg collapsed in his office in Windsor Castle and died in the King Edward VII Hospital in Windsor on 4 July, at the age of 74, where he had been the governor of the castle since 1953. He was buried on 10 July at St Martha's Churchyard, Chilworth, Surrey. His gravestone did not weather well and in recent years has been replaced. His widow lived on until 1973 and their son succeeded to the Peerage. In commemoration of this brilliant soldier and administrator there is a bust of his likeness in the Guildhall, London. There is a memorial and bronze in the crypt of St Paul's Cathedral, designed by Oscar Nemon, and a commemoration of him in St George's Chapel, Windsor. He is also commemorated in Auckland, New Zealand with a statue which shows him wearing a service cap and greatcoat. A memorial to the memory of the 63rd Royal Naval division was set up in Beaucourt after the war and unveiled on 12 November 1922 by General Sir Hubert Gough and Brigadier General Arthur Asquith. Freyberg had been one of the prime movers behind the project. It was possibly through him that Sir Edwin Lutyens was invited to design a memorial to the division which was set up in Horse Guards close to the then Admiralty building. It was unveiled by Major General Sir Archibald Paris on Gallipoli Day (25 April) 1925. His decorations are in private hands.

APPENDICES AND SOURCES

The Lummis Files in the care of the Military Historical Society at the National Army Museum and Imperial War Museum. Maps are taken from Marix-Evans, M., *Somme 1914–18: Lessons in War,* The History Press, 2010

E.N.F. Bell
National Archives WO 339/14809

G.S. Cather
National Archives WO 339/273
Hazelwood School, Limpsfield
English Heroes (*This England*, Summer 1986)

J.L. Green
Coin & Medal News
Hunts Post
Contemporary Biographies of Huntingdonshire

S.W. Loudoun-Shand
National Archives WO 128/13 and WO 339/14041
The Legion (July/August 1986)

W.F. McFadzean
Belfast Telegraph
Royal Ulster Rifles Association

R. Quigg
Bulletin, issue 35, page 12
Belfast Telegraph
Northern Constitutional
Daily Mail

W. Ritchie
War Diary of the 2nd Battalion, Seaforth Highlanders
Cabar Feidh
Glasgow Evening Times
R.H.Q. Queen's Own Highlanders
Maj. Gen. Sir John Laurie's experiences as adjutant of the 2nd
Battalion, Seaforth Highlanders, 1916 (IWM)

G. Sanders
Yorkshire Evening News
Yorkshire Evening Post
This England (n.d.)

J.Y. Turnbull
The Royal Highland Fusiliers
The Outpost (December 1916)
Glasgow Herald

A. Carton de Wiart
Lady Joan Carton de Wiart
Dictionary of National Biography 1961–1970 (1981)
Daily Sketch
Daily Telegraph
Evening News
The Sunday Times
The Times
Black Badge (1966)

T.G. Turrall
'Firm'
The late Dennis Gillard
Worcestershire Regimental Museum

T.O.L. Wilkinson
National Archives WO 339/5266
Stand To!, 70, p. 54
The Regimental Association, The Loyal Regiment (North Lancashire)
The Sphere

D.S. Bell
Gunfire 31
Oxford Dictionary of National Biography (ODNB)
National Archives WO 339/2902
Victoria Cross Society, volume 3, p. 27–30
Stand To!, 87, p. 58
Stand To!, 61, p. 31
Yorkshire Evening Post

W.E. Boulter
VC Society, vol. 9, p. 19–21
National Archives WO 339/88734
Leicester Mercury
Sir Ivor Maxse, 'Notes on the Somme Situation, 11 July 1916'
Irene Progin

W.F. Faulds
East Anglian Daily Times
S. Monick, 'W.F. Faulds VC, MC: A Uniquely South African Victoria
Cross Group' (*Museum Review,* vol. 1, no. 6, September 1987)
Graeme Swinney, 'The Capt W.F. Faulds VC, MC Centre: A New
Museum Function Facility Dedicated to a South African First
World War Hero' (*Military History Journal*, vol. 10, no. 3)
South African Museum of Military History

W. La T. Congreve
National Archive WO 339/7831
Royal Green Jackets Museum
The late Dennis Gillard
Country Life (1916)
Daily Mirror
Daily Telegraph

The Guardian
Cheshire Express
The Rifle Brigade Chronicle (1916)
The Suffolk Regimental Gazette (April 1926)
J. Fellows, 'For valour –Wirral Family's Double Distinction' (1966)

J.J. Davies
Bournemouth Evening Echo
The Times History and Encyclopaedia of the War

A. Hill
North Cheshire Herald and Hyde Reporter

T.W.H. Veale
VC Society, vol. 2, p. 49 and *Stand To!,* 89, pp. 18–21
Evening Standard
Brenda Ward
Western Morning News
Devonshire and Dorset Regimental Journal

J. Leak
Australian War Memorial, Canberra
Dictionary of Australian National Biography

A.S. Blackburn
Australian War Memorial, Canberra
Dictionary of Australian National Biography
10th Battalion, AIF War Diary

T. Cooke
Australian War Memorial, Canberra
Dictionary of Australian National Biography
G. Bryant, *Where the Prize is Highest: The Stories of the New Zealanders who won the Victoria Cross* (1972)

A. Gill
Stand To!, 37, p. 11
Evening News

C.C. Castleton
Stand To!, 70, p. 57
Australian War Memorial, Canberra
Lowestoft Journal

W.J.G. Evans
VC Society, no. 10, p. 14
Croydon Times & Advertiser
The Child's Guardian
Tameside Metropolitan Borough Council
The Manchester Museum Committee of the King's Regiment

J. Miller
Lancaster City Council
Lancaster Evening Post
J.M. Garwood

W.H. Short
Roger Chapman

G.G. Coury
National Archives WO 39/43771
VC Society, vol. 2, p. 17–20
The Stonyhurst Magazine
The South Lancashire Regiment Newsletter
The Liverpool Echo
The Warrington Guardian
Yorkshire Evening Newsletter

N.G. Chavasse
ODNB
Bulletin, 62, p. 19
Bulletin, 82, p. 3 & cover
VC Society, vol. 8, p. 25
VC Society, vol. 9, p. 48
D. Cargill, 'Serving the Outpatients in Hell' (*Medical*, January 1981)
Liverpool Daily Post

This England
Daily Mail
Ann Clayton

M.O'Meara
Australian War Memorial, Canberra
The West Australian
Australian Dictionary of Biography

W.B. Allen
Edinburgh Evening Newsletter
Daily Mail
Chichester Observer
The Star (Sheffield)
Yesterday, no. 22, February 1990
Article by Harold Ellis IWM 95/666K

T. Hughes
The Star
Daily Telegraph

J.V. Holland
The Mercury (Tasmania)
Clongowes College School Magazine
S. Lindsay, 'Merseyside Heroes' (unpublished)

D. Jones
National Museums and Galleries on Merseyside
Liverpool Echo
S. Lindsay, 'Merseyside Heroes' (unpublished)

L. Clarke
Department of Public Records and Archives, Toronto

D.F. Brown
Auckland Institute and Museum
G. Bryant, *Where the Prize is Highest The Stories of the New Zealanders who won the Victoria Cross* (1972)

J. Sanders, *New Zealand VC Winners* (1974)
A.E. Byrne MC, *Official History of the Otago Regiment in the Great War* (n.d.)

F. McNess
Yorkshire Evening Post
Yorkshire Post
Bournemouth Daily Echo
The Scots Guards Archives
The McNess Family

J.V. Campbell
Punch (1916)
W. Oliver Wicks
Daily Mail
Gloucestershire Gazette

J.C. Kerr
National Archives of Canada

T.A. Jones
Runcorn Guardian
Runcorn Weekly Newsletter
Wide World Magazine
Cheshire Chronicle
The Oak Tree (Cheshire Regiment Journal)
Bulletin, 28, p. 13
Stand To!, 41, p. 4
VC Society, vol. 2, p. 53

F.J. Edwards and R.E. Ryder
Star & Garter Newsletter
Soldier
The Die-Hards (Middlesex Regiment Journal)
Middlesex Regiment Museum
The Sunday Express

T.E. Adlam
D.A.B. Shardlow interview with daughter Mrs J. Swinstead, November 1990
Luton Museum & Gallery

A.C.T. White
Yorkshire Evening Post
The Green Howards Gazette
Stand To!, 87, p. 58
VC Society, vol. 3, pp. 27–30

R.B. Bradford
Jack Cavanagh
Brig. Gen. R.B. Bradford VC, MC and His Brothers (privately published, n.d.)
R. Bradford, 'The Attack made by the 50th Division on the Butte-de-Warlencourt and the Gird Line on November 5th 1916' (S. Shannon, DLI Museum)
ODNB
VC Society, vol. 5, p. 51

H. Kelly
Daily Herald
The Duke of Wellington's Regiment
The Iron Duke
10th Battalion, The Duke of Wellington's Regiment War Diary

J.C. Richardson
Directorate of National Defence Canada
D.A. Melville, *Canadians and the Victoria Cross* (n.d.)
National Archives of Canada
VC Society, vol. 3, p. 11

R. Downie
Glasgow Evening Herald

E.P. Bennett
W. Oliver Wicks, *History of Marling School*

Stroud and the Great War 1914–1919
Daily Mail

J. Cunningham
D.G. Woodhouse
Hull Daily Mail
Grimsby Daily Telegraph
Eastern Morning News
The Sapper
S. Kimberley, *Humberside in the First World War* (n.d.)

B.C. Freyberg
Royal Marines Museum
W.J. Marsh
D. Jerrold, *The Royal Naval Division* (1923)
Major, the Hon. Lionel S. Montagu, RMLI, letter to his mother
dated 20 November 1916, Arch 11/12/13 (33) RM Museum
H.E. Blumberg, *Royal Marines in the War of 1914–1919* (n.d.)
ODNB
Bulletin, 58, p. 29

BIBLIOGRAPHY

Arthur, M., *Symbol of Courage: Men Behind the Medal*, Pan 2005

Ashcroft, M., *Victoria Cross Heroes*, Revised Edition, Headline/ Review, 2007

Bailey, R., *Forgotten Voices of the Victoria Cross,* Ebury Press, 2010

Bancroft, J.W., *Devotion to Duty: Tributes to a Region's V.C.*, Aim High Publications, Manchester , 1990

– *The Victoria Cross Roll of Honour,* Aim High Productions, Manchester, 1989

Bean, C.E.W., *The Official History of Australia in the War of 1914–1918, volume 3, The A.I.F. in France 1916–1929*, Angus & Robertson, 1929

Brigadier-General R.B.Bradford, VC., M.C. and His Brothers, Ray Westlake Books, South Wales, n.d.

Brazier, K., *The Complete Victoria Cross: A Full Chronological Record of all Holders of Britain's Highest Award for Gallantry*, Pen & Sword, Barnsley, 2010

Chapman, R., *Beyond Their Duty: Heroes of the Green Howards*, The Green Howards Museum, Richmond, Yorkshire, 2001

Clark, B., *The Victoria Cross: A Register of Awards to Irish-born Officers and men,* The Irish Sword, 1986

Clayton, A., *Chavasse: Double VC,* Leo Cooper, 1992

– *Deeds that Thrilled the Empire: True Stories of the Most Glorious Acts of Heroism of the Empire's Soldiers and Sailors during the Great War*, Hutchinson, London, n.d.

De la Billiere, P., *Supreme Courage*: *Heroic Stories from 150 Years of the VC*, Abacus, 2005

Denman, T., *Ireland's Unknown Soldiers: The 16th (Irish)*

Division in the Great War, 1914–1918, Irish Academic Press, Dublin, 1992

Doherty, R. & Truesdale, D., *Irish Winners of the Victoria Cross*, Four Courts Press, Dublin, 2000

Edmonds, Sir J.E. (ed.), *Military Operations, France and Belgium*, Macmillan/HMSO, 1922–1949

Falls, C., *The History of the 36th (Ulster) Division,* McCaw, Stevenson & Orr, Belfast 1922

Gliddon, G., *Somme 1916:A Battlefield Companion*, The History Press, 2010

– *VCs Handbook: The Western Front 1914–1918*, Sutton Publishing, Stroud, 2005

Gummer, S., *The Chavasse Twins*, Hodder & Stoughton, London, 1963

Harvey, D., *Monuments to Courage: Victoria Cross Headstones & Memorials*, D. Harvey, 1999

Jebb, J., *Patrick Shaw Stewart*, Dovecote Press, 2010

Kelleher, J.P. Comp., *'Elegant Extracts': The Royal Fusiliers Recipients of The Victoria Cross* 'For Valour',The Royal Fusiliers Association, London, n.d.

The King's Regiment, 8th, 63rd, 96th: For Valour, Fleur de Lys Publishing, Cheshire, n.d.

Kirkby, H.L. & Walsh, R.R., *The Seven VCs of Stonyhurst College*, THCL Books, Blackburn, 1987

Levine, J., *Forgotten Voices of the Somme*, Ebury Press, 2008

The London Gazette, 1916–1920

McCrery, N., *For Conspicuous Gallantry: A Brief History of the Recipients of the Victoria Cross from Nottinghamshire and Derbyshire*, J. H. Hall & Sons, Derby, 1990

Maxwell, C. (ed.), *Brigadier General Frank Maxwell VC, CSI, DSO:* A memoir and some letters, Murray, 1921

The Medical Victoria Crosses, n.d.

Memorials of Rugbeians who Fell in the Great War, Volume 3, 1917.

Middlebrook, M., *The First Day on the Somme 1 July 1916*, Allen Lane, London, 1971

Moses, H., *The Fighting Bradfords: Northern Heroes of WWI*, County Durham Books, 2003

Murphy, J., *Liverpool VCs,* Pen & Sword, Barnsley, 2008

Napier, G., *The Sapper VCs: The Story of Valour in the Royal Engineers and its Associated Corps,* The Stationery Office,

London, 1998

Nicolson, G.W.L.N., *Canadian Expeditionary Force 1914–1919,* Queen's Printer, Ottawa, 1962

Norman, T. (ed.), *Armageddon Road: A VC's Diary 1914–16,* William Kimber, London, 1982

O' Moore, General Sir C. & Humphris, E.M., *The VC and DSO, Vol 1,* 1924

Orr, P., *The Road to the Somme: Men of the Ulster Division Tell Their Story,* Blackstaff Press, Belfast, 1987

Pearce, Sgt L., *A History of the Coldstream Guards Victoria and George Cross Holders,* Coldstream Guards, London, 1995

Pillinger, D. & Staunton, A., *Victoria Cross Presentations and Locations.* D. Pillinger & A. Staunton, Maidenhead, 2000

The Register of the Victoria Cross, This England Books, 1988

Shannon, S.D., *Beyond Praise: The Durham Light Infantrymen who were awarded the Victoria Cross,* County Durham Books, Durham, 1998

Smith, M. *Award for Valour*: A History of the Victoria Cross and the Evolution of British Heroism Palgrave Macmillan 2008

Smyth, Sir J. VC, *The Story of the Victoria Cross,* Frederick Muller, 1963

– *Thirty Canadian VCs,* 1918

Staunton, A., *Victoria Cross: Australia's Finest and the Battles they fought,* Hardie Grant Books, Victoria, 2005

Thompson, D., *I laughed like blazes! The Life of Private Thomas 'Todger' Jones VC, DCM,* Dave Thompson, 2002

Urquhart, H.M., *History of the 16th Battalion (the Canadian Scottish) Canadian Expeditionary Force in the Great War,* Macmillan of Canada, 1933

Uys, I., *For Valour: the History of Southern Africa's Victoria Cross Heroes,* self published, Johannesburg, 1973

– *Delville Wood,* Uys Publishers, 1983

Wasley, G., *Devon in the Great War 1914–1918,* Devon Books, 2000

Westlake, R., *British Battalion on the Somme,* Leo Cooper, 1994

Wiart, Lt Gen. Sir A. Carton de, *Happy Odyssey: The Memoirs of Lieutenant-General Sir Adrian Carton de Wiart VC, KBE, CB, CMG, DSO,* Jonathan Cape, 1950

Wigmore, L. & Harding, B., *They Dared Mightily,* Second Edition revised by Williams, J & Staunton, S., Australian War Memorial, Canberra, 1986

Williams, W. Alister *Heart of a Dragon:* The VCs of Wales & the Welsh Regiments, 1914- 1982 New Edition Bridge Books, Wrexham 2008

Divisional, Regimental and Battalion histories have all been consulted where appropriate but unfortunately are too numerous

INDEX

1st Australian Division (AIF)
   103-105, 107, 113, 115, 119
1st Canadian Division 221
2nd Australian Division (AIF) 119
2nd Division 116-117, 123
3rd Division 85-86, 88-89, 90, 233
4th Division 45, 61, 225
5th Division 187
6th Division 85, 175, 181, 187,
   214
7th Division 98, 164,
8th Division 68
11th (Northern) Division 207208
12th Division 149
16th (Irish) Division 18, 157, 159,
   160-161, 163, 164, 167
17th (Northern) Division 31, 33,
18th (Eastern) Division 77-78,
   201, 203
19th (Western) Division 59, 61, 64,
   68, 127
20th (Light) Division 157, 160,
   164, 165, 166
21st Division 31, 33
23rd Division 71, 130, 217
25th Division 208
29th Division 45, 241, 244
30th Division 77, 123,
31st Division 232
32nd Division 48, 54
33rd Division 228

34th Division 58, 71
35th Division 123
36th (Ulster) Division 17-18, 22,
   24, 36, 38, 39, 41, 42, 45, 48
39th Division 153
46th (North Midland) Division (TF)
   26, 213
47th Division 211, 217
49th (West Riding) Division 48-49,
   153, 193, 201
50th (Northumbrian) Division
   211, 213
51st Division 238
55th (West Lancashire) Division
   (TF) 133, 135, 140-141, 202
56th Division (TF) 28
62nd (West Riding) Division 215
63rd (Royal Naval) Division 238,
   242-243, 245

Abbey Road 172
Acheux 208
Adlam, Second Lieutenant T.E.,
   VC 201-206
Aigneville 134
Albert 58-59, 65, 66, 68, 71, 186,
Albert-Bapaume Road 58, 107,
   119, 130, 168
Albert-Pozières Road 58
Allen, Captain W.B., VC 153-156,
   234

Amiens 71, 197
Ancre Valley 18, 23
Arras 61, 136, 190
Arrow Head Copse 134
Auckland Regiment 171
Australia 20, 47, 103, 105-106,
    109-112, 117, 120, 122, 125,
    150-152, 242
Australian Infantry Force (AIF)
    103, 105, 107, 109, 110, 111,
    112, 114, 151
Australian War Memorial,
    Canberra 106, 112, 122, 151
Authuille 193
Authuille Wood 54, 56
Aveluy Wood 48-50, 54

Baizieux 71
Baker, Private George 81
Bapaume Road 71, 172, 213, 217,
    218
Batey, Private 72
Bazentin le Petit 82, 120, 127,
    128, 130
Bazentin Ridge 87
Beaucourt 22, 233, 238-242,
    244-245
Beaucourt Station 22, 41
Beaucourt Station Road 238
Beaulencourt 165
Beaumont Hamel 43, 45, 233, 238
Beaumont Hamel-Serre Road 46
Becourt 34, 58
Bécourt Wood 31, 34, 212
Bedfordshire Regiment 187, 193,
    201, 202,
Bell, Captain 223
Bell, Captain E.N.F., VC 17–21
Bell, Second Lieutenant D.S., VC
    71–76, 209
Bellacourt 27
Bennett, Lieutenant E.P., VC
    228–231, 232
Bennett's Trench 229
Bernafay Wood 32, 77
Bethune 56, 188

Bienvillers 27
Black Watch Alley 107
Blackburn, Lieutenant A.S., VC
    103, 107–112, 120
Blue Line 181
Bois des Tailles 91
Border Regiment 211
Boritzka Trench 225, 228–229
Bouleaux Wood 187
Boulter, W.E., VC 77–79
Bouzincourt 54
Bradford, Lieutenant Colonel R.B.,
    VC 211–216, 234
Brandhoek 142, 144, 147
Bray 81
Breslau Trench 91
Brick Lane 123
Brown, Sergeant D.F., VC
    171–173, 180
Buchanan Street 90
Butte de Warlencourt 213–214
Byers, Private J.W. 75

Cameron, Brigadier Genera 212
Campbell, Lieutenant Colonel J.V.,
    VC 180–183, 209
Campbell, Lieutenant General Sir
    W.P. 143
Canada 24, 70, 96, 170, 186, 199,
    224
Carnoy 86-87, 158, 160
Castleton, Sergeant C.C., VC
    119–122
Caterpillar Copse 194
Cather, G.S., VC 22–25, 41
Chapes Spur 72
Chavasse, Captain N.G., VC
    140-148, 176
Cheshire Regiment 187, 189, 220
Chimpanzee Trench 134
Circus Trench 172
Citadel Camp 124, 176, 181
Clarke, Corporal L., VC 168-170,
    171
Cloudy Trench 165
Coffee Trench 171

Coldstream Guards 180, 182, 209
Colston, Dr J.A.C. 142
Colwill, Corporal 72
Combles 77, 168, 187-188, 193
Commonwealth War Graves
    Commission 7, 9, 40, 200
Congreve, Lieutenant General Sir
    W., VC 86, 88
Congreve, Major W. La. T. 85-89
Contalmaison 72, 75, 76, 130,
    131
Cooke, Private T., VC 113-115,
    119
Courcelette 149, 170, 171, 184,
    186, 221
Coury, Sergeant G.G., VC
    133-139
Cox, Major General H.V. 149
Craig, Lieutenant Arthur 80-82
Crest Trench 171
Crucifix Corner 56
Crucifix Trench 31
Cunningham, Private J., VC
    232-237, 238
Currie, Major General 221

Davies, J.J., VC 85, 90-93, 94, 97
De Wiart, A. Carton, VC 58-63,
    64, 244
Delville Wood 44, 80, 82, 83, 85,
    87, 90, 92, 93, 94, 95, 97, 98,
    103, 116-118, 130, 171, 180
Dernancourt 31, 65
Devonshire Regiment 98, 100–102
Dotted Green Line 238
Downie, Sergeant R., VC
    225-227, 228
Drysdale, Lieutenant A.N. 56
Duff, Leiutenant 99
Duke of Wellington's (West
    Riding) Regiment 71, 131,
    207, 217–220
Duke Street 85

East Yorkshire (Duke of York's
    Own) Regiment 232–233, 237

Eaucourt 221
Eaucourt l'Abbaye 172, 211, 213,
    217
Edwards, Private F.J., VC
    193-198, 201
Edwards, Quartermaster Sergeant
    H.J. 196
Elgin Avenue 36
England 34, 38, 42, 60, 61, 62,
    63, 70, 78, 81, 83, 96, 104,
    120, 125, 137, 145, 161, 170,
    178, 185, 199, 231, 242, 244,
    245
Enquin-les-Mines 91, 95
Essex Regiment 85
Estment, Private Alexander 81
Evans, Company Sergeant Major
    W.J.G., VC 123-126, 241

Fabeck Graben 168, 184
Fabeck Trench 184, 185
Faffemont Farm 168, 187
Faulds, Private W.F., VC 80–84,
    90
Feilding, General R. 158, 181
Fellows, Corporal Harry 33, 34,
Flers 171, 211, 213, 217
Flers 1 218
Flers 2 218
Flers Line 171, 211
Flers Support Trench 217
Flers Trench 211, 217
Fludyer, Colonel 176
Fonquevillers 26, 29
Forceville 36
Fraser, Major the Hon. W., 88
Freyberg, Lieutenant Colonel B.,
    VC 238-245
Fricourt 31-34, 78, 176, 229

Gallipoli Peninsula 25, 103, 105,
    109, 121, 209, 238, 243
George V, King 17, 20, 25, 29, 33,
    38–39, 42, 47, 60, 70, 73, 78,
    82, 88, 92, 95, 100, 104, 109,
    117, 118, 120, 125, 128, 134,

141, 144, 150, 158, 161, 165, 166, 176, 182, 183, 185, 188, 190, 196, 199, 204, 208, 214, 218, 226, 227, 230, 233, 234, 241,

German First Line 181

German Second Line 77, 98, 108, 130, 184

German Third Line 181

German Trench 46, 114, 130, 175

Giles, Major F.G. 107

Gill, Sergeant A., VC 116-118

Gillespie, Private George 37

Ginchy 164, 168, 175, 179, 180, 187

Ginchy-Les Boeufs Road 180

Ginchy-Morval Road 187

Gird Trench 211

Gloucestershire (Glosters) Regiment 58–59, 61–62, 64, 127

Gommecourt 26

Gommecourt Park 26, 28

Gommecourt Wood 26

Goodlake, Major G., VC 200

Gordon Highlanders 85, 87, 88, 90

Gough, General H. 149, 245

Grandcourt 22, 40, 207, 241

Great Bear 140

Green Line 238

Green Street 160

Green, Captain J.L., VC 26–30

Green, Second Lieutenant E. 29

Green, Sergeant H. 94

Guards Division 174, 180, 187

Guedecourt 165

Guillemont 123-124, 130, 133-135, 140-141, 153, 157-159, 160-163, 164, 167, 229

Guillemont Road 140

Guillemont Station 123, 160

Guillemont-Ginchy Road 164

Haig, General Sir D. 11, 118, 168

Haldane, Major General J.A. 86, 89

Hamel 24, 153

Hamilton, Major General H. 88-89

Hampshire Regiment 225

Happy Valley 81

Harris, Second Lieutenant H. 218

Harrison, Second Lieutenant J., VC 237

Hébuterne 61, 232, 236, 238

Henencourt Wood 68, 71, 212

Hessian Trench 207-208

Heudecourt 83,

Hickie, Major General W.B. 161

High Wood 61, 80, 82, 98, 102, 103, 116, 127, 153, 168, 171, 180, 212, 213

Highland Light Infantry 54, 57

Hill, Private A., VC 85, 90-91, 94-97

Hoey, Lieutenant 169

Holland, Lieutenant J.V., VC 159, 160-163, 167

Hollebeke 105

Holmes, Colonel H.G. 74

Hooge 89, 145, 164

Hopkinson, Lieutenant Colonel J.O. 47

Horseshoe Trench 71–72, 74

Hughes, Private T., VC 157–159, 163, 167, 234

Hunter Weston, Lieutenant General Sir Aylmer 47

Hupfield, Lieutenant C.J. 95

Imperial War Museum 70, 132, 146, 147, 148, 200, 215

Inskip-Read, W.E. 198

Intermediate Line 58,

Intermediate Trench 127

Inwood, Sergeant R.M. 108, 111

Ireland 17–18, 63, 70, 150, 151, 161, 205, 219

Jacob, Lieutenant General Sir C. 209

Jardine, Brigadier General J.B. 56

INDEX

Jennings, Lieutenant R.W. 65

Jones, Private T.A., VC 187–192

Jones, Sergeant D., VC 159, 163, 164–167

Kelly, Second Lieutenant H., VC 217–220, 221

Kentish, Brigadier General R.J. 86, 91, 95

Kerr, Private J.C., VC 184–186

King's (Liverpool) Regiment 133, 125, 140, 143, 164, 166

King's Own (Royal Lancaster) Regiment 68, 85, 90, 127, 128, 133

King's Own Yorkshire Light Infantry 165, 217

King's Royal Rifle Corps (KRRC) 116, 157, 240

Kirk, Lieutenant Colonel A.E. 51

La Boiselle 32

Lambert, Brigadier General T.S. 74

Laurie, Captain J. 47

Le Havre 169, 189

Le Sars 180, 211, 217, 221,

Le Sars Line 221

Le Transloy 165, 187, 225, 228–229, 232,

Leak, Private J., VC 103–106, 107, 108, 120

Lee, Private A. 162

Leipzig Redoubt 56

Leipzig Salient 49, 54, 195

Les Boeufs 174, 181, 187, 193, 225, 228, 229

Leuze Wood 168

Lincoln Redoubt 71

Longueval 80, 82, 85, 87, 90, 103, 116

Loudoun-Shand, Major S.W., VC 31–35

Loyal North (LN) Lancashire Regiment 61, 68, 133

Lummis, Canon W.M. 95

Lynch, Major 223

Mackie, Company Sergeant Major 223

Macnaghten, Sir Harry 41–42, 44

Mailly-Maillet 47, 48,

Mailly-Maillet Wood 203

Maltz Horn Farm 123

Mametz 98

Mametz Wood 32, 34, 71, 77, 80, 82, 128, 212,

Manchester Regiment 123, 125, 126, 167, 219, 244

Mansell Camp 226

Mansell Copse 124

Marrieres Wood 83

Marseilles 105, 244

Martinpuich 110, 130, 168, 171

Martinsart Wood 23, 50–51

Mash Valley 62

Maxse, Major General F.I. 203

Maxwell, Lieutenant Colonel F.A. 194–195, 198, 203

May, Lieutenant H., VC 227

McCann, Lieutenant Colonel W.F.J. 107–108, 111

Mcfadzean, Private W.F., VC 36–40, 41,

McNess, Lance Sergeant F., VC 174–179, 180

Mellish, Reverend N., VC 89

Méricourt l'Abbé 165

Mesnil 153, 155

Middlesex Regiment 193–194, 197–200, 201

Millencourt 58–59

Miller, Private J., VC 127–129, 130

Mirage Trench 228

Montagu, Lieutenant Colonel The Hon. L.S. 240

Montauban 32, 78, 87, 90, 123–124

Morval 180, 187, 193, , 221

Mount Street 157

Mouquet Farm 103–105, 107, 110, 149, 168, 170, 184, 185, 207

Munich Trench 46
Munster Alley 108, 130–131, 153

New Zealand 20–21, 114–115, 172–173, 242, 245
New Zealand Division 171, 180
New Zealand Expeditionary Force 173, 244
Nicholls, Sergeant W.H. 169
Norfolk Regiment 187
Northamptonshire Regiment 77–79, 193, 194, 201
Northern Ireland 17, 19, 24, 42
Northumberland Fusiliers 31, 33, 211
Northumberland Fusiliers 31, 33, 211
Nottinghamshire and Derbyshire Regiment (Sherwood Foresters) 26–29, 69

O'Meara, Private M., VC 149–152
OG1 (Old German) 103–104, 107–108, 119
OG2 (Old German) 103, 107–108, 119, 130
Orchard Post 113
Otago Regiment 171
Oxford Copse 188

Park Lane 149
Partridge, Lieutenant 108
Passchendaele Ridge 61, 141, 241, 244
Peck, Major C.W. 224
Pereira, Brigadier General E.M. 161
Pommier 26
Pozières 103–104, 108, 110–111, 113, 116, 119–120, 130, 149, 153, 207
Pozieres Heights 119, 149
Pozières Mill 107
Pozières Ridge 168

Pozières Trench 104, 107–108, 130
Pozières Windmill 110, 113
Pozières-Bazentin Road 108
Pozières-Thiepval Road 149
Prince Albert's Somerset Light Infantry 101, 165
Prince Charlotte of Wales's Royal Berkshire Regiment 116
Prince of Wales' (North Staffordshire) Regiment 26, 59, 127
Prince of Wales' Own (West Yorkshire) Regiment 49, 52, 73, 201, 207
Prince of Wales's (Leinster) Regiment (Royal Canadians) 160–161
Prince of Wales's Own (Yorkshire) Regiment (Green Howards) 31, 33, 35, 71–72, 75–76, 132, 207–210
Prince of Wales's Volunteers (South Lancashire) Regiment 133, 135, 138
Princes Street 80, 90
Prior, Major H.A.S. 74

Queen Elizabeth II 44
Queen's Redoubt 31
Quigg, R., VC 41–45

Rainbow Trench 165
Rawlinson, General 228
Red Line 180, 239
Redan Ridge 46, 153
Regina Trench 169, 221, 223
Ricardo, Colonel (later Brig Gen) Ambrose 20
Richardson, Piper J.C., VC 221–224, 225
Rim Trench 157
Ritchie, Drummer W., VC 46–48, 227
River Ancre 22, 24, 36, 41, 49, 50, 153, 238,

River Somme 71, 81

Robertson, Colonel 108

Robinson, Captain F. 27

Rodgers, Sergeant J. 171

Royal Army Medical Corps (RAMC) 29, 140, 145, 147, 154–156, 175

Royal British Legion 40, 44, 129, 147

Royal Canadian Air Force 186

Royal Dublin Fusiliers 161, 225

Royal Field Artillery (RFA) 153, 154

Royal Flying Corps RFC 136–137

Royal Fusiliers (City of London) Regiment 116, 193, 201

Royal Inniskilling Fusiliers 18–21, 37

Royal Irish Fusiliers 18, 22, 24, 41, 47

Royal Irish Rifles 18, 22, 38, 41, 42, 51

Royal Scots Fusiliers 123

Royal Warwickshire regiment 59, 127

Royal Welsh Fusiliers (RWF) 85, 90, 94, 166, 228

Ruddle, Lieutenant C.H. 107

Ryder, Private R.E., VC 193–194, 196–200, 201

Ryecroft Avenue 65

Ryecroft Street 59

Sailly-Saillisel 187, 228

Sanctuary Wood 185

Sanders, G., VC 48-53

Sandilands, Lieutenant Colonel H.R. 217

Sandpit Camp 165

Sausage Valley 32, 58, 62

Savill, Lieutenant Sir E. 99–102

Scales, Captain 94

Schwaben Redoubt 18, 36, 49, 153, 194, 195, 202–203, 207, 221

Scot's Redoubt 71

Scotland 34, 183, 222

Seaforth Highlanders 46, 48, 224

Second World War 52, 62, 83, 92, 96, 132, 138, 147, 162, 183, 186, 191, 205, 220, 231

Serre 232–233, 238

Seven Elms 212

Shelter Wood 31

Sherbrooke, Lieutenant Colonel 69–70

Short, W.H., VC 130–132

Skyline Trench 149

Smith, Sergeant 99

South Africa 34, 60, 61, 80–81, 83–84, 125, 182

South Africa Memorial (Delville Wood) 83

South African Infantry (SAI) 80, 83

South Staffordshire Regiment 208

South Wales Borderers 127

Spencer Chichester, Lieutenant Colonel R.D. 38

St Andrew's Trench 59

St Eloi 89

St Jean 141

St Pierre Divion 153, 233, 238

St Pierre Vaast Wood 228

St Sauveur 71

Stafford, Second Lieutenant H. 218

Star Wood 233

Stockwell, Sir H. 210

Stubbs, Major G.C. 85

Stuff Redoubt 202, 207–209

Stuff Trench 221

Suffolk Regiment 85, 90

Sugar Refinery 184

Sunken Road 28, 180–181, 186

Suzanne 78

Swainson, Major J.L. 134

Switch Lane 98

Switch Line 127

Switch Trench 171, 213

Tara-Usna Line 59, 66, 68, 69

Tara-Usna Ridge 62, 64, 71

The Gun-Pits 225
The Quadrilateral 47, 174, 221
The Triangle 174
Thiepval 25, 39, 40, 44, 56,
    63, 78, 104, 149, 153, 168,
    193–195, 199, 200–204, 206,
    207, 210
Thiepval Chateau 194, 195
Thiepval Ridge 207
Thiepval Road 18
Thiepval-Authuille Road 194
Thipeval Memorial to the Missing
    19, 21, 23, 37, 39, 70
Thipeval Wood 18, 36, 40, 41, 49,
    50, 193–194, 201
Torr Trench 131
Transloy Ridges 165, 211
Trônes Wood 77, 80, 82,
    123–124, 140, 226
Turnbull, J.Y., VC 54–57
Turrall, T.G., VC 64–67

Ulster Volunteer Force 17, 38
United States of America 20, 24,
    242

Varennes 208
Vaughan, Major 180
Vaux 228

VC memorial, Queen Victoria
    Building, Sydney 106, 112,
    115, 122, 151
Veale, Private T.W.H., VC 98–102,
    197
Victoria Cross Park Memorial,
    Canberra 106, 122

Wales 93, 105, 162, 189, 214
Waterlot Farm 80
White, Captain A.C.T., VC 73–75,
    207–210, 234
Worcestershire Regiment 59, 64,
    127, 228
Wieltje 141, 143
Wilkinson, Major G.E. 211–212
Wilkinson, T.O.L., VC 68–70
Wood Lane 98

Y Ravine 43, 46
Yellow Line 239
York and Lancaster Regiment 208
Ypres 52, 91, 92, 135, 141, 142,
    145, 161, 164, 185, 219, 241,
    244,

Zollern Graben 184
Zollern Redoubt 207
Zollern Trench 207–208